Research Methodology

in

Accounting

Publications of Scholars Book Co.

Accounting: Its Principles and Problems
Henry Rand Hatfield

Truth in Accounting
Kenneth MacNeal

Financial Accounting: A Distillation of Experience
George O. May

Twenty-Five Years of Accounting Responsibility:
1911–1936, Essays and Discussions
George O. May

A Theory of Accounting to Investors
George Staubus

Asset Valuation and Income Determination:
A Consideration of the Alternatives
Robert R. Sterling (editor)

Research Methodology in Accounting

Papers and Responses from
Accounting Colloquium II

cosponsored by

The University of Kansas School of Business

and

The Arthur Young Foundation

Edited by Robert R. Sterling

Scholars Book Co.
P.O. Box 3344
Lawrence, Kansas 66044

Manufactured in the United States of America

CONTENTS

PREFACE

This volume contains the papers and responses presented at the second Arthur Young Accounting Colloquium held at the University of Kansas May 6, 1971. It serves double duty in that the Introduction and seven of the papers also constitute the report of the American Accounting Association Committee on Research Methodology. The charge of that Commitee was

To prepare a report which identifies, explains, and illustrates the various methodological approaches which are appropriate for research in accounting.

As explained in the Introduction, the Committee decided to present individual papers instead of a common report.

The idea of the Colloquium was to broaden the participation in the discussion of research methodology. This was accomplished by inviting representatives from other disciplines and from accounting practice to author additional papers and responses and by inviting about 40 professors and practitioners to join in the open discussion. As usual, we raised a good many more questions than we answered. However, we also managed to clarify some of those questions, which is often the first step toward an answer.

The Colloquia series is made possible by gifts from Arthur Young & Company personnel who are alumni of the University of Kansas. We are most grateful. Special thanks is due to Robert S. Mueller and Stanley P. Porter for their assistance with this year's Colloquium. We are grateful to James Don Edwards and Hector Anton, President and Research Director of the American Accounting Association, for providing liaison between the Committee and the Association.

Lawrence, Kansas   Robert R. Sterling
1971

chapter 1

Introduction

Robert R. Sterling

University of Kansas

A glance at the accounting literature reveals that there has been a broadening of what accountants perceive to be appropriate research questions. Previously, the predominant view seemed to be that the research questions of accounting should be severely circumscribed. Primary emphasis was placed on the questions of the proper method of cost allocation and the appropriate timing of revenue realization. Currently, the predominant view seems to be that anything which is affected by accounting and anything which affects accounting is an appropriate research question. Thus, the number of questions considered to be appropriate for accounting research has been greatly expanded in recent years.

Concurrent with the expansion of research questions has been an expansion of the research methods utilized by accounting researchers. Many of these new methods are borrowed from other disciplines and applied to the problems of accounting. This has come about in two ways:

First, there have been some attempts to redefine the purpose and the subject matter of accounting. For example, a previous definition of accounting included the terms "recording" and "reporting." A current definition replaces these terms with "measuring" and "communicating."

Although it can be argued that the terms have the same meaning, the point in regard to research methods is that the new terms suggest that the concepts and methods of measurement and communication theory are pertinent to accounting, and there has been research in this direction. Another example is the view that accounting should supply "relevant information" instead of "matching costs and revenues." This has resulted in the application of the concepts and methods of decision and information theory to the problems of accounting.

Second, there have been attempts to broaden the analysis of the accounting function. Previously, the analysis of the accounting function stopped with the issuance of financial statements. The current view is that the effects of financial statements is an appropriate research question. There have been investigations of the market effects of their issuance, and these investigations have utilized the concepts, methods, and previous findings of the disciplines of economics and finance. Others have investigated the effects of financial statements in laboratory settings, utilizing the concepts, methods, and previous findings of the behavioral sciences.

These two categories are not mutually exclusive but we may refer to them broadly as research *in* accounting as opposed to research *about* accounting. The former are efforts to establish what the subject matter of accounting ought to be and to discover attributes of that subject matter. The latter are efforts to discover how accounting fits into the total scheme of things. The investigators are attempting to find out how accounting inputs and outputs mesh, or clash, with the inputs and outputs of other disciplines.

Given these goals, there is an almost limitless number of other disciplines whose concepts, methods, and previous findings are pertinent to research in accounting. Since accounting provides information to management as well as information about management's performance, management science is pertinent. Since technology is a crucial factor in the establishment of a communication system, in addition to the fact that the computer is a powerful research tool, computer science is pertinent. Since the act of measuring is likely to affect the behavior of those receiving the results of the measurements, as well as the behavior of those being measured, the behavioral sciences are pertinent. And so forth.

The listed disciplines are intended to be suggestive, not exhaustive. The point that I want to make is that the expansion of research *questions* has resulted in an expansion of research *methods*. It is evident that if one wants to explore the behavioral effects of accounting, then the methods of the behavioral sciences are appropriate; if one wants to explore the mathematical characteristics of accounting, then the methods of mathematics are appropriate; etc. Thus, the appropriateness of a research method depends upon the research question to be investigated. One cannot judge the appropriateness of a research method without placing it in the context of the research question that is being explored.

Since the selection of a research method depends upon the research question, the basis for the selection of methods reduces to the basis for selection of questions. Ultimately, the criterion for selecting a research question is the importance of the answer to that question. But, we are unable to know the importance of the answer until that answer has been obtained, i.e., until after the research has been performed. Indeed, we cannot know that we will be able to obtain an answer until after the research has been per-

formed. Thus, one must address a research question because he *believes* that he can obtain an answer and that the answer is likely to be important. Since one cannot demonstrate the importance of the research results prior to performing the research, the selection of a research question requires a leap of faith. As Polanyi [7, p. 123] puts it, a scientific discovery requires the jumping of a "logical gap" and one can never be sure of his ability to make the jump until he has tried. Of course, the length of the leap will vary, since some research questions are more routine than others. Usually, but not always, the more routine the research question, the greater the chance of being able to answer the question but the smaller the chance that the answer to that particular research question will be important. The cumulative effect of routine research may result in an important break-through, but it is unlikely that the results of any single project will result in that break-through. Therefore, the length of the leap of faith and the importance of the results probably vary directly. Unfortunately, it is likely that the length of the leap of faith also varies directly with the probability of failure.

In discussing the advancement of science, Bernal distinguishes between "tactics" and "strategy." He defines "tactics" as the method of attacking a problem or question. By contrast,

The essential feature of a strategy of discovery lies in determining the sequence of choice of problems to solve. Now it is in fact very much more difficult to see a problem than to find a solution for it. The former requires imagination, the latter only ingenuity. (Bernal [2, p. 39])

Bernal's purpose is not to denigrate the solving of problems (by saying that they require "only" ingenuity), but, instead, to make the contrast between working within a well defined area and breaking new ground. The latter is much more difficult and risky but, if successful, the payoffs are much greater. He cites the cases of Newton, Darwin and Faraday as examples of researchers who "set themselves to find and solve problems of their own" [2, p. 39]. Cohen and Nagel [3, p. 392] make the same point when they write: "The ability to formulate problems whose solution may also help solve other problems is a rare gift, requiring extraordinary genius."

There is no reason to believe that accounting is different from science in general in this regard. How are we to know beforehand that research question X will yield more fruitful results than research question Y? The answer is that we cannot, and therefore, *each* researcher must select his research question on the basis of his belief about the importance of the answer to the question.[1]

Given the requirement of extraordinary genius for the selection of research questions, it would be most presumptuous if I were to attempt to argue that some questions are appropriate for research by accountants and that others are inappropriate. My view is quite the opposite. I think that the broadening of accounting research questions has been wholly beneficial and that any attempt to restrict the scope of the questions would be detrimental. In fact, I could list a number of questions which I think we should investigate. However, since these questions are based upon *my* interests and beliefs, the only way for me to demonstrate to you that these are fruitful lines of inquiry is for me to do at least some of the necessary research. Therefore, I will not importune you to do something that interests me nor will I attempt to restrain you from doing something that interests you.

Since the research methods depend upon the questions and since I am unwilling to place restrictions on questions, it follows that I am unwilling to place restrictions on methods. I conclude, therefore, that all of the research methods from all of these other disciplines are appropriate for accounting. To put it another way, the goal of research is to obtain results which will contribute to our knowledge. The danger of excluding a research method is that, in so doing, we will be excluding some research results which may contribute to our knowledge. To avoid this danger, I am unwilling to *ex*clude any research method, and therefore, I must *in*clude *all* research methods.

This rather sweeping conclusion is likely to be disappointing to those who had expected me to label some research methods as "unscientific" and to endorse others. I am sorry to disappoint, but that is precisely the attitude to which I am opposed.[2] I do not believe that it is possible to define "the scientific method" and thereby to delimit the set of research methods that are appropriate to accounting. Although the research methods of all of the scientific disciplines have some general properties in common, the more striking feature is their diversity. Kaplan [5, p. 27] has observed that any definition of the scientific method which is specific enough to be of use in methodology is not general enough to embrace all of the methods which scientists use or may come to use. I would only add that any definition which is general enough to embrace all of the methods is not specific enough to be of any use.

There have been a number of attempts over the years to provide a concise definition of "the scientific method." All of these attempts have failed. They have failed because, as the historians of science have shown, sometimes science progresses in one way and sometimes in another.[3] This is the basis for Kaplan's observation that no definition is general enough to embrace all use-

---

[1] Of course, we are speaking here of an idealized researcher. In actuality, there are a good many other factors involved in the selection of the research question. These include the interests, skills and perhaps prejudices of the researcher, as well as the overriding criterion of the availability of funds to support the research.

[2] In particular, I am opposed to those who provide a definition of the scientific method for the apparent purpose of criticizing the work of others as "unscientific." The definition that they provide is unbearably narrow and naive in the first place, and more importantly, it violates the basic tenet of science that *nothing* is indubitable and final, including the methods of science. "The canons of inquiry are themselves discovered in the process of reflection, and may themselves become modified in the course of study." (Cohen and Nagel [3, pp. 395–6])

[3] "Such an absolute conception of it [method of science] is belied by the whole history of science, with its continual development of a multiplicity of new methods. The method of science is not a fixed thing, it is a growing process. . . . Consequently scientific method, like science itself, defies definition. It is made up of a number of operations, some mental, some manual. Each of these, in its time, has been found useful, first in the formulation of questions that seem urgent at any stage and then in the finding, testing and using the answers to them." (Bernal [2, p. 35])

ful procedures. Since there are a variety of methods and since an attempt to restrict methods is likely to be harmful, he concludes (citing Conant) that it is "a public service" to emphasize "that there is no such thing as *the* scientific method." [5, p. 27] Another reason for failure is that if the procedures of science were reduced to rules so that one could systematically create knowledge, then we would not consider the results of the procedures to be scientific discoveries. As Polanyi [7, p. 123] puts it, "no solution of a problem can be accredited as a discovery if it is achieved by a procedure following definite rules." A major part of the scientific process is the scientist's creation of the method[4] which allows him to carry out his investigation. If discoveries could be made by following a routine procedure, such that any fool or machine could grind them out, then they would not be considered discoveries.

Of course, much of scientific enterprise is not concerned with making discoveries in the sense that Polanyi is using the term. Kuhn [6, p. 35] contrasts "normal science" with the making of discoveries and points out that "the most striking feature" of "normal research" is that it does not "aim to produce novelties, conceptual or phenomenal." He notes (p. 24) that practitioners of "normal science" spend most of their lives in "mopping-up operations." He likens mopping-up operations to "puzzle-solving" and argues that the framework of the normal science, or "paradigm," provides assurance that the puzzle has a solution (p. 37). As the terms suggest, these activities are much more routine than the activities required for making discoveries. In some cases, the method of a normal science can, at least in principle, be completely systematized. However, even in these more routine

activities, the systematic method is too inefficient to use. Consider, for example, the common children's puzzle consisting of a box with 15 sequentially numbered squares and one empty position. Turing [8, p. 9] calculated the total number of positions and found it to be finite but rather large, viz., 20,922,789,888,000. If one attempted to solve this puzzle by systematically surveying all of these positions, it would take over a million years, yet many children have solved it in a few minutes. The puzzles of normal science are much more complex, and therefore, the systematic method of solution is simply too inefficient to be used. Instead, as Kuhn says [6, p. 36], the solutions require "ingenuity" and "skill," and these two terms are clearly antonyms for "systematic solution."[5]

Thus, it is not possible or not efficient to use a systematic method for either making discoveries in science or for solving the puzzles of normal science. Perhaps considerations of this kind caused P. W. Bridgman to make his widely quoted remark: "The scientist has no other method than doing his damnedest." Doing one's damnedest neither restricts the scope of the questions to be investigated nor does it restrict the method of investigation to be utilized.

My quarrel, then, is only with those who attempt to make such restrictions. We can now begin to identify several separate schools of accounting by the way in which they attempt to make such restrictions. Representatives of each school have a tendency to claim that *their* particular research questions are the only important ones and that *their* methods are the only scientific ones and that the subject matter that *they* examine is the only pertinent evidence. To use only two broad categories, we can note that some empirists disparage analytical methods, and vice versa. This is a false issue. There are empirical questions and there are analytical questions, and it makes little

---

[4] A prime example of this is Glaser's invention of a device (bubble chamber) for measuring the paths of particles, i.e., the creation of a method of doing research on particles. Since its invention, the bubble chamber has been used in experiments which produced important results. However, it was Glaser who received the Nobel Prize, not the subsequent experimenters. The reason for this is that the process of using a bubble chamber is much more systematic or routine than the process of inventing it. Glaser, by his own account, got the idea while gazing at the bubbles rising in his beer.

[5] Turing [8, p. 23] makes the same point in different words in his concluding remarks. "These, and some other results of mathematical logic may be regarded as going some way towards a demonstration, within mathematics itself, of the inadequacy of 'reason' unsupported by common sense."

sense to try to answer an empirical question with analytical methods, or vice versa. For example, a paper by Ijiri, Jaedicke and Livingstone [4] addressed itself to the question of the effect of different inventory methods on full and direct costing. An analytical (mathematical) solution was presented. An empirical test of this question would have been entirely inappropriate, because, among other reasons, the empirical test would not have been able to provide a conclusive and general answer. On the other hand, a paper by Beaver [1] addressed itself to the question of investor reaction to earnings' announcements. Analytical methods would have been entirely inappropriate for much the same reasons, e.g., lack of conclusiveness, because there are *a priori* arguments that lead to contradictory conclusions.

Unfortunately, such internal strife seems to be one of those properties which is common to all disciplines. Kaplan [5, p. 30] has complained of the same thing in regard to the behavioral sciences. He notes that there are two tactics: (1) "defensive incorporation," in which each school says "everybody ought to work on ————," and (2) "exclusion," in which each school says "nobody ought to ————." He concludes:

These tactics lend themselves to rationalization by their identifying some particular phase or other of the complex process of inquiry as the core of "scientific method." For the experimentalist science progresses only in the laboratory; the theoretician views experiments rather as guides and tests for his models and theories; others see as the most important task making counts and measures, or arriving at predictions, or formulating explanations; the field worker and clinician have still other viewpoints. *All of them are right; what is wrong is only what they deny, not what they affirm.* [5, p. 30] (italics supplied)

The point can be stated in terms of the specialization of labor. Dividing science into disciplines by the subject matter which is examined is one form of specialization. Dividing the tasks within a particular discipline is another form of specialization. There are experiments to be performed, mathematical relations to be discovered, and concepts to be clarified. It is impossible for any one person to do all there is to be done, and it is likely that the productivity will be greater if individuals are permitted to specialize. Of course, an imbalance may result in the same way that bottlenecks develop in manufacturing. However, as in manufacturing, the solution is to try to maintain the proper balance, not to denigrate the importance of one of the specialties. Thus, the "data grubbing" of the empiricist, the "abstract meanderings" of the mathematician or logician, and the "idle dreaming" of the theorist are all appropriate methods. The only thing that is inappropriate is the pejorative terms used to describe them.

These observations are even more germane to accounting than to science in general. Accounting is currently in a state of flux; it does not have the paradigm necessary for it to be classified as a normal science in which only puzzle-solving is needed. We have not yet even decided what should be the subject matter of accounting. Many of the disputes in the current literature are, in essence, disagreements over what the subject matter of accounting ought to be.[6] For example, should the subject matter be costs or values or information? Should we focus on decision makers or on decision models? Should we study the reactions of individuals or their reactions aggregated by the market? Should we supply information relevant to decisions or confine ourselves to the stewardship function? Since we do not know how such questions will be resolved or which research methods will contribute to their resolution, we must tolerate, if not encourage, a variety of research questions from a variety of disciplines utilizing a variety of methods by a variety of specialists.

For this reason, my answer to the charge of identifying the methods appropriate for research in accounting can be stated quite simply: All methods are appropriate. Unfortunately, my answer to this part of the

---

[6] My critics unwittingly provided me with some empirical evidence for this assertion. Several of them denied that the subject matter of accounting was in dispute and then informed me of the nature of that subject matter. However, each critic had a different opinion of the nature of that subject matter. For example, one asserted that the economics of information is the basic subject matter of accounting, while another asserted that "accounting must be, in the final analysis, a behavioral science."

charge prohibits the fulfillment of the remainder of the charge. In addition to identifying the methods, the charge also specifies that the appropriate methods be explained and illustrated. Obviously, it is impossible to explain and illustrate all research methods. Therefore, the Committee was forced to select only a small subset of research issues for examination.

Given the views expressed above, a nondirective approach to the organization of the Committee seemed reasonable, and this approach was adopted. Each member of the Committee selected a topic on research methodology on the basis of his interests and his belief in the importance of that topic. Thus, the particular research methods and issues which are discussed in the following set of papers are a reflection of the interests of the members of the Committee, and the set is not intended to contain an exhaustive list of all methods that are appropriate for research in accounting nor even, necessarily, the methods that are most preferred for research in accounting. Had there been different members of the Committee with different interests, different research methods and research issues would have been selected for examination.

The result of this selection process is a rather diverse set of topics. Given the diversity of the members of the Committee, this is to be expected. About the only thing common to all the authors is that they have made significant research contributions. In making these contributions, their diversity of interests is evidenced by the diversity of research questions which they address and the concomitant diversity of research methods which they utilize. Such diversity would have made it difficult, if not impossible, for the Committee to prepare a useful common report. We would have had to try to discover the (probably null) intersection of eight different sets of ideas or else express the report in such general language that it said nothing or everything. I preferred to try to make use of each person's special skills by asking them to explore an issue which they believed to be important.

The Committee met three times. The first meeting was organizational, and the nondirective approach was adopted. The second meeting was for the purpose of discussing the preliminary drafts of the papers. This discussion was devoted to constructive criticism, not to an attempt to get agreement. The spirit of cooperation was such that members of the Committee offered suggestions for strengthening positions which they opposed. Thus, the ideas expressed in each paper are those of the author, not the Committee. There are disagreements, including, I am sure, disagreements with these introductory remarks. This is intentional. I prefer to expose and examine disagreements rather than to conceal them with delicate phraseology.

The third meeting was devoted to a presentation and discussion of the final drafts of the papers. This final meeting was combined with Accounting Colloquium II. This allowed us to invite nonmembers to author additional papers and discussion remarks, as well as to get immediate feedback from all of the conferees.

The Accounting Colloquia series of the University of Kansas is sponsored by the Arthur Young Foundation. The Committee instructed me to express their gratitude to the Foundation. It is a pleasure to carry out those instructions and to add my personal thanks, especially to Stanley P. Porter and Robert S. Mueller.

References

1. Beaver, William H., "The Information Content of Annual Earnings Announcements," *Empirical Research in Accounting: Selected Studies, 1968,* supplement to the *Journal of Accounting Research,* University of Chicago, 1968, pp. 67–92.

2. Bernal, J. D., *Science in History, Volume 1: The Emergence of Science,* The M.I.T. Press, 1971.

3. Cohen, Morris R., and Nagel, Ernest, *An Introduction to Logic and Scientific Method,* Harcourt, Brace & World, Inc., 1934.

4. Ijiri, Yuji, Jaedicke, Robert K., and Livingstone, John L., "The Effect of Inventory Costing Methods on Full and Direct Costing," *Journal of Accounting Research* (Spring, 1965), pp. 63–74.

5. Kaplan, Abraham, *The Conduct of Inquiry: Methodology for Behavioral Science,* Chandler Publishing Company, 1964.

6. Kuhn, Thomas S., *The Structure of Scientific Revolutions,* The University of Chicago Press, 1962.

7. Polanyi, Michael, *Personal Knowledge: Towards a Post-Critical Philosophy,* Harper & Row, Publishers, 1964.

8. Turing, A. M., "Solvable and Unsolvable Problems," in A. W. Haslett (ed.), *Science News,* Penguin Books, 1954, pp. 7–23.

chapter 2

The Behavior of Security Prices and Its Implications for Accounting Research (Methods)

WILLIAM H. BEAVER

Stanford University

1. Introduction

It has been noted that the scientist can be viewed as a decision maker, and hence, research issues are capable of being analyzed in a decision-theoretic context.[1] The term *research method* usually refers to some arbitrary subset of the action-choices available to the scientist. For example, in an empirical study, the issues of research method would involve questions of *experimental design*. However, the issue of research method is much broader. The scientist must also identify those research topics that potentially are worthy of a commitment of resources. Ultimately, the selection of research methods (in this narrow sense) depends upon a specification of what research topics (i.e., what relationships among phenomena in the environment) are of interest to scientists in a given discipline. In a complete formulation of the scientist's decision, the action-choices constitute a set of experiments, where an experiment is defined in terms of both topic and method.[2] A complete, formal

analysis is almost always too costly to conduct, and hence, the scientist's decisions (including those of research method) are made in a very informal, heuristic manner. Presumably, the specification of research methods available is a prerequisite for the selection of the optimal member of the set.[3]

This paper will explore recent research in security price behavior and its implications for research methods in accounting. This, in turn, will require a discussion of the related

---

[1]Ackoff [1] and Churchman [18], among others, have made such a suggestion.

[2]The scientist's decision is to select an optimal member from the set of experiments. This, of necessity, involves specification of a preference relationship for

possible outcomes of the experiments. These preference relations are, in turn, derived in part from the effects of actions taken by policy makers acting upon the outcomes of the experiment. The assessment of a preference function is too complex to adequately discuss here, but it is important to note that neither the experiments nor their outcomes, per se, are the objects of choice. Rather, they are at the end of a long chain of analysis which ultimately depends upon the overall level of well being attained by members of the society in which the scientist works. The role of the policy maker (e.g., the Accounting Principles Board) will be completely suppressed in the paper. This is an important omission, but the present length of the paper precluded inclusion of the additional issues which must be addressed if the policy maker is made explicit in the analysis.

[3]Hence, presumably this is the justification for the American Accounting Association to assign a committee to search for research methods that might be applicable to research in accounting. The implicit assumption is that knowledge of a larger set of action-choices available is expected to lead to better research decisions.

areas of portfolio theory and capital asset pricing. A danger in applying methods whose origins are in other disciplines is that they may not be particularly suited to providing information on topics that are relevant to accounting. The security price research was chosen because it not only provides a set of specific research methods, but also possesses both theoretical and empirical support for the relevance of such research methods for accounting research. For example, it not only provides methods for examining the relationship between accounting data and security prices, but it also establishes why such a topic (i.e., such a relationship) is a necessary part of any complete research program in accounting. As shall be indicated later in the paper, this latter function is lacking in many applications of research methods from other disciplines. It is essential that research issues be viewed in this broader context. Otherwise, the most important implications of this literature for accounting research will be lost. The paper will largely restrict itself to discussing the implications of this research for (accounting) information issues with respect to decision makers external to the firm, even though it will be obvious at several points that important implications exist for internal information issues as well. The scope was narrowed in this fashion for three reasons: (1) There appears to be a consensus in the accounting literature that a major use of financial statements is to "facilitate" investor decisions regarding purchase and sale of securities. (2) The literature on security price behavior and the related literature have been quite productive in recent years in developing a rich theoretical and empirical foundation. (3) There are many important implications of the literature for research into external information issues.

2. Relevance to Accounting Research

At the outset, it is important to distinguish between the securities market and the individual investors that compose the market, because the role of (accounting) information can be vastly different in each context. To a certain extent, the distinction is artificial, in the sense that the aggregate actions of the individuals determine market behavior. However, the process of aggregation is often deceptive, and if we fail to make the distinction, we may be subject to any one of a number of fallacies of composition. In many cases, what is "true" for the group as a whole is not "true" for any individual of that group, and conversely.[4] The role of a securities market is two-fold. First, the existence of an exchange market for securities is a mechanism for separating the ownership of assets and the management of those assets by agents who have a comparative advantage in making production decisions. Second, an exchange market provides a means whereby investors can exchange claims to present and future consumption in such a manner that each individual is able to attain a more optimal pattern of lifetime consumption than would have been possible if no exchange market existed.

Viewed in this light, the role of information is two-fold: (1) to aid in establishing a set of security prices, such that there exist an optimal allocation of resources among firms and an optimal allocation of securities among investors, and (2) to aid the individual investor, who faces a given set of prices, in the selection of an optimal portfolio of securities. These two functions reflect the two-fold distinction described above, and the behavior of security prices is an inherent part of both contexts.

For this reason, the behavior of security prices is a *necessary* consideration in a complete system of accounting research into external information issues. If we accept the premise that the purpose of accounting is to facilitate decision making, then accounting research can be defined, and in fact *must* be defined, to include any research efforts that help us to address the issue of providing the optimal information set for some defined class of decision makers. The use of the term "optimal" necessarily implies a "cost-benefit" or "value-cost" context in the eval-

---

[4]Economics abounds with such examples. For example, the demand facing all firms in the industry is not the same as the demand curves facing each firm in the industry under conditions of perfect competition.

uation of alternative information sets. Viewed in this light, it is apparent that the issue of information choice is itself a decision, and hence it can be structured in decision-theoretic terms. This has been made most explicit in papers by Feltham [31] and by Feltham and Demski [32], who have extended the research in information economics to the (accounting) information decision.

Within the context of external reporting, one class of decision makers has been viewed as the investors in the securities of firms for which financial statements are being prepared. Until recently, little was known in a formal way about the decision processes of investors. Pioneering works by Markowitz [49] and Tobin [69], drawing upon decision theory for their foundation, led to significant contributions in structuring the investment decision under uncertainty, particularly in the context of a single-period analysis. The most general statement of the problem is that of Hirshleifer [37], who combined the classic multi-period analysis by Fisher [34] under certainty with the work of Arrow [3] and Debreu [19] using state preference models. The result is a time-state preference theory which is extremely general and yet simple in specifying the nature of the multi-period consumption-investment decision process faced by investors. The effect of security price behavior upon the multi-period consumption-investment decision is immediately obvious when viewed within the context of the time-state preference formulation. In the Hirshleifer analysis, the investment decision is viewed as a decision to exchange current consumption for future consumption in such a manner that utility is maximized. The sole arguments of the utility function are time-dated, state-contingent consumption claims. However, the optimization problem is subject to the constraint that the present certainty equivalent value of all consumption (present and future) must be equal to the present certainty equivalent value of current wealth (which includes current and future endowments as well as securities).

The implications of security price changes (and hence, wealth changes) are clear. A price increase implies an increase in current wealth, which permits the investor to consume more. A decrease in prices (wealth) will result in a reduction in consumption opportunities. Hence, price changes induce a change in consumption decisions, even though the precise nature of the change will depend upon the individual's preference for time-dated, consumption claims in each state. Moreover, the change in consumption, as measured in present certainty equivalent value terms, is exactly equal to the change in current wealth (i.e., the change in price times the number of shares held). The net effect across all investors is the change in total market value of the firm's securities.

Given the importance of security prices upon the wealth and overall level of well being of investors, it is inconceivable that optimal information systems for investors can be selected without a knowledge of security price behavior. In particular, any complete analysis must specify the interaction between the information system and security price behavior and must be able to specify how security price behavior will be altered as the information system is altered. Hence, each information system will imply a set of equilibrium prices conditional upon that information system.[5] The choice among information systems then rests upon the effects of different sets of prices upon the multi-period consumption pattern of the individuals in the economy. The effect of the different consumption patterns will depend upon the nature of the investor preferences for consumption claims, and therefore, the effect may be measurable only in "utility" terms.[6]

At the level of the individual investor who faces a given set of security prices, the role

---

[5]If alternative information systems imply the identical set of security prices, then the issue reduces to that of the comparative cost of each system. Note that cost considerations must be incorporated into any complete analysis of alternative information systems. Both issues will be addressed later in the paper.

[6]Hence, in constructing an information system for a group of investors, the issue of interpersonal comparison of preference functions arises. Pareto-optimality is one solution to this problem. However, current research in cooperative decision making (see Wilson [71]) is exploring the properties of other solutions. In any event, the question of the existence and nature of a social welfare function must be addressed.

of information is to aid in the selection of the optimal portfolio of securities (i.e., consumption claims).[7] Portfolio theory provides a decision context within which to assess (accounting) information issues. In selecting the optimal information set for the individual investor, the information evaluator (i.e., the accountant) must specify how the decision maker will use the information in altering his investment behavior. The issue of security price behavior is also important at this level, because it is crucial in specifying what constitute plausible assumptions about investor uses of accounting data. The effect of accounting data on the decision behavior of investors will be influenced by what they can properly assume regarding the nature of the security price formation process.[8]

3. Review of the Research

Because of the complexity and nonoperationality associated with a complete formulation in a time-state preference context, some simplification must be made.[9] A common one is the two-parameter portfolio theory as represented by Markowitz [50], Tobin [69] and Sharpe [67], among others.[10] Most of the discussion will deal at this level of simplification. One member of this set is the market model, which has been employed extensively in the research methods to be described. The model (also sometimes referred to as the diagonal model) was first suggested by Markowitz [50] and later extended by Sharpe [62], and it defines the stochastic process generating security price changes (returns) in the following manner:

$$R_{it} = \alpha_i + \beta_i R'_{mt} + u_{it} \qquad E(u_{it}) = 0$$
$$E(R_{it}) = \alpha_i + \beta_i E(R'_{mt}) \qquad \sigma(R'_{mt}, u_{it}) = 0$$
$$E(R_{it} \mid R'_{mt}) = \alpha_i + \beta_i R'_{mt} \qquad \sigma(u_{it}, u_{jt}) = 0$$
$$R_{it} - E(R_{it} \mid R'_{mt}) = u_{it}$$

where

R_{it} = the return of security i in period t.
α_i, β_i = intercept and slope of linear relationship between R_{it} and R'_{mt}.
R'_{mt} = the market factor in period t.
u_{it} = stochastic portion of individualistic component of R_{it}.

The model asserts that there exists a linear relationship between the expected return on security i and the expected value of the market factor.[12] The model also states that the expected return on security i, conditional upon the *ex post* value of the market factor, is also a linear function of the market factor. The *ex post* return on security i differs from this conditional expectation by the amount, u_{it}. In this sense, u_{it} reflects the unexpected portion of the *ex post* return on security i, *conditional* upon the *ex post* value of the market factor. The expected value of u_{it} is zero, and hence, any trading scheme that implies a nonzero expectation for u_{it} would imply that abnormal returns are associated with such a stategy.

Intuitively, a rationale for the model can be provided by classifying events that affect a security's return into one of two categories: One class of events are those that have economy-wide impacts, which are reflected in the market factor. β_i reflects the respon-

[7]Note that securities, per se, are not the objects of choice, but rather they are desired because they represent complex bundles of time-dated, state-dependent consumption claims. This is obvious in the Hirshleifer analysis, where the sole arguments of the investor's preferences function are consumption claims. See also Fama [25] for a similar treatment of the investor's multi-period consumption decision.

[8]Another distinction between the market analysis and the individual analysis is that the latter is a partial equilibrium analysis. It is assumed that the individual will have no effect on price, and the analysis abstracts from any effect of the individual behavior upon the N-1 investors in the economy. For certain purposes, such an analysis is adequate for evaluating information issues, but as the paper indicates later, for many purposes, the analysis is seriously deficient.

[9]For example, the absence of a natural, agreed-upon, and manageably small set of state definitions is a major obstacle to the use of the model in empirical studies.

[10]The relationship between the complete formulation and the two-parameter simplification is discussed more fully in the Appendix.

[11]The return on a security can also be thought of as a price change adjusted for dividends. For purposes of consistency, the term "return" will be used throughout. More precisely, the return from t-1 to t shall be defined as

$$R_t = (\text{Price}_t - \text{Price}_{t-1} + \text{Dividends}_{t-1,t})/\text{Price}_{t-1}$$

[12]Operationally, the market factor can be closely approximated by computing the return on the market portfolio (i.e., a portfolio consisting of all securities in the market). This issue is discussed in greater detail in Fama [23] and Jensen [41]. It is worth noting, however, that they are distinct concepts.

siveness of security i to such events. A second class of events are those which have an impact only upon security i. Their effect on return is reflected in u_{it}, which is assumed to be uncorrelated with the market factor. The model permits us to abstract from the *ex post* behavior of the market and to focus only upon that portion of return that reflects events particular to security i. Being able to "control" for the effects of the movements of the market is an enormous advantage for several reasons. (1) A substantial portion of the variation in securities' *ex post* returns is due to variations in the movements of the market. King's [44] study of monthly returns from 1926 through 1960 found that, on the average, approximately 52 per cent of the variation in an individual security's returns could be explained by its comovement with a market factor. The percentage has been secularly declining, and in the final 101 months studied, the proportion explained was approximately 30 per cent. However, note that the above statistics are only averages. The relative importance of the market factor varies across securities, and the degree of responsiveness to the market factor (i.e., β_i) also varies across securities. Hence, the use of the market model in abstracting from market movements is more appealing than previous experimental designs, which either completely ignored the market factor or dealt with it by performing some naive transformation on R_{it} involving some measure of R_{mt}. Such transformations are usually equivalent to assuming that the β_i is the same for all firms in the sample, and moreover, they often assume all β_i's to be equal to the constant, one. (2) For many purposes, particularly those relevant to accounting, the use of the market model permits the researcher to pool data from different time periods, resulting in a substantial increase in the number of observations. (3) Because many of the information items of research interest are of the second category (i.e., individualistic in nature), being able to isolate the individualistic component of security returns increases the probability that the information effects can be detected. Otherwise, the "noise" created by market move-

ments might completely obscure the effects of the information item under study. (4) The individualistic component u_{it} is expressed in terms of *ex post* rather than *ex ante* returns, which makes it amenable to empirical testing.

The u's (and the α's and β's) can be empirically assessed from a time series, ordinary least squares regression. R_{it} and R_{mt} can be obtained from the Center for Research in Security Prices (CRSP) Tape developed at the University of Chicago. It contains monthly return and price data for all NYSE firms from January, 1926 through June, 1968. Most of the studies described in this portion of the paper rely upon the CRSP Tape in part or in full. The evidence of Fama, et al. [28], and Blume [13], among others, suggests that the time series regressions conform well to the assumptions of the least squares models and to the assumptions of the market model itself.[13]

The market model (or more precisely, the residual u_{it}) has been applied in the examination of the announcement effect of several types of information items. The method was first applied by Fama, et al. [28] to stock split and stock dividend announcements. The measure of abnormal return used in this study was a simple average of the u_{it}'s across securities to form u_t, the average abnormal return in month t. The u_t was then cumulated over several months, starting 29 months prior to the split date and ending 30 months after the split date to form U_t. Since the expected value of u_{it} is zero, the expected value of u_t and U_t is also zero. A nonzero value would imply abnormal returns. The evidence indicates that the values of u_t are essentially zero after the date of the stock splits and dividends. The implication is that once the news of a stock split or dividend has been made public, no abnormal returns can be earned.

Scholes [61] has also applied the method to an examination of the security price reaction to secondary distributions and rights offerings, with essentially the same results. Although there is a negative return associ-

---

[13]The details of the specification tests are discussed in the last section of the Appendix.

ated with the secondary offering, the magnitude of the price decline is unrelated to the size of the issue but is, in fact, related to the vendor of the secondary distribution. Scholes finds that offerings by corporate officers and the corporation itself (and to a lesser extent offerings by mutual funds) are associated with the largest price decline. However, Scholes' data indicate that once knowledge of the offering has become public, no abnormal returns can be earned thereafter.

This method has also been applied to accounting earnings announcements. Ball and Brown [5] examined the association between unexpected changes in earnings and unexpected changes in price (i.e., the u_{it}). Their earnings expectation model is a form of the market model, except that first differences in accounting earnings are inserted for R_{it}, and a market-wide index of first differences in earnings is the market factor. Their study found that once the annual earnings announcements have been released, no abnormal returns can be earned.[14] Moreover, their evidence indicates that the market is able to form unbiased assessments of the unexpected earnings component (the forecast error, to use their terminology) approximately one to two months prior to the announcement.

The Ball and Brown study extended the research method in a manner that has special relevance for accounting research. By examining the behavior of the u's in the months *prior* to the earnings announcement, Ball and Brown were able to construct an Abnormal Performance Index (API), which reflects the abnormal return associated with knowing the earnings figure in advance of the market.

The Abnormal Performance Index is computed in the following manner, where the strategy under study encompasses several time periods and several securities:

$$\text{API}_T = \frac{1}{N} \sum_{i=1}^{N} \prod_{t=1}^{T} (1 + u_{it})$$

where

T = number of time periods
N = number of securities
u_{it} = defined as before

Note that computation is similar to the computation of terminal wealth (assuming initial wealth equals one dollar) of a portfolio where $1/N$ dollars have been invested in each security at the beginning of period 1 and held to the end of period T. The only difference in the computation of API is that u_{it} has been inserted where R_{it} would normally appear.[15] While this is only one way in which the u_{it} could be aggregated over time across securities, the API is more appealing than simply summing the u_{it}'s over t and i, which is the aggregation procedure used in Fama, et al. [28]. The latter procedure implies an unusual portfolio policy of always having $1/N$ dollars invested in each security at the beginning of each period. At the very minimum, the existence of transactions costs makes such a policy less appealing than the buy and hold policy implied by the API.

The API has a convenient intuitive interpretation. Suppose a clairvoyant offered to provide the earnings number (actually the sign of the forecast error) T months prior to the release of the earnings report. What is the most an individual investor would be willing to pay for such information? The API is an *ex post* analogy to the concept of the value of perfect information (about the sign of the earnings forecast error), a concept commonly used in decision theory (see Howard [38]). It is not precisely clear how far the interpretation of the API can be extended to a complete value of information approach (see Feltham [31] and Feltham and Demski [32]). For example, competing sources of information (e.g., the information content of dividends) must also be considered. Hence, one must be careful in interpreting the API as the value of earn-

---

[14]The implications of these findings will be discussed later.

[15]See Fisher [35] for further discussion of the computation of portfolio returns.

ings information.[16] However, at the very least, the API can be interpreted as an operational index of association between accounting data and security prices.

Ball and Brown compute the earnings forecast error from a market model form. The coefficients of the model are assessed from a time series regression, and the model provides a basis for forming expectations about earnings conditional upon the observed *ex post* value of market earnings factor. The residual from the equation is the forecast error (or unexpected earnings component, assuming that the model properly specifies expectations). With knowledge of only the sign of the forecast error twelve months prior to the earnings announcement, it is possible to earn an abnormal return of approximately 8.5 per cent per year. It is interesting to compare this statistic with the abnormal return that could be earned, if the investor knew the sign of the API itself for each security twelve months in advance. The abnormal return earned would be 16.5 per cent, and the implication is that approximately one-half of the given security's API can be explained by the sign of the forecast error of accounting earnings.

The API analysis has been extended to a comparison of alternative earnings methods (specifically, controversy over the interperiod allocation of taxes) in a recent study by Beaver and Dukes[12]. This study examined a broader class of earnings expectations models and several methods of transforming earnings before placing the earnings' variables in the expectations models. The findings were that earnings with deferral (i.e., earnings as reported) had the largest API, earnings without deferral were next, and cash flow had the lowest API. This study illustrates how the API analysis

can be used to assess the relative degree of association between alternative accounting measures and security price changes. The precise implications of such associations for accounting research will be discussed in the next section of the paper. Incidentally, the Beaver and Dukes study also found that once the earnings report was released, no abnormal returns were associated with knowledge of the sign of the forecast error.

Two additional research methods for examining the information content of earnings have been developed by Beaver [8]. The first is an analysis of the volume of securities traded in periods surrounding the announcement of earnings. The second is an analysis of the return variability in periods surrounding the announcement date. The primary advantage of both methods is that they do not require any specification of investor expectation models concerning accounting earnings variables.

The major premise of the price variability test is that if accounting earnings lead to changes in the equilibrium prices of securities, then the variance of price changes (i.e., returns) should be greater in periods when earnings are reported than in nonreported periods. The price change variable used in the Beaver study was an estimate of the u_{it} from the market model. The variance of u_{it} during the week of the announcement was then compared with the variance during the nonreport periods. The variance, on the average, was 70 per cent higher in the report week than at other times during the year.

The finding was consistent with the hypothesis that earnings reports convey information in the sense of leading to changes in equilibrium prices. On the surface, this finding might appear to conflict with Brown and Ball's finding that investors are able to form unbiased estimates of the forecast error in advance of the announcement of the earnings. However, it is important here to distinguish between an unbiased forecast and an efficient forecast, in the statistical sense of the term.[17] Even though the earnings estimate may be unbiased in an *ex ante* sense, there still can be a great deal of "sur-

---

[16]Other differences are also immediately apparent. The value of information is an *ex ante* concept, while the API is derived from *ex post* relationships. Thus, the value of information is an expected value derived from summing over the entire state space, while the API reflects the realization of the *single* state which has occurred. Also, the value of information must be assessed in terms of the impact upon the multi-period consumption behavior and consequent effect upon the utility of investors. In this sense, the API constitutes neither an upper nor a lower bound on the value of information.

[17]See Beaver [8] for a more complete discussion.

prise" at the actual outcome (i.e., the actual earnings figure). The evidence on price variability also indicates that the adjustment to the earnings announcement is very rapid. In terms of the variability measure, the effect of the announcement is largely dissipated by the end of the week of the announcement, because there is virtually no abnormal price change variability in the weeks following the announcement.

The volume analysis examines the extent to which an event can alter individual investor expectations sufficiently, such that they incur transactions costs to alter their portfolio holdings. A market model was used to describe the process generating the percentage of shares traded in a given week. The parameters of the model were estimated using regression techniques. The residual from the model is a measure of the abnormal volume in a security given the market-wide volume that occurred that week. An analysis of the volume in the weeks surrounding the announcement of earnings indicated that volume is approximately 30 per cent higher in the week of the announcement than during other periods. The effect is largely dissipated by the end of the week of the announcement. The evidence is consistent with the contention that earnings reports alter investor expectations sufficiently that they will incur transactions costs to alter their portfolios.

A major difference between the price variability analysis and the volume analysis is that the former deals with the effect of an event at the market level (i.e., by examining changes in equilibrium prices), while the latter deals with the effects of an event upon the expectations of individual investors.[18] The volume analysis may provide some insight into the extent to which investors hold heterogeneous expectations, since an unusually large number of exchanges of shares at earnings report times in part reflects the fact that the buyer and sellers hold different expectations.[19] The issue of heterogeneous ex-

pectations is one of general interest in research into investor behavior, but it is of special interest to accounting. For example, a related topic is the extent to which accounting data induce heterogeneous expectations among investors and, hence, an exchange of shares without changing the equilibrium price of the security. The issue becomes important because nonzero transactions costs are incurred as a result of the exchange of shares, and such costs represent an external drain on the system, as opposed to a reallocation of wealth among the investors.

Although these two analyses are appealing because they do not require a specification of investors' expectations, for that reason they are limited in the scope of research topics they can address. They are particularly useful for exploring the announcement effects of a given event (e.g., annual earnings report) and can easily be extended to similar events such as interim reports (see May [51]) and to dividend announcements. However, they are not useful in discriminating between two events reported simultaneously (e.g., earnings with deferral versus earnings without deferral). Yet, the evaluation of alternative accounting methods involves precisely that problem (i.e., both measures are reported simultaneously).

The Beaver study also replicated the findings of the two previously discussed studies of earnings reports, but using weekly data. The expected abnormal return for the eight week period following the announcement of the earnings was essentially zero. Note that the three studies differed with respect to (a) firms studied, (b) years studied, and (c) interval over which return was computed (i.e., monthly vs. weekly returns). In all cases, the findings were the same—no abnormal return can be earned on publicly available earnings reports. The empirical evidence is remarkably consistent in this respect. The implications of this finding for accounting research will be explored in the next section.

---

[18]See Beaver [8] for a more complete discussion of this issue.

[19]It is possible that the earnings reports revealed changes in the riskiness of the security and that part of the volume is induced by this factor. However, the security in question would have to be a substantial

portion of the portfolio of some individuals before this would occur. The investors would have to be poorly diversified.

The studies discussed thus far have been concerned with rates of changes in security prices (i.e., returns) rather than with the level of prices per se. However, there is an extensive literature on valuation theory that expresses a direct relationship between accounting variables (e.g., earnings) and the value of the firm (or its securities). The Miller and Modigliani [54] theory is one prominent example. The theory postulates a relationship between value of the firm and permanent earnings. Miller and Modigliani (MM) also provide empirical evidence that reported earnings, adjusted for measurement error through the use of instrumental variables, are the most important explanatory variable in the prediction of the market value of electric utility firms (see Miller and Modigliani [52]).[20] The appeal of the MM approach is that the variables included in the regression model were supported by a tightly reasoned underlying theory that indicates precisely what variables should be included and what variables should be omitted from the valuation equation. A similar approach was adopted by Brown [16] in an examination of the valuation of railroad firms. In an extension of the MM approach, Brown [16] examined the relative ability of alternative income measures to predict the value of the firm. Currently, research is underway by Brooks [15], who is examining the relative predictive ability of alternative income methods with respect to the market value of steel firms.

This method also readily lends itself to a cross sectional analysis of differences in accounting methods. The significance of this is that the previous research was primarily concerned with examining the time series behavior of returns in a given security to see if abnormal returns could be earned in that security by using a trading scheme based on some information item. The results from different firms were pooled to obtain an "average" result, but there was no attempt to make cross sectional comparisons of the return behavior of different securities. In other words, these studies have not addressed the issue of whether the securities are "appropriately priced" vis-a-vis one another. In order to address this issue, an equilibrium model must be introduced to specify what "appropriately priced" means. Currently, there are three major models, the time-state preference approach of Hirshleifer [37], the two-parameter capital asset pricing model of Sharpe [63], Lintner [45], [46] and Mossin [55], and the MM "risk class" model. As indicated earlier, the time-state preference model is the most general, but at present, it is not operational. To date, neither the capital asset pricing model nor the MM model has been used to address the issue of appropriate security pricing in an accounting context. The appeal of the MM model is that it readily lends itself to specification in terms of accounting variables (e.g., see the MM electric utility study). The appeal of the capital asset pricing model is that it is more general and does not rely upon the operationally restrictive assumption of a "risk class." In the context of capital asset pricing model, there is only one risk class, and every security is a member of that class.

One promising application of the capital asset pricing model is the examination of the relationship between accounting variables and the riskiness of securities.[21] As will be shown later in the paper, the capital asset pricing model suggests that the β_i in the market model represents the contribution of security i to the riskiness of an investor's

---

[20]The errors-in-variables problem is a common one that is faced when using accounting data as independent variables. Hence, this problem and solutions to it (such as instrumental variables) are extremely relevant to accounting research. Another application is to use accounting variables themselves as instrumental variables for other variables, such as security risk (see Beaver, Kettler, Scholes[11]).

[21]The concept of risk is greatly altered in a simplified setting. For example, in a time-state preference world, the consumption-investment process can be explained without ever formally introducing the concept of risk, as it is defined in the two-parameter approach. The dispersion of outcomes across states takes on no particular significance in the more complete approach. Measuring something called "risk" in terms of variability of outcomes only arises when the objects of choice are simplified and described by statistics, such as the mean and standard deviation, that serve to summarize the complex bundle of claims that each security represents. In a u-σ approach, the standard deviation is used to capture the variety of outcomes and, as such, is referred to as the riskiness of the security. The Appendix describes this relationship in more detail.

portfolio (see the Appendix for details).[22] There also exist financial statement variables, which long have been viewed as reflecting some dimension of the risk of a security.

Recent research by Beaver, Kettler and Scholes [11] has investigated the association between accounting determined measures of security riskiness and β_i from the market model. There were two major findings in the study. (1) There is significant contemporaneous association between the accounting risk measures and the market determined risk measure β_i. The finding supports the contention that the accounting risk measures are consistent with the underlying information set used by the market in assessing the riskiness of securities. (2) The accounting risk measures can be used as instrumental variables in a way that will lead to superior forecasts of future market determined risk measures than would be possible from the use of models using past observed values.

The significance of this research method from the point of view of the market is that it provides some insight into what information is used in assessing the relative riskiness of securities. The assessment of relative risk in turn implies a setting of a price for the security, such that the expected return is commensurate with the risk. In this sense, examining the association of accounting variables with respect to market determined risk measures is merely the other side of the coin of examining the return behavior. The method is applicable to a time series analysis (i.e., changes in β over time) and to cross sectional comparisons (i.e., examining differences in β across firms). The method is also applicable from the point of view of the individual investor in assessing the risk of securities, such that he can select an optimal portfolio. The method can be extended to an examination of the relative predictive

ability of alternative accounting measures and to the question of appropriate security pricing in an accounting context. Moreover, later discussion will suggest that under appropriate conditions, security analysis reduces to an estimate of β_i, the systematic risk measure.

The implications of the research fall into three categories: (1) A set of research methods are provided that can be applied to a variety of research topics. (2) A set of findings are provided that have further implications for the type of research topics and methods that are appropriate for accounting research. Conversely, the findings also imply a set of topics and methods that are irrelevant or inappropriate for accounting research. (3) A theoretical and empirical foundation is provided with which the issue of information evaluation can be addressed; the result is a program for future research in accounting. Although item (1) is most directly related to the charge of the committee, items (2) and (3) must be discussed first.

4. Implications of Findings

The nature of the findings is two-fold. (1) Evidence is provided regarding the efficiency of the market in processing accounting information. (2) The evidence indicates an association exists between accounting data and security prices both in the context of returns and risk measures. The implication is that the market acts as if it uses accounting data in setting equilibrium prices. Alternatively stated, accounting data are consistent in many respects with the underlying information set used by the market. The consistency reflects either or both of two possible states of the world. The market literally uses accounting data, or the market uses other sources of information where these sources and accounting data reflect the same underlying relationships. Implications of this will be discussed in the final section. In this section, the discussion will be largely devoted to the issue of the efficiency of the market.

The Efficient Market Hypothesis. The efficiency of the market can be defined in a

[22]Even without relying upon the capital asset pricing model, it can be shown that an individual security's contribution to portfolio risk will be a function of β_i. However, in general, the function will be investor-specific and will depend upon the optimal proportion of security i in the portfolio. The capital asset pricing model states that the opportunity set for all investors is linear. Hence, β_i becomes an unambiguous measure of risk across individual investors.

variety of ways, including many definitions that would be nonoperational and, hence, would preclude empirical testing. For example, efficiency could be defined in terms of the relationship of the security price and the true (or intrinsic) value of the security. However, left to that form, the hypothesis would be too vague and would elude empirical testing unless the true value of the security could be made operational. Efficiency could also be defined directly in terms of prices, and, in fact, much of the discussion in the accounting literature concerning "functional fixation" by investors is expressed in terms of prices. However, it is important to note that most of the existing work has expressed tests of efficiency in terms of changes in price (i.e., returns). In a recent review of the literature, Fama [26] presented a thorough exposition of the definitions of market efficiency, the arguments supporting the efficient market hypothesis, and the existing research regarding the extent to which the evidence confirms or fails to confirm the efficient market hypothesis. His comments will be briefly discussed here, but the reader is referred to the Fama article for a more extensive treatment of the subject.

Fama defines the following expected return model (which he refers to as a "fair game" model): Let

$$z_{i,t+1} = (r_{i,t+1} | \lambda_{t+1}, \Phi_t) - E(r_{i,t+1} | \Phi_t) \quad (1)$$
$$E(z_{i,t+1} | \lambda_{t+1}, \Phi_t) = 0$$

where

λ_{t+1} = any trading scheme implemented in the interval t to t+1 based upon information Φ_t.

$z_{i,t+1}$ = the excess return for security i in period t+1 (i.e., the difference between the observed return and the equilibrium expected return)

$(r_{i,t+1} | \lambda_{t+1}, \Phi_t)$ = the observed return for security i in period t+1, conditional upon trading scheme λ_{t+1} and information Φ_t.

$E(r_{i,t+1} | \Phi_t)$ = the equilibrium expected return which is the return that fully reflects the information available in period t (Φ_t).

so that the sequence z_i is a "fair game" with respect to information Φ and trading scheme λ. There are two properties of the model worth noting: (1) Since the expected value of $z_{i,t+1}$ is zero, any trading scheme based on Φ_t has an expected *excess* return of zero. Note that the equilibrium expected return conditional upon the information set is determined from the particular expected return theory being used (e.g., the Sharpe capital asset pricing model [63]). (2) If it is further assumed that the equilibrium expected return is nonnegative, then the set of one-security-and-cash mechanical trading rules based only on information set Φ_t cannot have greater expected returns than a policy of buying-and-holding the security during the future period in question. Both properties of the "fair game" efficient market model are stated in such a manner that they can be subjected to empirical testing.

By defining the information set Φ_t in various ways, it is possible to distinguish between various degrees of market efficiency. Fama delineates three major forms. (1) The *weak* form states that equilibrium expected returns (prices) "fully reflect" the sequence of past returns (prices). This implies that there are no superior trading rules possible based solely upon a knowledge of past security returns (e.g., chartist techniques). It does permit the possibility that superior trading rules may exist based upon other information publicly available in period t. (2) The semi-strong form defines the relevant information set as all publicly available information (e.g., financial statements). If the market is efficient in this sense, no trading rules based upon publicly available information will permit the investor to earn an excess return. However, it is still possible to earn superior returns with "inside information" (i.e., information over which the decision maker has monopoly control or information not generally available to others). (3) The *strong* form of the efficient market asserts that no superior trading rules exist, even for those rules that incorporate inside information.

The sufficient conditions for an efficient market in the strictest sense of the term are extremely stringent and obviously are not met in practice.[23] However, it is important to note that they are *sufficient*, but not *necessary*, conditions for market efficiency. It is difficult to specify *a priori* the extent to which the presence of such factors as non-zero transactions cost and inside information induce inefficiency in the markets.

For example, consider inside information. How widely does information have to be disseminated in the market before it is no longer "inside information"? The answer will depend upon the nature of the arbitrage process that brings prices into equilibrium. Similarly, it is difficult to specify the impact of transactions costs. Hence, it is inappropriate to judge the merits of the efficient market hypothesis based upon the "realism" of its assumptions (i.e., the sufficient conditions needed for the model to hold). Ultimately, the model must be judged in the light of the extent to which its testable predictions conform to observed market price behavior. This is the task of empirical research, to which we now turn.

Tests of the weak form of the efficient market have taken two major forms. The first are tests of serial dependence in the return series. It can be shown that one implication of the fair game model is the serial correlation of the z_i's, for all lags must be zero. If one is further willing to assume a stationary expected return over the sample period, this property can be empirically examined by computing the serial correlation for the observed return series over the sample period. The second test is the use of filter rules to determine if, even though observed correlations are nonzero, the correlations are large enough to produce superior trading schemes. Research of these types has

a long history, of which the work by Fama [21] and Fama and Blume [27] are two recent examples.[24] The results strongly support the efficient market hypothesis particularly for returns of longer than a day. There does exist some small positive dependence in day-to-day returns. However, the filter rules needed to take advantage of such dependence generate so many transactions that the marginal profits fail to cover even the minimal transactions costs that would be incurred by a floor trader on the exchange.

Tests of the semi-strong form have also supported the efficient market hypothesis. In many respects this research is most relevant to accounting, because financial statements are contained in the information set, which includes all publicly available information. Hence, any evidence with respect to market efficiency for one type of publicly available information set is helpful to forming priors about the degree of efficiency one would expect to observe when examining another type of public information. In other words, if the market appears to be efficient with respect to one kind of publicly available information, this finding conditions our priors with respect to other kinds as well. Moreover, the research methods developed by this body of research can be applied, and in fact have been applied, to examining market efficiency with respect to accounting data.

The research discussed in the previous section dealt with efficiency in the semi-strong form. The evidence cited in that section dealt with a wide variety of information contexts, and the evidence was remarkably consistent in its support of the efficient market in its semi-strong form. In fact, to my knowledge, there is not a single prominent empirical study of security price behavior that has documented an inefficiency in the semi-strong form. Since accounting is most immediately concerned with market efficiency in this form, the existence of such evidence cannot be ignored when conducting research in accounting. The implications

[23]Fama lists three conditions: (1) all available information is costless and equally available to all market participants, (2) there are no transactions costs, and (3) all participants agree on the implications of information for current price and the distribution of future prices (i.e., homogeneous expectations). These assumptions are discussed in greater detail in the Appendix.

[24]Much of the earlier work appears in the text: Paul Cootner (ed.), *The Random Character of Stock Market Prices*. Cambridge: M.I.T., 1964.

will be drawn out more fully later.

With respect to the strong form, the evidence is sparse. As indicated earlier, Scholes' evidence with respect to the "vendor effect" in secondary distributions indicates inside information can be used to attain superior returns. There is also some evidence by Niederhoffer and Osborne [56] that on a transaction-to-transaction basis, there is a potential for superior returns if the investor had access to the specialists' book. The question arises as to how pervasive the opportunities for abnormal returns due to inside information are. There is no direct answer to the question, for by its very nature, inside information is difficult to isolate even on an *ex post* basis. However, there is some convincing evidence of an indirect nature that comes from a series of studies of mutual fund performance, of which the Jensen study is the most recent and more thorough member. Jensen [40] found that mutual fund returns fail to cover research costs and brokerage commissions in the sense that, after the deduction of the expense, the net return to the holder of a mutual fund share was below that which could be obtained from a simple strategy of buying-and-holding a portfolio of the same riskiness. These results not only apply in aggregate, but additional tests were conducted in an attempt to isolate superior individual funds. Jensen was unable to find any fund that had consistently superior performance over time. There are two interpretations of this evidence: (1) Even though inside information may exist, it is not pervasive enough for mutual funds to cover the incremental costs they incur in trying to attain access to and to act upon such information. (2) Inside information is pervasive, but mutual fund managers are not privy to it or do not have the financial resources to act upon the information once they have it. Given the sizable financial resources of mutual funds and the extent to which mutual fund personnel are continuously involved in all segments of the business and financial communities, the latter interpretation is not very persuasive.

Functional Fixation and the Efficient Market. The term *market efficiency* is not in popular usage in the accounting literature, where the issue has been raised in terms of functional fixation (see Ijiri, Jaidicke, and Knight [39] for one of the earlier, more explicit statements of the functional fixation hypothesis).[25] In essence, the implication of the functional fixation hypothesis is that two firms (securities) could be alike in all "real" economic respects and yet sell for different prices, simply because of the way the accountant reported the results of operations. The implication is that the market ignores the fact that observed signals are generated from different information systems. Hence, it does not distinguish between numbers generated by different accounting methods either over time or across firms. Needless to say, this implies market inefficiency. However, the interesting part of this hypothesis is that it is phrased in a context such that it is not directly confronted by the earlier empirical work cited.

The earlier work examined the possible existence of abnormal rates of returns (price changes), while the functional fixation hypothesis is stated in terms of prices. The advocates of functional fixation might contend that the return evidence does not directly bear on their hypothesis, because the prices might be out of equilibrium permanently. Hence, no abnormal rate of return would occur in the holding period returns for any finite period. The reply is that market inefficiency becomes more implausible the longer one posits that the inefficiency exists. For example, at one extreme, many would admit that securities could be improperly priced for some small instant in time until the next transaction is recorded reflecting the new information. However, fewer would agree that disequilibrium could exist for a day, even fewer would posit inefficiency for a week, and so on. The functional fixation hypothesis as described above is a rather extreme form of the market inefficiency argument, in that it implies

---

[25]Although the phenomenon was originally described in a management decision, time-series context (i.e., a change in measurement methods over time), Mlynarczyk [53] extended the implications of the phenomenon to an investor decision, cross sectional context.

that disequilibrium could exist indefinitely and presumably permanently.

Apart from the lack of *a priori* appeal that such an hypothesis may possess, the nature of the test implied by the hypothesis and the available, direct evidence should be examined. In this respect, the Jensen study [42] is one well known example. The findings of the study were based upon responses of financial analysts with respect to their price predictions on two hypothetical electronics firms. The findings were consistent with the functional fixation hypothesis. While the purpose of this paper is not to indict the research methods of others, there are two points worth mentioning: (1) There was no economic motivation for the analysts to conduct an intensive analysis and make "good" price predictions. It is difficult to see how an inherently economic decision setting (i.e., information processing) can be properly tested where no economic payoffs are involved. The lack of economic incentive is a point that has been raised before with respect to behavioral studies of this nature, and I do not wish to dwell on it here. However, I do have grave doubts that such findings (showing that individuals process data in a naive manner when there are no economic payoffs involved) can be reasonably extrapolated to actual market behavior. (2) Even if we assume that the study is a correct reflection of the manner in which analysts actually behave, we must further assume that the analysts' behavior affects the security price formation process, before we can extrapolate the findings to actual market behavior. There is considerable evidence by another Jensen [40], among others, to suggest that analysts may not be a relevant group upon whom to test this hypothesis. The evidence on mutual fund performance indicates that the analysts paid by the mutual funds are able to earn only normal returns on the portfolios, before considering management fees and transactions costs. After such costs, the return is actually below what would be the expected return for a randomly selected portfolio of the same degree of riskiness. Hence, analysts may not be very important in the price determination process. At the

very least, their role is unclear.[26]

Although the research by O'Donnell [57], [58] and Mlynarczyk [53] on the interperiod tax allocation issue for electric utilities generally supports market efficiency, it is difficult to interpret. The tax allocation issue is not purely an accounting measurement issue, since some rate making bodies (i.e., the state power commissions) make rate decisions based upon the reported numbers. Hence, the use of flow through versus normalized could have an economic impact as well (see Livingstone [47]). Industrial firms do not face this problem. Some preliminary findings by Beaver and Dukes [12] indicate that the market adjusts, both for the interperiod tax allocation differences and for depreciation method differences, when setting prices for securities. But additional research is needed, particularly in a cross sectional context.

5. The Role of Information and Issues of Information Evaluation

The discussion will start with an investor decision context that has been traditionally assumed in addressing external information issues and then will proceed to revise that context in the light of research discussed thus far.

The original context was that of intrinsic value analysis and is perhaps best illustrated in the approach to security analysis as postulated by Graham, Dodd, and Cottle [36]. However, there are at least three major deficiencies in the use of such an approach as a decision context to address external information issues.[27] (1) It is a *single security* analysis and does not adequately deal with portfolio aspects of the investment decision. (2) It implicitly assumes an inefficient market, which conflicts with the considerable

---

[26] An even more damaging criticism is that attempts to draw inferences regarding market efficiency from the observed behavior of individuals is committing the fallacy of composition alluded to earlier. More will be said about this later.

[27] The intrinsic value approach essentially involves a determination of the true (or intrinsic) worth of a security through an analysis of fundamentals and a comparison of the intrinsic value with the observed market price. Significant differences imply the existence of overvalued or undervalued securities, upon which a trading scheme is based.

evidence in favor of market efficiency. (3) It is a partial equilibrium analysis, in that it focuses only upon the return to a *single investor* and ignores his impact on the rest of the system. Hence, as a research method (i.e., as a decision context within which to assess information issues), such an approach is seriously deficient for all of the reasons cited above. However, an examination of these factors in detail will provide further insights into appropriate research methods.

Accounting Data and Portfolio Theory. Portfolio theory (e.g., Markowitz [49], [50] among others) provides an alternative (and more appealing) decision context within which to evaluate accounting information issues.[28] The Markowitz model (in and of itself) takes no position on the efficiency of the market. In fact, we can recast the intrinsic value approach within the framework of the Markowitz model. In this sense, the search for undervalued and overvalued securities is implicit in the search for portfolios that are members of the efficient set. More importantly, the portfolio model emphasizes that the relevant level of concern to the decision maker is the portfolio level, not the individual security level. Hence, the behavior of the individual securities' returns is relevant only to the extent to which it impacts on the portfolio parameters. For example, it is now well known that a measure of an individual security's riskiness is not its total variability but rather its systematic variability with other securities in the portfolio. In the context of the market model, the variance of the portfolio's return can be decomposed in the following manner.[29]

$$\sigma^2(R_{pt}) = 1/N \, \overline{\sigma^2(u_{it})} + \bar{\beta}^2 \, \sigma^2(R'_{mt})$$

The first factor is referred to as the individ-

ualistic factor or avoidable risk of a security, because its effect on $\sigma^2(R_p)$ can be effectively driven to zero by merely increasing N. The β_j reflects the systematic risk or unavoidable risk of a security, because it cannot be diversified away by increasing the number of securities in the portfolio. Hence, the decision maker clearly would be unwilling to pay anything for any data that only would permit him to reduce the variance of the individualistic factor.

This is an extremely important implication for accounting, because all of accounting's concern about errors in accounting data has stressed only the *individual security* level, with no consideration of the portfolio context. For example, suppose it was empirically demonstrated that the existing reporting rules led to prediction errors in the return distributions of several individual securities. Such evidence is insufficient to indict current reporting methods. The reason is that investors may be able to diversify out of the errors in securities, and hence, it is in the nature of an individualistic or avoidable risk.

Errors, independent in nature (i.e., uncorrelated with market factors), can be effectively diversified away and are not of major concern. Only systematic errors, which still persist at the portfolio level, are detrimental to optimal predictions and decisions. This implication substantially alters the entire context within which accounting has traditionally viewed errors in accounting data and issues of information alternative.

From the viewpoint of research methods, any method that is essentially a single security approach and ignores the portfolio aspects of investor decisions is seriously deficient. However, thus far we have not addressed the issue raised earlier—the role in accounting data in an efficient market.

Accounting Data, Portfolio Analysis, and Efficient Markets. If we introduce the notion of an efficient market, then securities are "properly priced" vis-a-vis each other, such that expected return and risk are commensurate. One such model that specifies the appropriate relationship between ex-

---

[28]Remember, however, that even the two-parameter portfolio theory referred to here is a simplification of a more complete process.

[29]$\sigma^2(u_{it})$ is the average variance of individualistic factors (u_{it}). $\sigma^2(R'_{mt})$ is the variance of the market factor. $\bar{\beta}^2$ is the average β squared. The variables for the market model were originally introduced on p. 12. Further details on the model are presented in the Appendix.

pected returns (and hence, prices) of securities is the capital asset pricing models of Sharpe [63], Lintner [45], [46], and Mossin [55]. The model states:

$$E(R_{it}) = R_{ft} + [E(R_{mt}) - R_{ft}]\frac{\sigma(R_{it}, R_{mt})}{\sigma^2(R_{mt})}$$

or with some simplifying assumptions[30]

$$E(R_{it}) \simeq R_{ft}(1 - \beta_i) + \beta_i E(R_{mt})$$

where

$$\beta_i \simeq \frac{\sigma(R_{it}, R_{mt})}{\sigma^2(R_{mt})}$$

Note that the expected return on an individual security is a linear function of its systematic risk (i.e., either its covariance with the market portfolio or its β, a measure of its responsiveness to the market factor). There are at least two implications worth noting: (1) The individualistic factor does not enter into the pricing of the asset (or equivalently, its expected return). This is consistent with our earlier discussion, where it was concluded that individualistic risk was irrelevant to the investor. It is not too surprising that the same result is obtained in an equilibrium model for all securities. The reason, of course, is the same. The individualistic component of return does not enter into the pricing of capital assets, because the variance of that component can be eliminated through diversification. The market will not compensate an investor for incurring a risk that could be trivially eliminated by merely increasing the number of securities in his portfolio. Hence, the capital asset pricing model states that the only variable that determines the differential riskiness among securities is the systematic risk coefficient, β_i. (2) The only variable on the RHS of the equation that is specific to security i is its systematic risk coefficient. In estimating the expected return for the security, several variables must be assessed, in-

cluding the return on the riskless asset, R_f, and the expected return on the market portfolio, $E(R_m)$. However, both of these parameters are economy-wide variables and are common to the valuation equations of all securities. Hence, within the context of the capital asset pricing model, security analysis (i.e., the assessment of security specific parameters for a decision model) reduces to the prediction of the value of the systematic risk coefficient. This sort of analysis replaces the intrinsic value approach as the major thrust of security analysis. Moreover, the role of accounting data becomes its predictive ability with respect to β.[31] Hence, the β analysis becomes extremely important as a research method, if the object is to assess the value of information to the *individual investor* and if market efficiency is accepted as a fact of life.

Moreover, in light of the research cited earlier regarding the evidence strongly in favor of market efficiency, particularly in its *semi-strong* form, any research method that relies upon the assumption of market inefficiency in addressing an information issue should be seriously questioned. It was stated earlier that within the context of information evaluation to the individual investor, the information evaluator must specify how the decision maker will use accounting data in altering his investment behavior. The scientist, in providing evidence, must conduct experiments that implicitly assume something about how the investors will use the data. The value of the experiment, in part, rests upon the plausibility of the scientist's assumption in this respect. One such assumption is that the investors use accounting data to search the market for undervalued and overvalued securities. In light of the available evidence, such a decision context is not a meaningful way in which to address the accounting information decision, because the set of erroneously priced securities is null. However, this statement does not preclude future testing of the efficiency hypotheses in new contexts and with different methods, and in

---

[30]The assumptions of the capital asset pricing model are discussed in the Appendix. Also, the reasons why β is only an approximation are discussed there.

[31]This argument is developed at greater length in Beaver, Kettler, Scholes [11].

fact, some suggestions for future research in this respect will be offered in the next section of the paper.

The foregoing discussion was not intended as an *a priori* argument for an efficient market.[32] However, if market efficiency is a "correct" statement about the world, then the accounting profession must be prepared to examine accounting issues in a substantially different light than it has thus far. There are at least two reasons for emphasizing the implications of the efficient market. (1) The accounting profession is quite familiar with the implications of market inefficiency. This is so because the preponderance of members of our profession are believers in the inefficient market. Hence, apart from questions of the empirical evidence regarding these two opposing views, I believe accounting must be prepared to evaluate its position, conditional upon each of these states of nature being true. (2) As indicated at the outset of the paper, there is a considerable body of empirical evidence to support the efficient market hypothesis. The purpose of this paper is not to engage in polemics about belief in market inefficiency, since the research has already been interpreted by its authors. There is little I can add of a persuasive nature that has not been discussed before. However, the purpose of the paper is to expose accounting researchers to a literature of which they may not be fully aware and whose implications they may not have fully explored.

Analysis of Information at the Social Level. The value of accounting information cannot be left entirely at the level of the individual investor. Rather, the value of information must be viewed within the context of the entire set of investors, and, in fact, must incorporate the entire society. For example, reconsider the intrinsic value approach. Even if the ability to earn excess returns is a legitimate consideration in the assessment of the value of information to an individual investor, such an analysis is not macro-consistent, because the aggregate return to all investors must be the same and, hence, the excess returns for one individual must be offset against the negative excess returns of those who transacted with the investor who earned the excess returns. In other words, from the point of view of society, total wealth is unchanged and intrinsic value analysis merely implies a reallocation of the wealth.[33] Hence, the ability to earn abnormal returns can never be a valid basis for "assessing the value of information."

Moreover, in an efficient market, the only potential value of accounting information to the individual investor would be the assessment of the risk (and hence, expected return) associated with a given portfolio, which in turn would involve estimation of the systematic risk component for the individual securities that constitute that portfolio. However, it is possible, with the number of securities large enough, that the investor can diversify out of any prediction errors on the individual β's, and hence, accounting is not of any value to the individual investor.[34]

In other words, it is conceivable that the value of accounting information exists only at the social level. The value of accounting information arises from its role in setting equilibrium prices. Of course, the members of society benefit from this function. However, once the information is impounded in the prices, the additional value of the information to the individual investor is zero.

If this is the case, accounting must be prepared to evaluate the value of accounting data in the context of the value of information to "the market as a whole," which is a totally different perspective from that typically adopted in addressing accounting issues. Moreover, it becomes essential that the relationship of accounting data and

---

[32] For example, it would be possible to discuss the precise mechanism that forces the market toward efficiency. Various sorts of mechanisms have been suggested, such as "The Arbitrager" and "The Sophisticated Investor."

[33] The statement refers to wealth, as defined in monetary terms. Of course, a reallocation of wealth may induce a change in the total overall well being of society (e.g., measured in utility terms). However, this merely indicates still another dimension in which the traditional analysis is deficient.

[34] In fact, if the investor literally interpreted the prescriptive implications of the capital asset pricing model, he would buy the market portfolio and lever that portfolio accordingly. This requires no estimation of β's whatsoever.

security prices be specified. From the viewpoint of research methods, it must be stressed that the studies cited in the previous section all adopt this point of view and are completely compatible with it. However, this is not true of any methods used in the accounting research.

The Market for Information. For the analysis to be complete, competing sources of information affecting security prices must also be incorporated into the analysis. Not even the most ardent supporter of accounting data would contend that accounting data is the only source of information available to the market. In other words, it becomes necessary to specify the structure of the market for information where information is viewed as an economic good, for which demand and supply factors must be considered. The specification would include: (1) specification of the competing sources of information, (2) specification of the comparative advantage that each source has in providing given types of information, (3) specification of the cost of each source providing given types of information, (4) any imperfections created in the market by governmental and institutional requirements to disclose or not to disclose certain types of data.

Moreover, there may be more than one information structure that could lead to the same set of equilibrium prices. The implication is that, if the accountant does not provide relevant data, other sources will. In fact, the efficient market hypothesis predicts precisely that. The issue then becomes—are excessive costs of providing that information incurred because of failure to report certain accounting data? This can only be answered by knowing the comparative advantages and costs of competing information sources.

In other words, does the accountant have a comparative advantage in providing any type of data? If he does not provide the optimal information, competing sources will remove such reporting deficiencies. However, there is the possibility that a more optimal solution would be obtained if the accountant can provide the data at a lower cost. Hence, in an efficient market, the central issue becomes one of assessing the costs of alternative methods of providing essentially the "same" information ("same"— the sense of leading to identical set of prices).

Such costs involve not only the direct, "out-of-pocket" costs of data collection, storage and reporting, but other costs as well. For example, arbitrage profits may be incurred because of reporting deficiencies (which is one special type of competing source of information, where the arbitrager must be compensated for the resources he expends in scanning the market for improperly priced securities). Note, the prices respond quickly to available information, but this does not imply that arbitrage profits are zero or even small. In assessing the magnitude of the arbitrage profits, the amount of resources expended must be specified.[35]

The cost issue is further complicated by the fact that alternative information systems may imply differing incidence of costs. For example, one cost of the system is the processing of accounting data by investors. Different systems may impose differing processing costs upon different individual investors, such that some individuals incur less cost under one alternative but others incur more. Problems of comparing these costs across individuals arise.[36]

If different information systems lead to different sets of equilibrium prices, then the problems of information evaluation becomes more complex. The effect of the differing equilibrium prices can only be assessed in terms of their impact upon the multi-period consumption behavior of the

[35]When we view the external reporting problem in the context of a market for information, other insights emerge. For example, note that the value of information is subject potentially to a substantial amount of externalities. The value that one firm reports a given data item may be greatly affected by how many (and which) other firms also report the same data item. Also, the cost structure of providing accounting data is such that there is a large fixed cost associated with preparing the "first" report, but the incremental costs of providing additional copies of that report are virtually zero.

[36]A related issue is that of deciding what portion of the data "processing" will be performed in a uniform manner by some central agent (e.g., the firm) versus what portion will be shifted to the individual investor. At the first level, the anwer will depend upon (1) the extent to which individual investors would process the data in a uniform manner, and (2) the relative cost of processing by a centralized agent versus the individual decision makers.

investors. Hence, a complete analysis of the value of alternative information systems must assess the effect on the underlying preference functions of investors for lifetime consumption patterns. Moreover, the problem of interpersonal comparison or preference function arises, or alternatively, the problem of specifying a social welfare function. Pareto-optimality has been a common solution to problems of this sort. However, research in cooperative decision making (see Wilson [71], [72], [73], [74]) is exploring the properties of alternative solutions.

The Sophisticated versus the Naive Investor. Thus far, little has been said of which or how many investors make the market efficient. In particular, how is the previous analysis affected, if only a small fraction of the total investing public in effect determines the market price, even though it is "efficient"? If the market is efficient and only a few "sophisticated" investors are required to make it efficient, then the remaining investing public can assume that the security price "fully reflects" information available and can make investment decisions on that basis. In an efficient market, all securities will be priced such that there is a single, market determined relationship between risk and return. Hence, the naive investor can get "harmed" in an efficient market in only two ways. (1) He could select a portfolio with risk-return characteristics that are not optimal, given his preference function. This is essentially equivalent to incurring prediction errors with respect to the systematic risk component of the individual securities, which was discussed earlier.[37] (2) He may incur unnecessary transactions costs, altering his portfolio position when such an alteration was not needed. Hence, the volume analysis may provide some insights, as suggested earlier.

To restate the issue, in an efficient market, the naive investor becomes a "price taker" and acts as if the price is an unbiased assessment of the intrinsic value of the security. The naive investor has no comparative advantage in information processing and, hence, he implicitly delegates that task to those that do. The theory of specialization and comparative advantage predicts precisely this, and we should not expect everyone to perform the information processing task. (see Ball [4] for a more detailed discussion).

This insight has important implications for research methods used in accounting. In particular, it demonstrates the fallacy inherent in failing to distinguish between the individuals who comprise the market and the behavior of the market itself. For example, consider some recent application of behavioral methods in accounting to investigate the manner in which individuals process data. The method commits the fallacy of attempting to predict properties of market behavior based upon the behavior of the individuals. As pointed out at the outset of the paper, the aggregation process is seldom that simple. In particular, in the case of securities markets, there is good reason to believe that such evidence is of little value to predicting the behavior of market prices.

6. Implications for Future Research

The research methods described here can be applied to two topics: (1) the efficiency of the market in impounding accounting information in security prices, and (2) the association between alternative accounting measures and security price behavior.

The issue of market efficiency is by no means closed, although the preponderance of empirical evidence supports it. One application of these research methods is a direct extension to an examination of the abnormal return behavior associated with various accounting events. For example, the works by Ball [4] and by Kaplan and Roll [43] directly address the issue of functional fixation in a time series context (i.e., does the market act as if it ignores the fact that the earnings signals come from different generating systems). Potentially a β analysis could also be applied to the issue of changes in accounting methods. One area

---

[37]Within the context of the more complete model, this is essentially equivalent to an investor erroneously stating his wealth constraint, because he believes the intrinsic value of his portfolio is greater than its current market value.

that is particularly lacking is a cross sectional analysis of the functional fixation hypotheses. Beaver and Dukes [12] are currently working in this area, using a β analysis to see if the market assesses differential security risk in a manner that reflects the underlying measurement differences across firms. Another model applicable to a cross sectional context is the MM valuation model.

With respect to the other topic, the association between alternative accounting methods and security price behavior, it is important to point out that the necessity for such research can be established at two levels: (1) Apart from the issue of market efficiency, knowledge of the association between alternative accounting measurement and security prices is an essential part of knowledge of what information is impounded in security prices. The reasons why such knowledge is important to accounting were established earlier. We must specify how prices behave with respect to alternative information systems. One important member of the set of information systems is the one currently used. Hence, the relationship between the current information set and security prices constitutes part of the knowledge we need for a complete analysis. Since this is the only observable relationship we can obtain, it is also likely to be important for specifying how prices would change (if at all) as the system is altered. (2) If the efficient market hypothesis is adopted, then the association with security prices provides a simplified preference ordering with which alternative measurement methods can be ranked. That method which is more highly associated with security prices is more consistent with the underlying information set used in setting equilibrium prices. Hence, subject to a more complete analysis involving competing sources of information and costs of alternative methods, the finding provides prima facie evidence that the method which is more highly impounded ought to be the method reported in the financial statements.[38] In fact, such a reporting policy

would reduce the probability of nonoptimal decisions being made by individuals through prediction errors or through misspecification of the wealth constraint.

However, the ultimate issue is the extent to which this simplified preference ordering is consistent with ordering obtained under a complete analysis. Our current state of knowledge provides little basis for answering that issue at the present time. Essentially, what is needed is a general equilibrium theory under uncertainty that specifies the optimal amount of the economic good *information* that society should produce. Such a theory must be dynamic, in the sense of permitting the probability distributions of actors in the market to be revised in the light of new data. Presently, the general equilibrium theories under uncertainty are static, in the sense that probability distributions remain intact throughout the analysis. In such a context, information has no role. Until general equilibrium theory is extended to the dynamic case, the analysis of the value of information is incomplete in a very fundamental sense.[39]

7. Summary and Conclusions

The major points raised in the paper are:

(1) Any complete program of research into external reporting issues must include research into the relationship between accounting data and security price behavior. Its importance arises from the fact that the multi-period consumption, investment decisions of individuals are inherently affected by their wealth. Since security prices, in part, determine wealth, it is inconceivable that optimal information sets

---

[38]Inevitably, the issue of the relative visibility of the alternative measures arises. The essence of the argument is that the more visible measures will tend to be more highly impounded to security prices. It should be

obvious at this stage that such an argument implies market inefficiency of some form (i.e., semi-strong or strong) depending upon how obscure the nonreported measure is. Incidentally, the visibility issue would not arise where the alternative methods were equally visible or where the nonreported method had a higher association with the market price variable. In the latter instance, the finding would be convincing evidence against functional fixation.

[39]This issue has been discussed in Diamond [20], Hirshleifer [37, Chapter 11], and in Arrow [3]. In part, it involves the concept of transactions or price certainty, as opposed to technological uncertainty which is incorporated into the models.

for investors can be provided by accounting without a knowledge of how accounting data are impounded in security prices.

(2) An examination of portfolio theory suggests that the appropriate context within which to examine information issues is at the portfolio level, not at the level of individual securities. Hence, individual security return errors that are random or independent in nature are not of concern because they can be diversified away. Only errors that are systematic and still persist at the portfolio level are of major concern. This context constitutes a major alteration in the way that measurement errors in accounting have been traditionally viewed.

(3) There is a substantial body of empirical evidence which suggests that the securities markets are efficient, especially in the sense most relevant to accounting (i.e., the semi-strong form). This research is relevant to accounting in two respects, the implications of the findings themselves and the application of the research methods.

(4) If the market is efficient, the economic justification for the existence of accounting and for accounting research must be substantially re-examined in a new context. The traditional "intrinsic value" approach as a prediction-decision context is no longer appealing. In fact, portfolio theory, together with the capital asset pricing models, suggests security analysis reduces to the prediction of the systematic risk coefficient of the individual securities.

(5) Moreover, it is possible that prediction errors on the systematic risk component are avoidable and can be diversified away. If so, then the only purpose of accounting data is to help bring prices into equilibrium. Apart from that task, the accounting data may be valueless to the individual investor. This is an important implication, because the sole role of account-

ing data would be a social, not an individual one.

(6) A complete analysis of the value of accounting data at the social level will, of necessity, require an incorporation of competing sources of information and comparative costs of providing essentially the same information. The central issue is—in what areas, if any, does accounting have comparative advantage in providing information? The problem must be viewed in the context of a market for information, where accounting is only one supplier.

(7) Apart from the implications of the findings, the previous studies provide accounting with a set of research methods that can be used for several purposes.

(a) The research methods can be used to explore the issue of market efficiency in greater depth. Additional elements of the information set can be isolated, and it can be determined whether the market is efficient with respect to that information element. In particular, cross sectional as well as time series tests are needed.

(b) The research methods can be used to examine the relative association between accounting alternatives and security prices. Knowledge of such association is a prerequisite to specifying what data are impounded in prices and how prices might be altered if the information set were altered.

APPENDIX

Brief Review of Market Model and Capital Asset Pricing Model

1. Assumptions

The empirical research has relied heavily upon the "market" model (see Markowitz [49] and Sharpe [62]) and the capital asset pricing models of Sharpe [63], Lintner [45], and Mossin [55]. They are simplifications of a more general model, such as Hirshleifer's [37]. In this sense, the models make the following assumptions.

(1) The multi-period consumption-investment decision can be reduced to a one-period decision involving current consumption and terminal wealth at the end of the first period.[40] Fama [25] has shown that the multi-period problem can be reduced to a one-period decision under very general conditions. The resulting pseudo "one period" utility function (whose arguments are current consumption and terminal wealth) has implicitly imbedded in it the effects of the preference function and opportunity set for the remaining N − 1 decision periods. Hence, the individual can act *as if* he is solving a one-period problem, when, in fact, it is only one step in a recursive process. The conditions are quite general, and hence, the one period formulation does not appear to be a restrictive one.

(2) The objectives of choice can be defined in terms of two-parameters of the probability distribution of returns. In the finite variance case, the two parameters are assumed to be the mean (u) and the standard deviation (σ). This assumption actually involves several additional assumptions.

  (a) The utility of the outcome is independent of its state labeling. This constitutes a major difference between the time-state preference approach and the u-σ approach. To use Hirshleifer's terminology, the u-σ approach assumes a unique utility function for wealth (time-dated, state-labeled consumption claims) that is the same for all possible states. In principle, this assumption appears to be severe, since casual observation will generate many counterexamples. Basically, there is much intuitive evidence that a conditional claim to one unit of consumption in "good" times (e.g., boom) is not of the same value as a conditional claim to a unit of consumption in "bad" times (e.g., depression). Insurance provides one example where even a risk averse individual will accept an "unfair gamble" in order to provide a conditional consumption claim for his family if the state "death" occurs. However, until the state-preference approach is made operational it is virtually impossible to assess the importance of ignoring state labeling, because the ultimate test of a theory is its comparative predictive ability with a u-σ approach.

  (b) The first derivative of the utility function for wealth is assumed to be positive, and the second derivative is assumed to be negative. That is, the individual is assumed to be risk averse.

  (c) The probability distribution of all possible portfolios is assumed to be of the same form.[41] Note that one-security portfolios are a proper subset of all possible portfolios. Since the portfolio returns are a summation of the individual security returns, this assumption requires stability under addition. This implies that each individual security's returns must be a member of the stable family. Moreover, most proofs have relied upon the additional assumptions that the return distributions are symmetric and all securities have the same characteristic exponent (see Fama [21], [22], [30]).

  (d) The original exposition of the models assumed that two parameters of interest were the expected

---

[40]More precisely, the "one period" models actually involve two periods, now and one period from now (e.g., see Fama and Miller [29]).

[41]This is an extremely stringent assumption. Potentially, it could be weakened, but there have been no attempts to do so. Hence, assumption may not be necessary but sufficient.

value and the standard deviation (or in some cases, the variance (Markowitz [49])). This assumes that the variance exists, which is true for only one member of the stable family, the normal distribution. However, Fama [22], [24] has shown that the market model and the capital asset pricing model can be extended to the infinite variance case, of stable, symmetric distributions where the characteristic exponent is greater than one. This extension is important since there is considerable evidence (Fama [21], Mandelbrot [48], Roll [59]) that the characteristic exponent for many classes of securities is less than two, which implies the variance does not exist (i.e., normality does not hold).[42]

(3) Most specifications omit current consumption as an argument of the utility function, which is then stated solely in terms of terminal wealth. Again, in principle, this is an important abstraction of the process, since the underlying multi-period utility is stated solely in terms of consumption. However, Fama and Miller [29] have formulated the one-period problem with current consumption explicitly introduced as a variable, and the results of the model are essentially the same as that of the earlier treatments.

(4) The capital pricing models derive certain conditions for equilibrium in the pricing of securities. In order to obtain such results, the pricing models require additional assumptions not required by the portfolio models of Markowitz or the market model. These assumptions are perfect capital markets and homogeneous expectations. The properties of perfect capital markets are:

(a) no buyer or seller of securities is large enough to affect price,

(b) no external drains on wealth (e.g., transactions costs) from the system exist, and

(c) all actors have equal and costless access to information.[43]

(5) The capital asset models, in extending the earlier work by Tobin [69], also assume the existence of a riskless rate at which all individuals can borrow and lend. The introduction of a riskless rate produces an opportunity set that is linear. Hence, there exist unequivocal measures of risk, and the slope of the risk-return capital market line is the same (i.e., a constant) for all investors at their optimum regardless of the form of their preference functions.

2. The Market Model

The market model is a specification of the stochastic process generating the individual security returns. Simply, the model asserts that security returns are a linear function of a general "market" factor. More precisely, the return on security i is expressed as:

$$R_{it} = \alpha_i + \beta_i R'_{Mt} + u_{it} \qquad (2)$$

where

$$E(u_{it}) = 0.$$
$$\sigma(R'_{mt}, u_{it}) = 0.$$
$$\sigma(u_{it}, u_{jt}) = 0.$$

R_{it} = return on security i in period t.

R'_{mt} = general market factor (hereafter referred to as the market factor) in period t.

u_{it} = the stochastic portion of the individualistic factor reflecting that portion of security i's return which varies independently of R'_{mt}.

---

[42]The characteristic exponent (α) is a measure of the height of the distribution in the tail areas, with a lower α indicating fatter tails. The range of α is, $0 < \alpha \leq 2$. The α for a normal distribution is two. For $\alpha < 2$, the variance is undefined. For $\alpha \leq 1$, the expected value also does not exist.

[43]In other contexts, additional assumptions about the effect of external drains, such as taxes and costs of reorganization upon bankruptcy, have received attention (see Miller and Modigliani [52], [54]).

α_i, β_i = intercept and slope associated with the linear relationship.

The market model asserts that the stochastic portion of a security's return can be decomposed into two elements, a systematic component ($\beta_i R'_{mt}$), which reflects common movement of a single security's return with the market factor, and an individualistic component, u_{it}, which reflects that portion of a security's return that varies independently of the market factor. Intuitively, a motivation for the model can be provided by viewing events as being classified into one of two categories: (1) those events that have economy-wide impacts, which are reflected in the market factor, and (2) those events which have an impact only upon one particular security. Dichotomizing events in this fashion is obviously highly abstractive. In fact, a third class of events immediately would come to mind—industry-wide events. However, previous empirical evidence (King [44]) suggests that omission of an explicit industry factor in the equation is not a serious misspecification of the model.[44]

Within the context of the market model, the variance of portfolio return is defined as (assuming, for simplicity, that equal amounts are invested in each security):

$$\sigma^2(R_p) = \frac{1}{N} \bar{\sigma}_i^2 + (\bar{\beta})^2 \sigma^2(R'_m) \qquad (3)$$

where

$\bar{\sigma}_i^2$ = mean of the variance of the individualistic factor,

$$\bar{\sigma}_i^2 = 1/N \sum_{i=1}^{N} \sigma^2(u_i)$$

$\bar{\beta}$ = mean of β_i's, $\bar{\beta} = 1/N \sum_{i=1}^{N} \beta_i$

$\sigma^2(R'_m)$ = variance of the market factor.

The variance $\sigma^2(R_p)$ is composed of two elements.[45] As N increases, the first term goes to zero and the portfolio variance becomes equal to the second term, $\beta^2 \sigma^2(R'_m)$. Portfolio variances will differ solely according to the magnitude of β, the average of the β_i's of the securities comprising the portfolio. Hence, an individual security's contribution to the riskiness of the portfolio is measured by its β_i, not $\sigma^2(u_i)$.

As equation (3a) shows, the variance of a security's return can differ from that of other securities because of one of two factors, either $\sigma^2(u_i)$ or β_i. The first factor is referred to as the individualistic or avoidable risk of a security, because that risk can be driven to zero through diversification (i.e., by increasing N). For a risk-averse investor (i.e, one who prefers less risk to more risk for a given expected return), it is optimal behavior to select a portfolio where the individualistic riskiness is essentially zero.[46] The β_i is the systematic or unavoidable risk of the security and measures the security's sensitivity to market-wide events. It is called the systematic or unavoidable risk because it is that portion of the variance of the security's return that cannot be diversified away by increasing the number of securities in the portfolio.

The original motivation for the market model was to reduce the number of parameters to estimate. The variance of a portfolio, using the diagonal model, requires an estimation of 2N + 1, which for N = 1000 is 2001 (as compared with 500,500 for the Markowitz model). Another advantage of the market model is that it can be extended to the general case where security return distributions are characterized by the symmetric, stable family of distributions, of which the normal distribution is a special case. Fama [22] has shown that the β_i can still be interpreted as a measure of systematic risk, even in cases where the covariance and variance, strictly speaking, are undefined.

[45]For N = 1 (i.e., for an individual security),

$$\sigma^2(R_i) = \sigma^2(u_i) + \beta_i^2 \sigma^2(R'_m) \qquad (3a)$$

[46]This statement implicitly assumes that the capital asset pricing model holds.

[44]King's [44] study of monthly returns from 1926 through 1960 indicates that the industry factors account for only 10 to 15 per cent of the variation of security returns.

3. The Capital Asset Pricing Models

Sharpe [63], Lintner [45], and Mossin [55] have extended the earlier work on portfolio models to capital asset pricing models, which determine the equilibrium prices for all securities in the market. Essentially, the models start from the assumption that investors are generally risk averse and show that, in equilibrium, capital assets will be priced such that

$$E(R_{it}) = R_{ft} + [(R_{mt}) - R_f] \frac{\sigma(R_{it}, R_{mt})}{\sigma^2(R_{mt})} \quad (4)$$

or alternatively stated

$$R_{it} = R_{ft} + [E(R_{mt}) - R_f] \lambda_{it}$$
$$R_{it} = R_{ft}(1 - \lambda_{it}) + \lambda_{it} E(R_{mt}) \quad (4a)$$

where

$E(R_{it})$ = expected return of asset i for period t.

R_{ft} = rate of return on a riskless asset in period t.

$E(R_{mt})$ = expected return on the market portfolio in period t.

$\lambda_{it} = \dfrac{\sigma(R_{it}, R_{mt})}{\sigma^2(R_{mt})}$.

The capital asset model states that the only variable which determines differential expected returns among securities is the risk coefficient, λ_i. The model further asserts that there is a linear relationship between λ_i and expected return, such that the greater the risk the higher the expected return. In his empirical research on mutual fund performance, Sharpe [64] found that the relationship between risk and return is linear and significant. The rank correlation coefficient between average ex post return and variance of return was +.836. For large portfolios, such as mutual funds, ranking by the variance is equivalent to ranking by λ. Although the models were originally developed under the assumption of finite variance and covariance, Fama [24] has shown that the results extend to the broader class of symmetric stable distributions with finite expected values but infinite variances and covariances.

4. Relationship Between Market Model and Capital Asset Pricing Models

In one sense, there is no necessary relationship between the market model and the capital asset models. The market model is a specification of the stochastic prices generating security returns, and presumably, it is consistent with several equilibrium pricing models of which the Sharpe, Lintner, Mossin models are a subset. By the same token, the capital asset pricing model makes few assumptions about the stochastic process generating returns over time. Hence, acceptance of the market model does not necessarily imply acceptance of the capital assets pricing models, and the converse also holds. However, the similarity in models structure raises the issue of what assumptions are needed to make the two models compatible.

Under some simplifying assumptions, the β_i from the market model will be approximately equal to the λ_{it} from the capital asset pricing model. The assumptions are: (1) $\sigma^2(R'_{mt})$, the variance of the market factor, is essentially equal to $\sigma^2(R_{mt})$, the variance of the return on the market portfolio. (2) Every security constitutes a small fraction of the market portfolio. (3) The variance $\sigma^2(u_{it})$ is not too much larger than $\sigma^2(R_{mt})$.[47] (4) λ_{it} (and β_i) are stationary over time. Under these assumptions,

$$\beta_i \simeq \lambda_i = \frac{\sigma(R_i, R_m)}{\sigma^2(R_m)} .$$

There is not much concern about assumptions (1) through (3) because they are very likely to hold. Assumption (4) is a far less trivial assumption.

Evidence by Blume [13], Jensen [40], and Beaver, Kettler, Scholes [11], suggests that there exists significant cross sectional correlation between security β's computed from

---

[47]In fact, evidence by King [44] and Blume [13] suggests that $\sigma^2(u_{it}) \simeq \sigma^2(R_{mt})$. The precise relationship is

$$\lambda_i = \frac{\beta_i \sigma^2(R'_m) + x_i \sigma^2(u_i)}{\sigma^2(R_m)}$$

where x_i equals the proportion of security i held in the market portfolio.

adjacent, nonoverlapping time periods. The correlation coefficient approaches one for portfolio β's, even for moderate size portfolios. This evidence is consistent with the assumption of underlying stationarity, but much more research is needed before the issue will be sufficiently resolved.

If it is further assumed that R_{ft} is stationary over time, then there will be virtually complete compatibility between the two models, if $\alpha_i = R_f(1 - \beta_i)$. R_{ft} is not strictly stationary over time, but changes in R_{ft} may be small when compared with other sources of variation in R_{it}. Until these issues are finally resolved the distinction between the market model and any particular capital asset pricing model must be kept in mind.

Recently, Roll [60] showed that nontrivial estimation errors for the coefficients of the market model can occur, if R_{ft} and β_i are not stationary over time. Alternative estimation procedures can be used, including the estimation of equation (4a) directly by using exogeneous estimates of R_{ft}. However, evidence by Scholes [61] suggests that this estimation equation does not differ essentially from a direct estimation of (2), for at least the contexts of the information content studies testing the semi-strong form of the efficient market hypothesis.

5. Empirical Estimation of Market Model

Empirical assessments of equation (2) can be obtained from a time series, least-squares regression of the following form:

$$R_{it} = a_i + b_i R_{mt} + e_{it} \quad t = 1, T. \quad (6)$$

where R_{it} and R_{mt} are *ex post* returns for security i and the market, respectively, and where e_{it} is the disturbance term in the equation.

The assessment of β_i from a time series regression assumes that β_i was stationary during that period. Evidence cited above is consistent with the stationary assumption. The empirical evidence (Fama, et al., [28]) also indicates that the resulting equation conforms well to other assumptions of the linear regression model (i.e., linearity, serial independence of the disturbance terms and

homoscedasticity).[48] However, the distribution of the estimated residuals is leptokurtic (i.e., has fatter tails than would be expected under normality). This departure from normality is consistent with Fama's [21] findings that security return are members of the symmetric, stable family of distributions with finite means but infinite variances. However, Wise [25] has shown that for stable distributions with finite expected values, least square estimates of β_i are unbiased and consistent, although not efficient.

References

1. Ackoff, R. L., *Scientific Method: Optimizing Applied Research Decisions*, Wiley, 1962.

2. Archibald, T. Ross, "The Return to Straight-Line Depreciation: An Analyses of a Change in Accounting Methods," *Empirical Research in Accounting: Selected Studies, 1968*, supplement to the *Journal of Accounting Research*, 1967, pp. 164–180.

3. Arrow, K. J., *Essays in the Theory of Risk Bearing*, Markham Publishing, 1971.

4. Ball, Ray, "Changes in Accounting Techniques and Stock Prices," presented at Workshop in Accounting Research, University of Chicago, 1971 (unpublished).

5. _____, and Brown, Philip, "An Empirical Evaluation of Accounting Income Numbers," *Journal of Accounting Research* (Autumn, 1968), pp. 159–178.

6. _____, and Watts, Ross, "Predictions of Earnings," University of Chicago, 1968 (unpublished).

7. Barrett, M. E., "A Study of Some Effects of Alternative Methods of Accounting for Intercorporate Investments," unpublished Ph.D. dissertation, Stanford University, 1970.

8. Beaver, William, "The Information Content of Annual Earnings Announcements," *Empirical Research in Accounting: Selected Studies, 1968*, supplement to the *Journal of Accounting Research*, 1968, pp. 67–92.

9. _____, "The Time Series Behavior of Earnings Variables," *Empirical Research in Accounting: Selected Studies, 1970*, supple-

---

[48]Although residuals exhibit slight negative correlation, Fisher [35] has advanced an argument that the estimated residuals would exhibit slight negative correlation, even though the "true" residuals were uncorrelated.

ment to the *Journal of Accounting Research,* forthcoming.

10. _____, Kennelly, J., and Voss, W., "Predictive Ability as a Criterion for the Evaluation of Accounting Data," *Accounting Review* (October, 1968), pp. 675–683.

11. _____, Kettler, Paul, and Scholes, Myron, "The Association Between Market Determined and Accounting Determined Risk Measures," *Accounting Review* (October, 1970), pp. 654–682.

12. _____, and Dukes, Roland E., "Interperiod Tax Allocation and the Behavior of Security Prices," Research Paper No. 7, Graduate School of Business, Stanford University, 1970.

13. Blume, Marshall, "The Assessment of Portfolio Performance," unpublished Ph.D. dissertation, University of Chicago, 1968.

14. Borch, Karl, *The Economics of Uncertainty,* Princeton University Press, 1968.

15. Brooks, Gene, "Depreciation Methods and Market Values of Securities in The Steel Industry," Ph.D. dissertation proposal, Graduate School of Business, Stanford University, 1970.

16. Brown, Philip, "Some Aspects of Valuation in the Railroad Industry," unpublished Ph.D. dissertation, University of Chicago, 1968.

17. _____, and Ball, Ray, "Some Preliminary Findings on the Association Between the Earnings of a Firm, Its Industry, and the Economy," *Empirical Research in Accounting: Selected Studies, 1967,* supplement to the *Journal of Accounting Research, 1967,* pp. 55–77.

18. Churchman, C. West, *Prediction and Optimal Decision,* Prentice-Hall, 1961.

19. Debreu, G., *Theory of Value,* Wiley, 1959.

20. Diamond, Peter A., "The Role of a Stock Market in a General Equilibrium Model with Technological Uncertainty," *American Economic Review* (September, 1967), pp. 759–76.

21. Fama, Eugene, "The Behavior of Stock-Market Prices," *Journal of Business* (January, 1965), pp. 34–105.

22. _____, "Portfolio Analysis in a Stable Paretian Market," *Management Science,* (January, 1965), pp. 404–419.

23. _____, "Risk Return, and Equilibrium: Some Clarifying Comments," *Journal of Finance* (March, 1968), pp. 29–40.

24. _____, "Risk Return, and Equilibrium," Report No. 6831, Center for Mathematical

Studies in Business and Economics, University of Chicago, June, 1968.

25. _____, "Multi-Period Consumption-Investment Decisions," *American Economic Review,* (March, 1970), pp. 163–174.

26. _____, "Efficient Capital Markets: A Review of Theory and Empirical Work," *Journal of Finance* (May, 1970), pp. 303–417.

27. _____, and Blume, Marshall, "Filter Rules and Stock-Market Trading," *Journal of Business* (January, 1966), pp. 226–241.

28. _____, Fisher, Lawrence, Jensen, Michael, and Roll, Richard, "The Adjustment of Stock Prices to New Information," *International Economic Review* (February, 1969), pp. 1–21.

29. _____, and Miller, Merton, *The Theory of Finance* (forthcoming text).

30. _____, and Roll, Richard, "Some Properties of Symmetric Stable Distributions," *Journal of American Statistical Association* (September, 1968), pp. 817–36.

31. Feltham, Gerald A., "The Value of Information," *Accounting Review* (October, 1968), pp. 684–696.

32. _____, and Demski, Joel, "The Use of Models in Information Evaluation," *Accounting Review* (October, 1970), pp. 623–640.

33. Fisher, Irving, *The Rate of Interest,* Macmillan, 1907.

34. _____, *The Theory of Interest,* Macmillan, 1930.

35. Fisher, Lawrence, "Some New Stock Market Indexes," *Journal of Business* (January, 1966), pp. 191–225.

36. Graham, Benjamin, Dodd, David L. and Cottle, Sidney, *Security Analysis,* McGraw-Hill, 1962.

37. Hirshleifer, J., *Investment, Interest and Capital,* Prentice-Hall, 1970.

38. Howard, R. A., "The Foundations of Decision Analysis," *IEEE Transactions of Systems Science and Cybernetics* (September, 1968), pp. 211–219.

39. Ijiri, Y., Jaedicke, R., and Knight, K., "The Effects of Accounting Alternatives on Management Decisions," *Research in Accounting Measurement,* American Accounting Association, 1966, pp. 186–199.

40. Jensen, Michael C., "Risk, the Pricing of Capital Assets, and the Evaluation of Investment Portfolios," *Journal of Business* (April, 1969), pp. 167–247.

41. Jensen, M., Black, F., and Scholes, M., "The Capital Asset Pricing Model: Some Empirical Tests," 1970 (unpublished).

42. Jensen, R., "An Experimental Design for Study of Effects of Accounting Variations in Decision Making," *Journal of Accounting Research* (Autumn, 1966), pp. 224–238.

43. Kaplan, Robert and Roll, Richard, "Investor Evaluation of Accounting Information: Some Empirical Evidence," Working Paper, Carnegie-Mellon University, 1970.

44. King, Benjamin, "Market and Industry Factors in Stock Price Behavior," *Journal of Business* (January, 1966), pp. 139–190.

45. Lintner, John, "The Valuation of Risk Assets and the Selection of Risky Investments in Stock Portfolios and Capital Budgets," *Review of Economics and Statistics* (February, 1965), pp. 13–37.

46. _____, "Security Prices, Risk and Maximal Gains from Diversification," *Journal of Finance* (December, 1965), pp. 587–616.

47. Livingstone, J. L., "The Effects of Alternative Accounting Methods on Regulatory Rate of Return Decisions in the Electric Utility Industry," unpublished Ph.D. dissertation, Stanford University, 1965.

48. Mandelbrot, Benoit, "The Variation of Certain Speculative Prices," *Journal of Business* (October, 1963), pp. 394–419.

49. Markowitz, Harry, "Portfolio Selection," *Journal of Finance* (March, 1952), pp. 77–91.

50. _____, *Portfolio Selection: Efficient Diversification of Investments,* Wiley, 1959.

51. May, Robert G., "The Influence of Quarterly Earnings Announcements on Investor Decisions as Reflected in Common Stock Price Changes," unpublished Ph.D. dissertation, Michigan State University, 1970.

52. Miller, Merton, H., and Modigliani, Franco, "Some Estimates of the Cost of Capital to the Electric Utility Industry, 1954–1957," *American Economic Review* (June, 1966), pp. 333–391.

53. Mlynarczyk, F. A., "An Empirical Study of Accounting Methods and Stock Prices," *Empirical Research in Accounting: Selected Studies, 1969,* supplement to *Journal of Accounting Research,* 1969, pp. 63–81.

54. Modigliani, Franco, and Miller, Merton H., "The Cost of Capital, Corporation Finance, and the Theory of Investment," *American Economic Review* (June, 1958), pp. 261–297.

55. Mossin, Jan, "Equilibrium in a Capital Asset Market," *Econometrica* (October, 1966), pp. 768–782.

56. Niederhoffer and Osborne, M.F.M., "Market Making and Reversal on the Stock Exchange," *Journal of the American Statistical Association* (December, 1966), pp. 897–916.

57. O'Donnell, J. L., "Relationships between Reported Earnings and Stock Prices in the Electric Utility Industry," *Accounting Review* (January, 1965), pp. 135–143.

58. _____, "Further Observations on Reported Earnings and Stock Prices," *Accounting Review* (July, 1968), pp. 549–553.

59. Roll, Richard, "The Efficient Market Model Applied to U.S. Treasury Bill Rates," unpublished Ph.D. dissertation, University of Chicago, 1968.

60. Roll, Richard, "Bias in Fitting the Sharpe Model to Time Series Data," *The Journal of Quantitative and Financial Research* (September, 1969), pp. 271–289.

61. Scholes, Myron, "A Test of the Competitive Market Hypothesis: An Examination of the Market for New Issues and Secondary Offerings," unpublished Ph.D. dissertation, University of Chicago, 1969.

62. Sharpe, William F., "A Simplified Model for Portfolio Analysis," *Management Science* (January, 1963), pp. 377–392.

63. _____, "Capital Asset Prices: A Theory of Market Equilibrium Under Conditions of Risk," *Journal of Finance* (September, 1964), pp. 425–442.

64. _____, "Risk Aversion in the Stock Market," *Journal of Finance* (September, 1965), pp. 416–422.

65. _____, "Mutual Fund Performance," *Journal of Business* (January, 1966), pp. 119–138.

66. _____, "Mean-Absolute-Deviation Characteristic Lines for Securities and Portfolios," Working Paper No. 185, Graduate School of Business, Stanford University, September 1970.

67. _____, *Portfolio Theory and Capital Markets,* McGraw-Hill, 1970.

68. Staubus, George, "The Association of Financial Accounting Variables with Common Stock Values," *Accounting Review* (January, 1965), pp. 119–134.

69. Tobin, James, "Liquidity Preference as Behavior Towards Risk," *Review of Economic Studies* (February, 1958), pp. 74–76.

70. Watts, Ross, "The Informational Content of Dividends," presented at the Seminar for Research in Security Prices at the University of Chicago, 1970 (unpublished, University of Chicago).

71. Wilson, R., "On the Theory of Syndicates," *Econometrica* (January, 1968), pp. 119–132.

72. _____, "The Structure of Incentives Decentralization under Uncertainty," in M. Guilbaud (ed. paus), *La Decision,* Centre National de la Recherche Scientifique (1969).

73. _____, "A Pareto Optimal Dividend Policy," *Management Science* (May, 1967), pp. 756–764.

74. _____, "Decision Analysis in a Corporation," *IEEE Transactions on Systems Science and Cybernetics* (September, 1968), pp. 220–226.

75. Wise, John, "Linear Estimation for Linear Regressions Systems Having Infinite Variances," presented at Berkeley-Stanford Mathematical Economics Seminar, October, 1963, (unpublished).

chapter 3

External Reporting, Security Prices, and Accounting Research

FERDINAND K. LEVY

Georgia Institute of Technology

This essay's major purpose is to comment on a paper by Professor William Beaver. As shall become apparent, I regard Beaver's efforts as scholarly but excessively narrow. The latter assertion is based on the fact that Beaver concentrates on the implications of security prices for accounting research from only one viewpoint, namely from the demand side of private investors. If this is true, then Professor Beaver's suggestions for research of accountants may form an "empty box."[1] Thus, the present essay is devoted to defending my position and providing evidence for it.

There are four major areas where I believe Beaver's work needs broadening, namely:

1. The question, who uses the accounting data provided by external reporting of firms.
2. The realization that equities and private securities in general are only a few possible alternatives in the range of investment opportunities.

3. An expansion of the idea that time series data rather than cross section studies are of little use in examining the efficiency of markets.
4. The realization of the "law of comparative advantage," specifically with regard to what research *economists* and *behavioral scientists* as opposed to accountants can undertake in this area.

I shall discuss each of these points at length in the following sections.

External Reporting—For Whom?

The function of a financial investment market in a hypothetical economy is to allocate real capital such that its marginal social products in all uses are identical. If the market is "efficient,"[2] the marginal social product of capital will equal its marginal social benefit, and a socially optimal accumulation of capital will obtain. Investors affected by the information emanating from this market include individuals, the

---

[1]Clapham defines an empty box as one in which a point may be well made but of little significance. See J. H. Clapham, "Of Empty Economic Boxes," *The Economic Journal*, 32 (1922), pp. 306–314.

[2]We use Fama's definition, as does Beaver. See E. Fama, "Efficient Capital Markets: A Review of Theory and Empirical Work," *Journal of Finance*, 25 (May 1970), pp. 383–417.

government and business, in general.

We shall examine the relationships between the equities security market and each of these groups sequentially. As will become obvious, it is not possible to separate the groups entirely.

Individual Investors. It is the consumption-investment decision of consumers, referred to by Beaver, that partially determines the type and ownership of accumulated capital. Why only partial? Obviously, the alternatives for financial investment open to consumers affect their saving decisions and their transfers of funds among assets.[3] Moreover, the actions of consumers affect both government and business. If government[4] decides capital is being allocated improperly, it has the facilities[5] and support to alter the allocation through tax and expenditure policy. Businesses are on both the supply and demand sides in the financial market. As new real investment opportunities arise, firms add to the supply of financial instruments; when firms perceive profitable opportunities occurring from other firms' inefficiencies in allocating capital, mergers and acquisitions take place. These actions of both government and business, each affected by the reporting practices of firms, in turn influence the consumer's investment decision. Thus, reporting practices of firms have general rather than partial equilibrium implications.

Government. External reporting also affects the various governments' tax and subsidy, expenditure, monetary, regulatory and antitrust policies. The question here is what type of reporting[6] is sufficient for the government to pursue an optimal[7] role in the economy. Examples illustrate this point most efficiently. The current controversy

over "value added taxation" can be lessened by looking at the economic evidence on the shifting of corporation income tax.[8] The evidence comes from studies based on external reports of large firms. The "shifting" must be verified by a model embracing the various goals of firms as well as accounting data. The allocation of overhead by public utilities affects their external reports and this in turn affects their profitability and rate structures, set by government. The lack of private economic returns on the SST as perceived by investors influenced the government's decision to aid in its development. The existence of monopoly profits as evidenced by annual reports provides a basis for antitrust proceedings. Abnormal stock price behavior leads an SEC investigation into stock manipulation, etc. The point here is, again, that reporting practices of firms may affect more sectors of the economy than just the private investor.

Business. Some of the economic reasons for conglomerates include the following:

A) Conglomerates reduce variability in earnings by trying to dovetail cyclical and anticyclical rises and falls in profits of their various components.
B) Conglomerates have a better overview of investment opportunities; hence they try to acquire firms which are investing in particular physical assets and use these firms' assets to purchase capital with higher rates of return than the firms buy when independent.
C) The various divisions of a conglomerate must compete with each other for capital funds. Thus there is a better allocation of capital because of this "extra check," than would occur if the market allocated funds to each of the conglomerate's individual divisions rather than the firm as a whole.

All of the above justifications, and the motivation for firms to acquire one another, depend upon accounting reports and securi-

---

[3]Perhaps the best elementary discussion of portfolio balance and the availability of a spectrum of assets is J. Tobin, "Money, Capital, and Other Stores of Value," *American Economic Review,* 51 (May 1961), pp. 26–37.

[4]This includes state and local as well as the federal government.

[5]After all the government can print money.

[6]Reporting includes special reports to various agencies, e.g., SEC, BLS, OBE, etc., as well as to stockholders.

[7]The economic literature on the "Theory of the Second Best" is germane here.

[8]See, for example, M. Krzyzaniak and R. Musgrave, *The Shifting of the Corporation Income Tax: An Empirical Study of Its Short-Run Effect upon the Rate of Return* (Johns Hopkins Press, 1963).

ty prices as reflected by these data. Moreover there is a whole class of firms known as financial intermediaries and banks charged with converting savings in the economy into investment. These include investment managers, mutual funds, trust officers, savings and loan associations, etc. Consumers buy assets in these rather than make investment decisions by themselves. Hence, they can often diversify out of risk in this manner. Again, the point here is that accounting reporting and its subsequent effect on capital allocation is useful to more than just the individual saver. The latter makes the initial investment-consumption decisions, but his investment decision is translated into capital allocation in many cases by other entities.

Accounting Reports of Firms—Relative to Other Data and Information Content

At any point in time, consumers are faced with a broad spectrum of potential investments, only a fraction of which is in private corporate assets. These opportunities include near money savings accounts of various types, federal and state local obligations, and money, in addition to corporate securities, durables, and non-durable goods. On a rational basis, the consumer's allocation takes place in a manner such that his marginal returns are equal in all assets. His calculations are based on expected returns from each of the possibilities. Thus, security prices should be efficient in the sense that they reflect all available information. Nevertheless, the concept of information is a relative one. Note that the security price reflects not only the intrinsic worth of the business based on accounting data, but also its relative worth among a complete spectrum of assets.

In terms of the econometric models that Beaver presents, regressions involving security prices are generally in reduced form and are heavily underidentified. Moreover, it is questionable whether these models are the supply equations or demand functions for corporate assets. The interesting point for accountants is how the market factor included in these models is derived. In part, it must arise from accounting data from the other firms in addition to expectations of investors and the supply and demand for non-private securities. In short, Beaver's discussion of these market models may tell us nothing about the type of external reporting needed unless he expands them to their structural equations, showing all factors that influence both the supply and demand for each type of asset.

Beaver pays a good deal of attention to the effect of company announcements of earnings, stock splits, dividends, deferrals, etc., on security prices. The major point is how additional information affects investors' behavior and concomitantly security prices and the allocation of resources. Here, accountants can find some clues to research in a political science paper by H. A. Simon.[9]

Simon investigated the effects of the publication of a political poll before an election. In particular, he was interested in knowing whether the publication automatically invalidated the results of the poll through "underdog" and "bandwagon" effects. The accounting analogy is obvious: Is there a possible predictive model of security price behavior and hence resource allocation based in part on company announcements and changes in accounting procedures?

The answer is yes in Simon's analysis. But, to obtain this result, the accountant must not start with the reduced form predictive equation but rather with a structural hypothesis showing the perception of information by the investor and its ultimate effect on his decision. Again, the point is that reduced form models are of little use in telling accountants what type of reporting and announcements are needed to assure efficiency in resource allocation. What is needed is a set of structural equations.

What Type of Data for Analysis?

Most of the empirical work cited by Beaver is based on time series data. From an economic efficiency point of view, the money, as opposed to real, returns on individual corporate securities are important at a given point in time. Particularly, the spectrum of relative money rate of returns available at a

[9]H. A. Simon, "Bandwagon and Underdog Effects and the Possibility of Election Predictions," *Public Opinion Quarterly*, 18 (1954), pp. 245–253.

specific time determines how the economy relatively values its capital resources and provides insights into future returns from various uses of capital. Thus, the explanation of how all investors distribute their assets must lie in cross section data analysis or, in a more general sense, in analysis derived from pooling cross section with time series data.

This point and its relevance to accounting is perhaps best illustrated in Beaver's discussion of Ijiri et al.'s "functional fixation hypothesis." Here differing money rates of return are due to accounting practice rather than to differing claims on real resources in the economy. Cross section analysis would make this difference between similar firms more apparent than time series analysis and demonstrate a more correct real return on both relative to the complete spectrum of other investment possibilities. Time series analysis would confound the non-real differences between the firms with changing investor preferences and market opportunities.

The major conclusion here, of course, is that while "non-real" differences in returns may exist between two firms due to different accounting practices, the accountant's job is to provide the proper type of reporting that will equalize these firms' returns and simultaneously align them with the balance of the market. The type of accounting research necessary to accomplish this has to be based in large part on cross section analysis of external reporting by firms.

Summary—The Law of Comparative Advantage

The major points in this paper include:

1. Accounting data and reports are of interest to businesses and governments as well as to the private investor. Any research on the external reporting by firms must be directed toward determining its effects on the three entities above and must include an analysis of the interactions among these groups.
2. Consumer saving is channeled into corporate assets directly, and indirect-

ly through financial intermediaries. The relationships between security prices, riskiness and external reporting, and consumers' direct or indirect investing has to be investigated. More specifically, should corporate reporting change so that more consumers would invest directly? Would this lead to a better allocation of capital resources? Etc.

3. The construction of structural models of the savings-investment process pointing out the differences in all economic entities competing for funds and encompassing investor decisions must be undertaken. If these models are examined from an economic efficiency point of view, insights for accountants into what type of external reporting data are necessary to assure proper capital allocation will be provided.
4. Hypotheses relating the effects of various information on investors' behavior must be devised and tested. Again, in this instance, clues for proper type of reporting which will lead to allocative efficiency will result.
5. Cross section data of firms within an industry and data between industries must be effected to understand how accounting reports may influence "real returns and opportunities."

All of the above, as pointed out by Beaver, call for interdisciplinary research among accountants, economists, and behaviorists. *Each* of these groups has a *comparative advantage* in some facets of the suggested research. It would seem unwise and uneconomic for any to undertake this type of research alone.

I should like to close with a point of personal privilege. Even though I have intimated that Beaver's work may be myopic and might be paying attention to the wrong previous research, I am quite impressed by it. His paper brings to the forefront the crucial idea that accounting affects resource allocation, and thus accounting research must be directed toward understanding the relationships between external reporting and this allocation process. Nothing is more important than this allocation process in assuring the viability of our economy. I am overjoyed to learn that such excellent accountants are also concerned with the vital concept of economic efficiency.

chapter 4

Accounting Research as an Information Source for Theory Construction

EDWIN H. CAPLAN

University of New Mexico

1. Introduction

One of the most interesting aspects of accounting evolution in the past few decades relates to attempts to develop basic accounting theory. The American Accounting Association Committee on the subject defined basic theory as "a coherent set of concepts explaining and guiding the accountant's action in identifying, measuring, and communicating economic information" [1, p.2]. If we concur in this definition, then we are forced to conclude that to date the various attempts to formulate basic theory have not been particularly successful; at least according to the "market test" of gaining wide acceptance. Accountants have been far more productive in applying experience from practice to improving and sharpening their procedures than they have been in establishing theoretical foundations for the discipline. While this "ad hoc" approach to improvement has facilitated some progress, especially in terms of specific technical problem areas, the lack of appropriate basic theory has placed the profession in a position that is rapidly becoming untenable.

2. Consequences of the Lack of Basic Theory

The present fragmentary state of accounting theory has precluded the development of conceptual standards by which existing and proposed practices can be evaluated. Further, few valid operational criteria exist for selecting from among conflicting practices. As a result, we are currently faced with the dilemma of numerous alternative practices —each capable of producing substantially different results—all of which are considered "acceptable." Perhaps, even more significantly, many practices—direct costing is an obvious example—which might represent desirable improvements continue to be considered "unacceptable."

Sterling [22] has noted that the role of theory in accounting is to specify (a) what is to be measured, (b) how the measurements are to be manipulated, and (c) what measurable outcomes can be expected. The absence of theory which is suitable for these purposes means that we lack the capability to effectively evaluate what we are now doing and to provide innovation in response to new demands as they arise. In times of relative stability, this situation would probably not be disastrous, but in the dynamic and rapidly changing environment which characterizes modern society, the ability to survive is largely dependent on the ability to adapt and change. Change is difficult, however, when the existing structure is based on authoritarian principles, and "generally accepted accounting principles" are justified solely on the grounds that they are "generally accepted." Thus, today, perhaps more than at any time in the history of accounting, we are in need of theoretical concepts which can provide the basis for a logical, consistent, and articulated set (or sets) of accounting practices.

3. "Theorizing" in Accounting

While we may lack theory in accounting, we have had an abundance of "theorizing" —i.e., statements of opinion. Some of this theorizing has been excellent and has provided new and important insights into the nature and role of accounting. Good theorizing is essential in helping to identify significant problem areas and to suggest possible solutions to the problems. But, there is a difference between theorizing (in the accounting sense) and theory construction (in the scientific sense). Theorizing is a necessary, but not a sufficient, element of theory construction. It is *necessary* because the first stages of theory construction involve identifying the problem and defining the relevant issues. It is *insufficient* because it represents only one step in the process of theory construction. Theorizing by itself has tended to result in untested and often untestable value judgments about the subject matter of accounting. Thus, theorizing, no matter how good in its own right, has not been very successful in eliminating or reducing the existing deficiencies and voids in basic accounting theory.

In my view, a major source of our difficulties in the development of accounting theory can be traced to two related problems—inappropriate research scope and lack of proper research methodology. The purpose of this paper is to examine the relationships between theory construction and research methodology and scope.

4. Attempts to Develop Normative Theory

In any discipline, theory can take one of two forms. Descriptive (or positive) theory attempts to explain that which exists. Normative theory, on the other hand, is principally concerned with what "should be."

Since the current range of acceptable accounting practices is so broad and so internally inconsistent, it seems unlikely that attempts to develop a logical and internally consistent descriptive theory of accounting will ever be very productive. Thus, while any valid theory will necessarily contain elements which describe the real world, it appears reasonable to reject at the outset the concept of pure descriptive theory in accounting. Instead, it seems appropriate to concentrate on the development of normative theory. The need for normative theory in accounting should be self-evident. Not only would it facilitate an evaluation of existing and proposed practices, but it would assist in focusing attention on those areas in which additional research is necessary. Further, it would provide accountants with a rational basis for explaining to the nonaccounting world what we do and why we do it.

There have been numerous efforts to develop normative accounting theory in recent years, but none of them have gained sufficient acceptance to be considered totally successful. I have discussed several of these efforts elsewhere [5] and will only briefly summarize them here. Essentially they fall into two basic groups. The first group attempts to identify the best of present practice and to integrate it into a unified whole, e.g., Grady [10]. Whatever the particular form these syntheses of practice happen to take, they have one characteristic in common—they are not able to deal effectively with conflicting practices. This is not surprising, since the approach itself provides no basis for resolving such conflicts. Rather, it is left to the "professional judgment" of the accountant to select the appropriate alternative in specific situations. Since an important function of theory is to furnish the basis for such judgments, the "synthesis of current practice" approach has accomplished little beyond providing inventories of current procedures.

I have termed the second group of efforts to develop normative accounting theory "global," because these efforts represent attempts to formulate in one great "happening" a single all-encompassing unified framework of accounting.[1] Global efforts are usually deductive in nature. The author(s) begins with one or more "fundamental premises" or "assumptions" and from these assumptions attempts to deduce a series of principles dealing with the specifics of accounting. Deductive logic is an acceptable and widely used method of scientific inquiry, but when applied to these global efforts in accounting, it has been relatively unsuccessful.

Let me emphasize my personal view that despite the recognized competence of the authors (indeed, they include some of the best minds in accounting), all of the efforts to set forth a unified theory of accounting have failed. They have failed, in part at least, because they have neglected a fundamental aspect of scientific reasoning—they provide no evidence to support their logic except the opinions of the authors. Although these theory formulations often contain valuable insights about accounting, in the final analysis, they represent only "armchair" theorizing which the reader can accept or reject depending on his own preconceptions. They simply do not stand by themselves as convincing and compelling works of research. The essential difficulty is, of course, one of methodology. Most of the "principles" and relationships contained in these theoretical formulations are either nonoperational statements of obvious truths or assertions, which, if they are to be accepted at all, must be accepted on faith.

5. Dogma Versus Science

Statements of authoritarian opinion which must be accepted on faith are called dogma. Now, I would not argue that all dogma is bad. There are certain advantages to a dogmatic approach. In situations of uncertainty it reduces the uncertainty. In the case of a profession, dogma permits respected leaders to exercise influence over practice and thereby serves as a unifying and cohesive force. Dogma is effective in this manner, however, only as long as the members of the profession (and ultimately the public)

are willing to accept and be bound by the respected opinions. But, the more we learn about our world, the less we are willing to accept statements of opinion which cannot be verified, no matter how respected the source of those statements.

I believe that we have reached the stage in the evolution of accounting theory where at least some academic accountants are no longer willing to accept respected authority as the basis for theoretical statements. One need only examine a current issue of the leading academic journals in accounting to recognize that there has been a significant change in research methodology in the last few years. The thrust of this change is in the direction of replacing opinions with facts and assertions with hypothesis-testing. It seems clear to me that a trend is developing—a trend which promises to open new vistas with respect to the development of accounting theory. The following paragraphs will attempt to summarize what I believe to be the major characteristics of this trend.

6. Empirical Research in Accounting

First, academic accounting has started to produce researchers who have been trained in statistics, quantitative methods, and behavioral science, as well as in the more traditional areas. These individuals have the perspective and the tools to formulate and investigate research problems according to the rules of scientific methodology. At the risk of stating the obvious, let me mention the elements of scientific methodology. They are (a) the identification of a problem, (b) the accumulation of relevant data, (c) the formulation of hypotheses from the data, and (d) empirical testing of the hypothesis. Thus, we are beginning to see a new kind of researcher in accounting—one who is capable of applying the same kind of research techniques to the problems of our discipline as are now being utilized in other areas of knowledge.

It appears that we are undergoing a major shift in emphasis toward empirical research (including laboratory experimentation and simulation). In my opinion, it would be dif-

[1] A recent example of this approach is *A Statement of Basic Accounting Theory* [1].

ficult to overstate the importance of this developing emphasis on empirical research.[2] "Research" is really two words—"re" and "search." It means to search *again*. Empirical studies that are well designed to test limited and clearly stated hypotheses should facilitate and encourage additional studies to substantiate as well as build on the earlier work. It is reasonable to anticipate that this approach will enable accounting research to progress slowly but surely in the direction of developing and testing an increasing range of hypotheses. Verified (or rejected) hypotheses should, in turn, provide the basis for validating theoretical statements concerning the nature and consequences of various accounting practices.

The important point to note regarding empirical research is that evidence from such research cannot be ignored simply because one disagrees with the findings. The individual who chooses to reject an empirical finding must do so either by attacking the methodology of the study or by conducting a similar study and obtaining different results. Thus, each properly conducted and properly reported investigation, as well as each effort to reconcile conflicting findings, make an incremental contribution to the development of a solid body of knowledge about accounting. One cannot avoid the somewhat trite analogy of the fable of the tortoise and the hare. Global theoretical endeavors are spectacular and thought-provoking. They attempt to move us rapidly forward in the area of theory formulation. Theory construction based on good empirical research, on the other hand, will move us forward very slowly—a small step at a time. But in the long-run, this kind of research appears much more likely to win the race in building a basic theory of accounting.

7. The Impracticability of a Unified Theory

A second characteristic of the new trend is that future research will be less likely to concentrate on attempts to develop a single unified theory of accounting. Our new breed of researchers seems to recognize that such a unified theory is no more practical than a single unified theory of history, psychology or economics. The field of psychology, for example, consists of numerous theories. Many of these theories deal with different areas of psychology and have not yet been conceptually related to each other. Others are concerned with the same area and represent conflicting views of the theoretical substance of that area. In time, as research progresses, it can be expected that the weaker of these conflicting theories will disappear. But for the present, each has its own school of supporters.

Similarly, in accounting, we can anticipate that there will continue to be different opinions about the role of accounting in society and about the most appropriate manner in which to perform that role. These opinions will lead to the identification of different problems and to different theoretical formulations. Eventually, through empirical research, it can be expected that certain theories will be demonstrated to have superior validity, in that they are better able to explain and predict real world phenomena. Perhaps, in the distant future, it will even be possible to relate these surviving theories into one conceptual structure. Then, and only then, we may finally arrive at that elusive unified theory. In the meantime, we can expect to see research concentrating on rather narrow problem areas that lend themselves to appropriate scientific analysis. In short, it seems that the era has passed when our best research potential was devoted largely to the development of broad, all-encompassing statements of theory.

Of course, this does not mean that productive research can occur in a theoretical vacuum. We need theoretical models to provide a conceptual basis for empirical research. However, in contrast to the global efforts mentioned earlier, these models will not attempt to provide answers to the major theoretical problems of accounting. Rather, their function will be to identify problems and possible solutions; to establish the parameters of various problem areas; to suggest possible relationships among variables; and to highlight specific questions which need to be investigated. An example of the kind of

---

[2] For an excellent discussion of empirical research in accounting see Green [11].

conceptual model to which I am referring can be found in the behavioral model of the decision process developed by Ijiri, Jaedicke, and Knight [16].

Also, there will always be a need for accounting "philosophers"—individuals who, because of their ability to explore new areas as well as cast new light on old problem areas, are able to widen our horizons and provoke us to more incisive analysis. I would not for a moment argue against this need, but I seriously doubt that the major thrust of productive research in accounting should be or will be in this direction.

8. An Interdisciplinary Approach to Accounting Theory

A third characteristic of the new trend is that researchers will not be content to view accounting as a self-contained discipline. Rather, they will investigate the possibility that the roots of accounting theory are to be found in the behavioral sciences, communications theory and measurement theory. We can expect, therefore, that a significant amount of accounting research efforts will be devoted to exploring the interface between these areas and accounting.

For example, I find it somewhat disconcerting that although financial accountants have for a number of years placed a substantial emphasis on the needs of the investor, relatively little research has been done *by accountants* on such questions as the behavioral characteristics of investors, the perceptions of investors concerning financial statements, the investor decision-process, and so forth. Similarly, if management accounting is primarily concerned with providing information for managerial decision-making, then it seems obvious than an essential step in building a theory of management accounting is to study the nature of the managerial decision-process.

9. Examples of Empirical Research

What will be the nature of good empirical research in accounting? Fortunately, we now have a number of examples of such research. In a recent study, based on an analysis of questionnaire data, Dyckman [6] investigated the reactions of financial analysts to financial statements adjusted for price level changes. While the Dyckman study necessarily leaves many questions unanswered, his findings strongly suggest that, after more than three decades of theorizing on the subject of price level adjustments, we still have a great deal to learn about the effects of such adjustments on investor decision making.

A second example of worthwhile empirical research can be found in Beaver's [3] investigation of the value of published accounting information in predicting insolvency. This study was based on an historical comparison of published financial statement data and the actual performance over time of selected firms. Beaver concludes that accounting indicators may be useful in predicting insolvency several years in advance of the actual occurrence. An important aspect of this research is that it represents one of the few pieces of hard evidence in support of the conventional wisdom that published financial statements are, or can be, useful to investors.

For a third example of good empirical research in accounting, I have selected Stedry's [20] experiment on the budget process. This work differs from the studies just discussed in two respects. First, it deals with a managerial rather than a financial accounting area, and second, the methodology of the study involved a laboratory experiment. The results of Stedry's investigation emphasize the interrelationship between budgets, aspiration levels, and performance, suggesting that these relationships are both significant and complex.

The preceding examples need not be discussed in great detail, since they are all widely known and accountants with an interest in theory construction can be expected to be familiar with them. But I do want to emphasize certain attributes that they share. First, each of these studies is based on some theoretical assumptions about accounting and its function in the real world. Second, these assumptions are formalized into hypotheses which appear to be testable. Third, real world data is gathered. Finally, the empirical data is analyzed in an effort to determine if the hypotheses should be accepted, rejected or modified in terms of their ability to explain and predict the empirical results. Thus, regardless of the specific methodology employed, each of these studies represents an application of accepted scientific methods to accounting research.

10. Conclusion

Earlier it was noted that we have an abundance of opinions in accounting. Unfortunately, these opinions are often called theories, and so we may tend to mistakenly believe that we have an abundance of theory. This does not mean that opinions are unimportant to theory formulation. Indeed, the first step in developing theory is to have an idea or opinion on the subject. But meaningful progress in theory construction requires that some method be available for identifying those opinions which are valid and for selecting the appropriate opinion from among conflicting views on a particular issue. Because accounting is pragmatic and can be justified only in terms of its usefulness in the real world, the test of what is valid and appropriate in accounting must relate to real world phenomena and behavior. In turn, the relationship between such phenomena and behavior and various accounting concepts and procedures can only be determined by empirical research.

While most individual empirical studies cannot, by themselves, be expected to provide definitive answers to the subject examined, each study should contribute to our understanding of the issue. The most important aspect of empirical research is that it is a method of obtaining agreement. Empirical research leads to conclusions which cannot be rejected simply because they do not coincide with our personal opinions. The nature of the methodology gives empirical studies a status and validity unmatched by non-empirical theorizing. Of course, any empirical finding may ultimately be disproved, but if this happens, it will usually be the result of additional empirical research.

There is always a danger of overstating the issue. Clearly, it is possible to have poor empirical research as well as good empirical research on trivial matters. It is also possible to place excessive emphasis on methodological tools, to the point that we are more concerned with techniques than with substance. Further, we have already noted that productive empirical research cannot occur in a theoretical vacuum. Perhaps the pendulum may swing too far, with the result that insufficient attention will be paid to the non-empirical aspects of theory construction. Nevertheless, I believe that as a profession, we are capable of avoiding these pitfalls and that the increasing interest in empirical research—together with a more specific and problem-oriented research focus as well as the application of techniques and findings from related disciplines—promises to add a new and essential dimension to theory construction in accounting.

References

1. American Accounting Association, Committee to Prepare a Statement of Basic Accounting Theory, *A Statement of Basic Accounting Theory*, 1966.

2. Bakan, David, *On Method: Toward a Reconstruction of Psychological Investigation*, Jossey-Bass, Inc., 1969.

3. Beaver, William, "Financial Ratios as Predictors of Failure," *Empirical Research in Accounting: Selected Studies, 1966*, Supplement to the *Journal of Accounting Research*, (1967), pp. 71–111.

4. Campbell, D. T., and Stanley, J. C., *Experimental and Quasi-experimental Designs for Research*, Rand McNally, 1966.

5. Caplan, Edwin H., "Relevance—A 'Will-O'-the Wisp'," *Abacus* (Winter, 1969), pp. 48–54.

6. Dyckman, T. R., *Investment Analysis and General Price-level Adjustments: A Behavioral Study*, American Accounting Association, 1969.

7. Ferber, Robert, and Verdoorn, P. J., *Research Methods in Economics and Business*, Macmillan, 1962.

8. Festinger, Leon, and Katz, Daniel, *Research Methods in the Behavioral Sciences*, Holt, Rinehart and Winston, Inc., 1953.

9. Goode, W. J., and Hatt, P. K., *Methods in Social Research*, McGraw-Hill Book Company, Inc., 1952.

10. Grady, Paul, *Inventory of Generally Accepted Accounting Principles for Business Enterprises,* Accounting Research Study No. 7, American Institute of Certified Public Accountants, 1965.

11. Green, David, Jr., "Evaluating the Accounting Literature," *The Accounting Review* (January, 1966), pp. 54–57.

12. Hempel, Carl, *Aspects of Scientific Explanation,* The Free Press, 1965.

13. _____, *Philosophy of Natural Science,* N.J.: Prentice-Hall, Inc., 1966.

14. _____, *Fundamentals of Concept Formation in Empirical Science,* The University of Chicago Press, 1967.

15. Ijiri, Yuji, "Logic and Sanctions in Accounting," R. Sterling (ed.), *Accounting in Perspective,* Southwestern Publishing Co., 1970.

16. _____, Jaedicke, Robert K., and Knight, Kenneth E., "The Effects of Accounting Alternatives on Management Decisions," in *Research in Accounting Measurement,* American Accounting Association, 1966, pp. 186–199.

17. Kaplan, Abraham, *The Conduct of Inquiry, Methodology for Behavioral Science,* Chandler Publishing Co., 1964.

18. Popper, Karl, *The Logic of Scientific Discovery,* Basic Books, 1959.

19. Simon, J. L., *Basic Research Methods in Social Science: The Art of Empirical Investigation,* Random House, 1969.

20. Stedry, Andrew C., *Budget Control and Cost Behavior,* Prentice-Hall, Inc., 1960.

21. Sterling, Robert R., "Elements of Pure Accounting Theory," *The Accounting Review* (January, 1967), pp. 62–73.

22. _____, "On Theory Construction and Verification," *The Accounting Review* (July, 1970), pp. 449–454.

23. Williams, Thomas H., and Griffin, Charles H., "On the Nature of Empirical Verification in Accounting," *Abacus* (December, 1969), pp. 157–178.

chapter 5

The Relationship of Empirical Research
to Accounting Theory

Thomas H. Williams

University of Texas at Austin

In commenting on a research or—perhaps following the line of argument of Professor Caplan—an "opinion" paper, it appears to me that it is incumbent upon a discussant to evaluate the propriety and relevance of the implicit or explicit objective(s) of the paper, as well as the "correctness" or reasonableness of the assertions and conclusions. Since a paper on methodology is necessarily non-empirical in character, the evaluation must ultimately rely on such factors as the cogency of the arguments, the completeness of the development, and the consistency of assertions. Because these criteria are at best inexact in nature, I explicitly recognize that this evaluation is influenced by my personal biases and predispositions in the same manner that the assertions of the author are undoubtedly affected by his. To the extent that the Chairman of this Colloquium was successful in selecting individuals with significantly different perspectives on this subject, the audience is provided an opportunity to evaluate the subject from two distinct points of view. Hopefully, this will aid their own evaluation of the paper.

Purpose and Major Thrust of the Paper

The purpose of the paper, as implicitly reflected in its title, would seem to be to identify the manner in which accounting research functions as an information source for theory construction. At first glance, this would appear to be a singularly desirable, topical subject to investigate. However, meaningful development of this subject requires explicit specification of what one means by the term "accounting research," and what is meant by "information source for theory construction." In my opinion, the author does not provide these specifications, and thus, if the conclusions that are reached in the paper do, in fact, bear upon this subject, the linkage is not adequately described for the reader. A more explicit statement of purpose is offered by the author in the following terms: "The purpose of this paper is to examine the relationships between theory construction and research methodology and scope." This expressed purpose is, to a limited extent, developed in the paper. I would suggest, however, that the major, albeit implicit, purpose of the

53

paper is to advance the thesis that empirical research is the primary research methodology toward which the resources and efforts of the accounting researcher should be directed if a scientifically based, operational set of theories is to be developed. In providing support for this thesis, however, it appears to me that the author has both overstated the merits of empirical research, as well as the limitations of what he describes as "theorizing." I should now like to address myself to several of these areas of the paper.

Evaluation of Arguments and Propositions

First, since the paper focuses upon the relationship between theory construction and research methodology and scope, it would appear appropriate to provide some rather definitive notion of what constitutes *theory*. Yet, Caplan provides us with only two abbreviated definitions. One such definition is gleaned from *A Statement of Basic Accounting Theory* (in itself a deductively oriented document), and a second from a paper by Professor Robert R. Sterling (a rather strong supporter of the application of the deductive method in accounting research). While each of these brief statements appears reasonable, Caplan does not provide us elaborative commentary in such a manner as would enable us to argue for a particular research methodology as the primary, or sole, relevant tool.

Some further notion of Caplan's concept of theory can be inferred from his assessment that we lack basic theory, wherein he seems to characterize the role of theory as providing *standards* by which existing and proposed practices can be evaluated. However, subsequently he refers to more valid theories as those which "are better able to explain and predict real world phenomena." While these two conceptions may indeed not be irreconcilable, it would seem desirable in a methodological paper to offer a more explicit notion of the basic object of investigation or the basic referent source.[1]

Second, Caplan early, and I might note rather consistently throughout the paper, categorizes most non-empirical approaches to theory construction as "theorizing—i.e., statements of opinion." He does acknowledge that individuals engaged in this activity may *occasionally* provide "new and important insights"; or, even if no "useful" theory results, he seems to suggest that we can perhaps indulge a few of what I might characterize as—using a variation of his descriptors—the "old breed of researchers." Notwithstanding these minor concessions, it is my opinion that Caplan advances a case against non-empirical research which is not supported by reasoned arguments.

Third, in dichotomizing theory (as noted before, essentially a primitive term) Caplan chooses to contrast descriptive and normative theories. In general, he argues strongly for a rejection of descriptive theories, and for the concentration of efforts on the development of normative theories. However, as is pointed out in Professor Ijiri's "The Nature of Accounting Research," most research that might be characterized as empirical in nature is essentially subsumed under the descriptive theory category, and that research which Caplan would seem to disparage falls under the normative theory class. While I would not argue that this apparent inconsistency should provoke Caplan to defect his strong support for empirical research, it might suggest that there is a role for additional types of research methodology of a non-empirical character.

One or two additional assertions in the author's development of normative accounting theories deserve brief comment. In illustrating existing normative theories, Paul Grady's inventory of generally accepted accounting principles for business enterprises is proposed as exemplar of one basic class thereunder. I would reject this example, and indeed the entire class, as attempts rather to provide some type of descriptive, not normative, theory. In outlining a second

[1]On this matter, see R. R. Sterling, "On Theory Construction and Verification," *The Accounting Review*, 46 (July 1970), pp. 444–464; T. H. Williams and C. H. Griffin, "On the Nature of Empirical Verification in Accounting," *Abacus*, 5 (December 1969), pp. 143–178; and Committee on Accounting Theory Construction and Verification, American Accounting Association, "Report of the Committee on Accounting Theory Construction and Verification," *The Accounting Review*, Supplement to Vol. XLVI (1971), pp. 51–79.

class of "normative" research in accounting, Caplan refers to the "global" theories, such as *A Statement of Basic Accounting Theory*. He then rejects this class with the argument that while the various researchers have all been competent and possessing of some of the best minds in accounting, they have failed to set forth a unified theory of accounting. While this conclusion may indeed be true, it seems to me that it identifies a problem of scope, not one of methodology or nature of the theory.[2]

Fourth, in a brief section entitled "Dogma versus Science," there is an indictment of statements of authoritative opinion (which implicitly, if not explicitly, seem to be identified with most deductive theories). Caplan recognizes that dogma "permits respected leaders to exercise influence over practice and thereby serves as a unifying and cohesive force. . . . But, the more we learn about our world, the less we are willing to accept statements of opinion which cannot be verified, no matter how respected the source of those statements." While I agree with this proposition insofar as it applies to accounting research, I feel that this discussion inadequately distinguishes between the day-to-day administration and coordination of accounting practice and the longer run accounting research and theory construction performed by individuals not engaged in the world of practice. Indeed, there are those in academia who believe that, within accounting practice, dogma and authoritarianism are perhaps the only ways of making ultimate choices, and that research serves to provide them some additional evidence (hopefully strong evidence) for these choices. In any event, this question would seem to be a separate issue unrelated to research methodology.

Fifth, in commenting on the first of three major characteristics which he perceives to

represent a new trend in accounting (i.e., (1) emergence of empirical research, (2) recognition of impracticality of a unified theory, and (3) expansion of the scope of accounting), Caplan sanguinely observes that we are now beginning "to produce researchers who have been trained in statistics, quantitative methods and behavioral science, as well as in the more traditional areas." Apropos of this appraisal, I would suggest two caveats. First, I presume the traditional areas would include logic and methods of theory construction; otherwise, the researcher may be inappropriately prepared for much more than data manipulation. Secondly, the training in quantitative methods, as opposed to statistics, prepares the researcher for model building of a deductive character rather than for empirical research.

In elaborating on the emergence of empirical research, Caplan apologizes for stating what he feels may be obvious when he lists the "elements of scientific methodology." In his view, these elements are "(a) the identification of a problem, (b) the accumulation of relevant data, (c) the formulation of hypotheses from the data, and (d) empirical testing of the hypothesis." To the extent that this enumeration, which essentially outlines the empirical phase of research, is the complete one, then it was indeed not obvious to me. Since one's conception of appropriate "scientific methodology" frequently derives from one's conception of a "scientific theory," I would offer the following description as a more general, and to me more acceptable, basis from which a scientific discipline defines appropriate methodology:

A scientific theory might therefore be likened to a complex spatial network: Its terms are represented by the knots, while the threads connecting the latter correspond, in part, to the definitions and, in part, to the fundamental and derivative hypotheses included in the theory. The whole system floats, as it were, above the plane of observation and is anchored to it by rules of interpretation. These might be viewed as strings which are not part of the network but link certain points of the latter with specific places in the plane of observation. By virtue of those interpretive connections, the network can

---

[2]I also have strong reservations regarding the appropriateness of *A Statement of Basic Accounting Theory* as exemplar of "global theories." Although this document contains a set of propositions that might be categorized as accounting theory, much of it is devoted to other matters—e.g., implementing standards, description of future areas of development, etc. Perhaps Paton & Littleton, Chambers or Sterling would have been better choices to illustrate this class of theories.

function as a scientific theory: From certain observational data, we may ascend, via an interpretive string, to some point in the theoretical network, thence proceed, via definitions and hypotheses, to other points, from which another interpretive string permits a descent to the plane of observation.

In this manner an interpreted theory makes it possible to infer the occurrence of certain phenomena which can be described in observational terms and which may belong to the past or the future, on the basis of other such phenomena, whose occurrence has been previously ascertained. But the theoretical apparatus which provides these predictive and postdictive bridges from observational data to potential observational findings cannot, in general, be formulated in terms of observables alone. The entire history of scientific endeavor appears to show that in our world comprehensive, simple, and dependable principles for the explanation and prediction of observable phenomena cannot be obtained by merely summarizing and inductively generalizing observational findings. A hypothetico-deductive-observational procedure is called for and is indeed followed in the more advanced branches of empirical science: Guided by his knowledge of observational data, the scientist has to invent a set of concepts—theoretical constructs, which lack immediate experiential significance, a system of hypotheses couched in terms of them, and an interpretation for the resulting theoretical network; and all this in a manner which will establish explanatory and predictive connections between the data of direct observation.[3]

While this concept of the theory construction/verification process seems to me to give due weight to the need for observational data, it does not limit the research process to this single phase. Furthermore, it suggests the explicit need for deductive theories. Further elaboration of this role is, I believe, contained in numerous sources.

I have one final comment on the description of the empirical research that is emerging in accounting: in my judgment, unwarranted emphasis is placed on the factual nature of the results from such research. Most of us have observed, I am sure, instances in which a researcher is inclined to redefine, remeasure and reclassify factual data until statistically significant results are achieved.[4] Such manipulation is, in my opinion, many times not evident in the reported results of research findings. Furthermore, I might propose that this phenomenon is correlated most highly with the absence of sound theoretical models of a deductive character which give purpose and direction to the data analysis.

Sixth, in commenting on the impracticality of unified theory, Caplan essentially despairs of developing such a theory and points to the recognition of this fact in other areas such as history, psychology, and economics. While this observation of the author may be a correct judgment, it does not in my opinion support the proposition that we reduce our efforts to continually integrate and generalize to higher levels various models and theoretical constructs. Furthermore, the lack of an overall unified theory does not, in my assessment, support sole reliance upon empirical methods. Caplan has noted that empirical research cannot occur in a theoretical vacuum. Thus, it seems that this section of his paper merely pleads for a reduction in the scope of our research problems (a point with which I would agree for most of our researchers, but not all), rather than a change in our research methodology.

Seventh, in describing the third characteristic of the new trend—interdisciplinary approach to accounting theory—Caplan suggests "that the roots of accounting theory are to be found in the behavioral sciences, communications theory and measurement theory." These do seem to be potentially fertile areas for investigation. Indeed, they have been suggested as such for approximately ten years. To date, however,

---

[3]C. G. Hempel, *Fundamentals of Concept Formation in Empirical Science* (University of Chicago Press, 1952), pp. 36–37. This presumes, of course, that accounting theory is a "scientific" theory. It may be that a more productive line of reasoning would start from a conception of accounting theory as an "operative technological theory." See Mario Bunge, *Scientific Research II: The Search for Truth* (Springer-Verlag New York, Inc., 1967), Chapter 11 for a general discussion of this notion.

[4]Bunge (p. 323) comments on this matter as follows: ". . . a high degree of confirmation can be attained by tampering either with the hypothesis or experience. In fact, any of the following tricks would enhance a degree of confirmation to practically any desired extent: (i) reinterpreting unfavorable evidence as favorable by introducing *ad hoc* hypotheses; (ii) reformulating the hypothesis in a loose (semantically weak) way so that it will span almost any evidence; (iii) disregarding (hiding) unfavorable evidence, i.e., selecting the data; (iv) subjecting the hypothesis to slack tests."

communications and measurement theory have not yet produced much in the way of helpful insights for accountants. More importantly, I presume that Caplan does not mean to exclude other areas, such as finance, economics, law, logic, ethics, etc., from this definition of root sources for accounting theory. If he does, I would dispute these contentions, and would ask for some evidence for his unsupported argument.

Eighth, and finally, the paper concludes with several examples of empirical research. The purpose of these illustrations, I presume, is to indicate to the reader more specifically what it is that constitutes the kind of thing that should be our major effort in the forthcoming years (research prototypes of a sort). While I do not wish to quarrel with his selection of research projects, particularly as illustrations of excellent methodology, I do believe that it is useful to draw attention to the types of conclusions Caplan sees flowing from these efforts. From the Dyckman study, Caplan concludes that "while the . . . study necessarily leaves many questions unanswered, his findings strongly suggest that, after more than three decades of theorizing on the subject of price level adjustments, we still have a great deal to learn about the effects of such adjustments on investor decision making." This conclusion hardly moves me to cast aside non-empirical models and rush to the side of those proposing exclusive emphasis on empirical studies. In appraising the Stedry experiment, Caplan notes that "The results of Stedry's investigation emphasize the interrelationship between budgets, aspiration levels, and performance, suggesting that these relationships are both significant and complex." While perhaps slightly more informative than the preceding conclusion, this hardly represents a "breakthrough" in knowledge. One additional comment on these studies may be in order. In enumerating the attributes that they share, Caplan indicates that "real world data is gathered." I recall that the Stedry experiment used students solving problems requiring allocation of water between water jars as a surrogate for managers preparing budgets, which only reinforces my previous comment on the somewhat soft, and not so manifestly factual, nature of the "real world data."

CONCLUSION

I remarked in the introduction to these comments that it is my understanding that the role of the discussant is to provide, where applicable, a different perspective concerning the arguments and propositions offered by the author. In doing this, particularly as it relates to areas of weakness rather than strength in the paper, a misleading impression is often conveyed. I do not intend that these comments should be interpreted to mean a rejection on my part of empirical research. We have not had enough empirical research in accounting, and can usefully employ much more. However, I conceive of this research as accommodating to an overall pattern of theory construction/verification more in the Hempel mold than that proposed by Caplan. Even in this context there remain major conceptual problems to be resolved, including the nature of accounting referents. It is to this issue which I would urge those interested in doing metatheoretical papers on empirical research to direct their attention.

chapter 6

The Nature of Accounting Research

YUJI IJIRI

Carnegie-Mellon University

1. Introduction

Among many unsolved problems in mathematics, one of the most famous and mysterious problems is the so-called "four-color problem." The problem is: How many colors are needed to color any map so that no two adjacent regions have the same color?[1]

It has been proven that five colors are sufficient. It has also been proven that four colors are sufficient for any map with 38 regions or less. But, despite the effort by numerous mathematicians since the problem was originally stated in 1852, no one has succeeded in proving that four colors are sufficient for any map regardless of the number of regions, nor has anyone been able to demonstrate a map which requires more than four colors.[2]

A problem like this is truly challenging. There are a large number of mathematicians who are most anxious to solve the problem. Its solution would mean a significant breakthrough in the field of topology. Such exciting and difficult problems are not rare in science, however. Many histories of science use the "great problems" as focal points. The histories explain how the problem came to be recognized and, if solved, how its solution came about, as well as the honor bestowed upon the person who solved it.

But what about research in accounting? Are there any research problems in accounting which may be as exciting and as challenging intellectually as the four-color problem?

I believe there are. Before I attempt to support this assertion, however, it will be necessary to review the characteristics of research findings in science in general and then to compare the nature of accounting research to the characteristics of research in science in general. This will help us to comprehend the basic structure of accounting research as it now exists. Thus, the following section will start with a review of the characteristics of research findings.

2. Characteristics of Research Findings

Generally speaking, research findings possess three essential characteristics, namely, novelty, defensibility and availability.[3]

[1] See Gardener [13, pp. 113–123] for an introductory description of the four-color problem. One of the most comprehensive studies on this problem is given in Ore [23].

[2] It is a trivial exercise to create a map which requires four colors.

[3] These characteristics were analyzed in Ijiri [19]. A brief summary of the discussion there is reproduced here. For a general discussion of research methodology, see Beveridge [4] and Kaplan [22]. For research methodology in accounting, see, e.g., Devine [9], [10], Chambers [6], Wheeler [27], Hendriksen [17, Ch. 1].

Clearly, research findings must be *novel*. This factor permits us to distinguish research activities from production activities. The effort to produce a television set is valuable even if an identical set has already been produced elsewhere. However, once a solution to the four-color problem has been developed, an effort to develop an identical solution is worthless from a research standpoint. What we are pursuing in research are "ideas" which can be applied by others. However, there is no need for someone else to come up with the *same* idea.

The second characteristic of research findings is that they must be *defensible*. The method of defense may vary from logical proofs to empirical verifications. Defensibility also means reproducibility of research findings by others. When they are successfully defended, the research findings can be used by anyone, without involvement of the researchers who produced them. They become independent of the researchers in this sense. For this reason, research findings are different from "opinions," which cannot be evaluated independently from the persons expressing them.

Finally, research findings must be made *available* to others. Researchers are expected to make every effort to let other people know about their results. It is crucial for researchers to understand that what is important in research is not what was discovered but how the world is influenced by what was discovered.

Because of these three characteristics, novelty, defensibility and availability, research findings may be considered analogous to the researchers' children. Certainly, research findings are the result of considerable time and effort expended by the researchers, similar to that expended in raising their children. But the analogy is more important in another way, viz., research findings have a life of their own independent from the life of the researcher.

Although a theory may be named after the researcher who developed it, the name does not seem to have any more significance than a father and his son having the same surname. From the viewpoint of society, the important question is "what was developed and how the world is influenced by it?" and not "who developed it?" Of course, a researcher often attempts to rescue his theory whenever it is in danger, but this is because the theory has not yet been fully accepted by the society. Ideally, he should be able to sit back and enjoy the reputation as "the father of the great son," with perhaps a touch of loneliness.

3. The Nature of Accounting Research

Having observed the general characteristics of research findings, let us now analyze the nature of accounting research in view of these characteristics.

Generally speaking, the objects of accounting research may be characterized as the relationship between economic events of an entity and information recorded and reported about them.[4] The relationship is mutual, in the sense that research may be directed toward the process in which information is generated from economic events or it may be directed toward the reverse process, in which economic events are affected by information.

Centered around the empirical phenomena concerning the mutual relationship between economic events and information about them, accounting research has been directed at various issues. Models (or theories) are developed in order to describe the existing accounting systems or in order to improve accounting systems.[5]

In general, models are representations of real-world phenomena as they exist or as they ought to exist. The former types of models are called "descriptive models" and the latter types, "normative models".[6] This distinction between descriptive models and normative models plays an important role in understanding the nature of accounting research, as we shall see later.

[4] See the definition of accounting as provided in, for example, American Accounting Association [1]. See also Ijiri [18] on representation problems involved in relating economic events and information.
[5] Here, the term "models" and the term "theories" are synonymous. See the discussion on this point in Cohen and Cyert [7, Ch. 2].
[6] For a stimulating discussion on this subject, see Friedman [12, Pt. I].

It may be worthwhile to point out here that this distinction does not exactly coincide with the distinction between "inductive models" and "deductive models." An "inductive model" is a model derived from a set of elementary factors by an inductive process, and a "deductive model" is a model derived from a set of assumptions by a deductive process. A descriptive model is an inductive model which is derived from a set of *empirical observations*, while a normative model is a deductive model which is derived from a set of *goal assumptions.* Thus, a descriptive model emphasizes the fact that it has a base in the empirical phenomena, while a normative model emphasizes its goal-oriented nature.

In either case, models may be constructed based on other models, which in turn may be models of other models, and so on. Thus, a model may be remotely related to the empirical accounting phenomena with which we are ultimately concerned, but the nature of accounting research appears to be such that models are all aimed at understanding existing accounting phenomena as well as improving them.

The distinction between descriptive models and normative models may not be clear-cut in every empirical situation. A descriptive model cannot represent all of the existing accounting phenomena, hence, there are likely to be some empirical observations which do not correspond to the model. On the other hand, a normative model can be a representation of some empirical phenomena, if the idea in the model has already been applied in practice. Also, a descriptive model can be normative, and a normative model can be descriptive, if the existing system is considered to be at optimum.

Nevertheless, the distinction between the two is important in terms of selecting the methods of defense. A defense of a descriptive model consists of showing that the model essentially represents what it is supposed to represent. A normative model, by contrast, is often developed deductively and may not have any counterpart in the empirical world. Thus, its defense is primarily concerned with demonstrating that the consequences of using the model will lead to a

better state of accounting, judged from a given set of goals.

The differences between the two types of models, may, therefore, be worth exploring further. Let us start with descriptive models in accounting and analyze the essential factors involved in constructing such models.[7]

The basic aim of descriptive models is to represent complicated empirical phenomena by simple models without losing the essentials. Models may be verbal, mathematical, or simply a set of tables, charts, etc., which represent the results of observations in simple form. In this sense, a map, a time schedule, a picture, etc. can also be considered as models of empirical phenomena.

If a model is an accurate representation of empirical phenomena, it has predictive power. Using a map, we can predict which street is next. An airline schedule enables us to predict arrival and departure times. *Accounting Trends and Techniques* can be used to predict, for example, the proportion of the companies who received qualified opinions from their auditors. A regression model relating accounting profits with stock prices enables us to predict the prices of stock in the market. An axiomatic system of current accounting procedures makes it possible for us to predict whether a certain procedure is accepted of not. Of course, prediction may or may not be accurate, depending upon how well the model represents the reality. But in any case, predictability is one of the benefits that may be derived from descriptive models.[8]

---

[7] The analysis of the structure of models in general is rather peripheral to the main subject of this paper. Hence, the reader is referred to other literature which specifically deals with this topic, such as Hempel and Oppeheim [16], Cyert and Grunberg [8], Cohen and Cyert [7], etc. Also, an important issue involved in model building is the issue of measurement. This is also not elaborated here for the same reason. For an interesting discussion on measurement in accounting from a methodological viewpoint, see Devine [11].

[8] Beaver, Kennelly, and Voss [3] emphasizes the predictive ability as the basis for evaluating accounting data. Although predictability is an important benefit, it must be remembered that predictability is only one possible consequence of having been able to comprehend complicated phenomena by means of a simple model. It is dangerous to emphasize predictability too much, since a high degree of predictability may result from a spurious correlation. The essential question to be answered by a scientific investigation is not just a question of what but of why.

Research methodology involved in developing descriptive models is two-fold, namely, (1) *empirical observations* and (2) *induction*. The process of constructing descriptive models starts with observations of empirical phenomena. There are many research methods used for this purpose.

Questionnaires, laboratory experiments, depth interviews, etc. are methods often used to obtain data about empirical phenomena. However, methods of observations are not limited to these. Reading literature is an indirect but often effective way of observing the phenomena. Also, putting oneself in the enviornment to gain experience about the problem is often a very useful way.

Observations may be statistical or judgmental. Statistical observations are those made under a statistical sampling scheme so that certain statistical inductions can be made from the observations. Judgmental observations are those which do not have such possibilities. Although statistical observations have advantages over judgmental observations, to meet the requirements for statistical sampling, the quality of observations may have to be lowered or the cost of observations may have to be increased. Thus, the trade-off must be considered. If the problem can be stated unambiguously and can be answered easily, questionnaires under a well designed sampling scheme may be ideal. On the other hand, if the problem involves an intricate psychological process (e.g., an auditor's decision process in selecting accounts), a depth interview may be superior to questionnaires, although it may not be possible to analyze statistically. In such a case, if the researcher happens to have auditing experience, there is no reason why he cannot analyze the psychological process which goes on in his own mind. Actually, the researcher himself is the only one who can analyze this process without going through his own perceptive mechanisms. This has the advantage of avoiding possible errors which may be associated with perception. Compared with a depth interview, the researcher can avoid not only his perceptive errors but also the errors which may be involved when the subject converts his inner feeling to his overt behavior. It is, therefore, not a coincidence that insightful research is often made by an expert in the field relying on his own experiences. Sometimes, a researcher spends a portion of his life to gain such experiences in order to enable him to analyze the phenomena first hand.[9]

Although such a method often carries with it a risk of being totally subjective, the depth of understanding that can be obtained by such a method often outweighs the risk. Statistical observations have desirable properties, but their results may be superficial. One should not neglect the power of penetrating observations involving "a sample of size one".

In developing descriptive models, the process of induction follows observations. A researcher does not normally have a set of observations covering the whole area of his interest. He must, therefore, induce the state of the entire area from a set of sample observations. Research findings must be reproducible if they are to be successfully defended. This means that the findings must have some generality. If the findings are concerned with only a particular observation at a particular point in time, it does not have reproducibility. In order to gain reproducibility, the process of induction must follow observations so that essentials are separated from peripherals.

Induction involves some degree of abstraction, focusing on essentials and neglecting peripherals, but what are essentials is determined with an aim toward generalization. Thus, induction may be considered as abstraction with an aim toward generalization.

Induction may be a very simple process, such as connecting two observed points in a cost chart to induce a cost curve, or may be a very elaborate process, such as those observed in regression analysis, factor analysis, etc. It may be qualitative or quantitative, statistical or judgmental. It may be well supported or poorly supported. Naturally, the more observations one has to induce

---

[9] A good example may be seen in Whyte [28] where he joined a group of a gang and lived together with them to study the social structure of a slum.

from, the better supported the induction will be.

The result of induction from observations is a model.[10] As discussed before, a model may be stated verbally, graphically, mathematically, etc. A model may be verified by deducing from it logically and checking with observations to see whether they agree with what is deduced from the model, or it may be verified by checking the size of observations, the method of selecting them, and the process of induction.[11]

In contrast to the processes of observations and induction that are involved in constructing descriptive models, the processes involved in constructing normative models may be characterized by (1) *goal-assumptions* and (2) *deduction*. Since a normative model is goal-oriented, the assumed goals must be clearly stated. In order to say that accounting practices should be such and such, one must agree on the goals to be served by changing the existing accounting practices toward the normative direction. Then, one must develop a model, deducing from the goals some of the properties that the model must have. The deductive process is also observed in applying the model to empirical phenomena in order to change the reality toward a more preferred state in terms of the assumed goals.

While a defense for a descriptive model is made by verifying the accuracy of representation, a defense for a normative model is made by demonstrating that certain benefits are derived if the reality is changed so that it fits the specifications of the model, where benefits are defined in relation to the assumed goals. A defense for a normative model may be made by logically showing the superiority of the state that can be created by using the model, or it may be made by demonstrating this superiority empirically.

Since goals are concerned with improving reality, it must be feasible to apply a model in an empirical situation. Thus, *feasibility* of

a model becomes an important part of a defense for a normative model. This has an important implication in dealing with normative models in accounting, as elaborated below.

Many normative models in accounting are concerned with methods of providing data for some given uses. Depending upon the uses of the data, the characteristics required of the accounting data may be quite different. Such characteristics may be concerned with the required degree of accuracy of data, which can vary depending upon uses. Timing, verifiability, objectivity, etc. may be other examples of such characteristics. One characteristic which is often neglected, however, in the discussion of normative models in accounting is what may be called "hardness" of the data. An important use of accounting data in this respect is to solve conflicts between two or more interested parties. Income taxes, determination of fair returns in regulated industries, and bonuses to employees under a profit-sharing plan, are a few examples where accounting profit figures are used to solve conflicts of interest in allocating the proceeds from business operations.[12] We often see the struggle between two parties, one trying to push the figure as high as possible and the other trying to push the figure as low as possible. We may thus define "hard figures" to be ones which can possess reasonable stability despite such pressures to make them move up or down. "Soft figures" are then defined as those which do not have such a property. Hard figures are not just objective figures which simply mean that neutral people will generally agree with the figures. Hard figures are such that even people whose interest is strongly affected by the figures find it difficult to disagree with them.

For many uses of accounting data, soft figures may be sufficient. This is the case when accounting data are used for manage-

---

[10] The process by which accounting models are constructed is compared with the same process involved in theory of language in Sterling [25] and Ijiri [20]. See also Hempel [15] on the process by which concepts are developed inductively.

[11] On the issue of verification of a model or a theory, see Grunberg [14], Sterling [25], etc.

[12] On the use of accounting data for solving conflicts of interest, see American Accounting Association [2], where a distinction is made between equity accounting (accounting used for solving conflicts of interest) and operational accounting (accounting for decision making). See also Ijiri [21], where the superiority of historical cost accounting is emphasized in equity accounting in this respect.

rial decisions aimed at increasing the profit of the firm. As we move from generation of profit to its allocation among interested parties, the hardness of the figures becomes more and more important.

When we talk about the feasibility of a new accounting model, it is important for us to question whether the model is capable of producing figures with a required degree of hardness. It must be remembered that almost any kind of model would become feasible if there were no constraints imposed upon the quality of outputs from the model. Hardness appears to be an important, yet often neglected, quality of outputs from such a normative model.

Finally, a distinction must be made between normative models and *policies*. Although a normative model is based upon certain assumptions as to the goals to be served, it does not necessarily mean that the researcher who created the model subscribes to the assumed goals. Thus, a normative model has policy implications but it is different from a policy judgment, which involves a commitment to goals. Whether it is a descriptive model or a normative model, a model is a theory which can be scientifically verified. It is different from policy judgments which have their base on "opinions."

We have now seen the nature of accounting research, which was analyzed based on two types of models, descriptive and normative.[13] Let us now go back to the question raised at the beginning of this paper and ask

what factors are needed to make accounting research as challenging intellectually as those observed in other areas of science. This is the topic of the next section.

4. Creating Challenges in Accounting Research

It is convenient to discuss descriptive models and normative models separately in describing factors needed to create more intellectual challenges for accounting researchers. Let us start with descriptive models.

What is most needed in descriptive models in accounting is *generality*. When we compare accounting models to those of science in general, this is the element that is most striking as being absent from accounting models. For example, when a Nobel prize winner, James Watson, discovered the structure of DNA, the heredity molecule deoxyribonucleic acid, he did not have any doubt about the generality of his findings to all DNA.[14] Such generalization is based on the scientist's confidence in the homogeneity of the phenomena in biochemistry. But suppose an accounting researcher runs an experiment, using students as subjects, to test, say, whether or not a change in an accounting method affects managers' decisions. To what extent can the results be generalized?

There have been almost no rules in accounting research which regulate the extent to which the researcher is entitled to generalize from his findings. Statistical methods are, in many cases, not much help here, since the population characteristics or the sampling method often fail to satisfy the required conditions, although such methods are frequently applied superficially just to meet the formality of research presentation. As a result, it is not unusual that wildest speculations are made from a tiny result. Although conjectures or speculations are necessary ingredients for scientific development, they are like personal opinions, which must be separated clearly from scientific results. Otherwise, discussions on account-

---

[13] As a means of understanding the nature of accounting research, a number of articles published in *The Accounting Review* and *Journal of Accounting Research* in recent years were surveyed with an aim toward obtaining some classification schemes based on the research methods used. The following seven categories were tentatively arrived at and reported in "Methodological Taxonomy of Accounting Research" (abstract) which formed a basis for this present paper. The seven categories are: (1) Goal-setting (A should exist), (2) Engineering (A is developed for B), (3) Feasibility (A is feasible), (4) Evaluation (A is a preference ordering of B), (5) Fact-finding (A exists), (6) Deductive (A is deduced from B), (7) Inductive (A is induced from B). Here, A represents the essential focus of research, whereas B is something that has already been established before. Upon a closer review of this classification and a further study of more accounting articles, these categories are merged together, due to their close interactions, and fitted into the standard classification of descriptive and normative models as presented above. For an interesting classificatory survey on accounting research and methodology, see Buckley, Kircher, and Mathews [5].

[14] For an interesting story by Watson about his personal account of the process of this discovery, see Watson [26].

ing research will become something like political debates.

In order to maintain accounting research on the scientific foundation, there must be some control over the degree of generalization one can make from research findings. As a possible way of achieving such control, we propose what may be called the *contrapositive method*.

When a researcher observes β and induces a generalized statement B, in many cases what he ought to say is not an unqualified B but rather a qualified B in the form of "A implies B," where A is a set of conditions under which the researcher believes that B will hold. Unfortunately, under the present practices in accounting research, A is often ambiguously stated or is totally omitted, as if the researcher had found a truly universal model unconditionally applicable. It should, therefore, be imposed as a requirement in any model induced from empirical observations that the conditions A, under which the generalized statement B is supposed to hold, must be explicitly stated. Furthermore, it may be desirable to require that the researcher state his conviction that observations contradictory to B will *not* be found if A is satisfied. In other words, in presenting his model (if A is satisfied, B is true), the researcher is asked to commit himself to another model which says that if not B, then not A. In fact the latter model is said to be *contrapositive* to the former model and two are logically equivalent.[15] But this gives him a chance to review his model from a different angle.

Moreover, such a conviction (observations contradictory to B will never be found under the conditions A) will provide an important challenge to future researchers and will make empirical research more stimulating. At the same time, this will make the original researcher more careful in stating the condi-

tions A. If he states A too loosely, he runs a risk that his conviction may be overturned easily. On the other hand, if he makes A too stringent, this will expose the lack of generality in his research findings.[16] In this way, the process of generalization seems to be effectively controlled by this contrapositive method.

Although wild generalization must be controlled, the lack of generalization must also be avoided. It is, perhaps, true that accounting phenomena are much more heterogeneous than phenomena in natural science, making generalization more difficult in accounting research. However, since reproducibility is essential as a part of the defense of research findings, generalizability must be more emphasized in accounting research.

It is true that accounting practices are not the results of logical and systematic development. Hence, it may be quite natural for us to regard accounting practices on inventories as being quite different from those on fixed assets, and we may accept contradictions among them. However, unless we force ourselves to find consistency among seemingly heterogeneous or even contradictory phenomena, descriptive models will be simply collections of bits and pieces of observations.[17] The models' predictive powers will also be greatly reduced, since few rules are induced from observations to fill the gaps among them.

On the other hand, as a model becomes more and more general, it is almost inevitable that the conclusions (as well as predic-

---

[15] "If A then B" means that it is not possible to have A and *not B*, both hold. Similarly, its contrapositive, "If *not B* then *not A*", means, by substituting *not B* for A and *not A* for B, that it is not possible to have *not B* and *not (not A)* = A, both hold, which is equivalent to the previous statement. However, note the so-called Hempel's paradox involved in empirical verification of a contrapositive statement. See Gardner [13a, pp. 52–53].

[16] Few people will be interested in the results of an experiment if the researcher states that an accounting method affects decisions, only if these particular subjects are used and these particular data sheets are used in this particular laboratory.

[17] A simpler model is more desirable than a complicated model for describing the same phenomena. The reason for this is that, in general, observations that appear more frequently in our experience tend to be given simpler names. Therefore, a simple model means that observations in question are related to known phenomena which have been frequently observed. Since we tend to believe that events observed frequently in the past have a higher chance of being observed in the future than events observed less frequently, a simple model appears to be more reliable in prediction than a complicated model which is often viewed with suspicion. In this sense, scientists' belief that nature is essentially simple is synonymous with the belief that nature is repetitive.

tions) derived from the model become more and more general (or ambiguous), losing the specificity one might like to have in using the model. Since accounting research deals with very pragmatic subject matter, emphasis on the "usefulness" of a model often results in pressure to make models less abstract and general.

Such pressure, however, can be a serious cause for making accounting research less scientific and less challenging intellectually. If Newton's only purpose in studying physics had been to make his horse carriage run more smoothly, would he have been able to develop such a beautiful structure of Newtonian physics? Any automobile mechanic knows that there are many more "useful" tricks of the trade than Newton's law of motion. But does this mean Newton's law is useless? Certainly not. Significant scientific findings of such magnitude cannot be obtained by pursuing cheap "usefulness" or trivial predictability.

Of course, this does not mean that the pragmatic value of scientific studies in accounting should be totally neglected. The above argument is presented only to emphasize the point that too much emphasis on immediate usefulness of accounting research can be a great impediment to the development of a profound structure of scientific theories in accounting, similar to those observed in other fields of science.

Let us now move to normative models to see what factors might be needed there to make the process of constructing normative models as challenging as solving the four-color problem or developing medicine to cure disease.

There have been numerous proposals on how accounting practices should be changed. Some deal with a small segment of practices, say, on how an adjustment to prior year's income ought to be handled on the income statement. Some deal with a large segment of practices, such as proposals for current cost accounting.

If there were no constraints to be imposed upon the properties that a normative model must satisfy, it would be very easy to develop a model on whatever segment of practices one is concerned with. In fact, it is trivial to develop a normative model under no constraints.

However, just as a descriptive model is constrained by empirical observations (in the sense that the model must fit the observations), a normative model is contrained by the goals to be served. It must be demonstrated that a normative model serves the goals better than other existing models.

Here, however, we see the same kind of ambiguity in specifying the goals to be served by a normative model as we saw in specifying the conditions under which a descriptive model was applicable. As pointed out in the previous section, the lack of attention to the required degree of hardness of figures generated from a model is one of many examples which show the ambiguity of goals.

The process of developing a normative model is like the engineering process involved in building a bridge over a river. The challenge involved in the process stems solely from the fact that specifications must be met by using limited resources and technology. Thus, in developing a normative model, the ambiguity of goals to be served (or the lack of detailed specification) seems to be the central obstacle that should be removed to make accounting research more challenging.

In addition, a strict separation of theories and policies seems to be essential to make evaluation of normative models more scientific. A normative model should be evaluated based on how well it meets the goal specifications and should never be evaluated based on whether or not one likes the goals. The latter is a policy issue, which must be distinguished from evaluation of the scientific and engineering achievement of the normative model.

In summary, it appears that the processes of accounting research (descriptive or normative) need to be constrained and tightened. The four-color problem is challenging because the solution must be derived following strict rules of logic. The discovery of the structure of DNA is exciting because the structure had to simultaneously satisfy a number of constraints derived from X-ray analyses and other empirical observations.

Just as beautiful love stories in classic literature all have in common some constraints overcome by the two lovers, scientific discoveries are praised because of the constraint that the scientist had to overcome.

In many parts of accounting, present research processes are so loosely constructed that nobody seems to be able to prove or disprove anything scientifically. This seems to be the essential factor to be remedied in making accounting research more intellectually challenging.

5. An Unsolved Problem: Triple-Entry Bookkeeping

To stimulate accounting research in another way, it seems to be worthwhile to prepare a list of unsolved problems in accounting. They can provide a great challenge to present and future accounting researchers. An accounting Nobel prize may be established and awarded to any researcher who is first to solve such a problem. Of course, in providing a problem, not only the rules of solving the problem but the criteria for judging whether or not the problem was solved must be explicitly and objectively stated.

As one example of an unsolved problem, I would like to contribute the following problem to the list. As everyone in accounting knows, the basic double-entry scheme of bookkeeping has remained unchanged over the past 500 years. Considering the enormous changes that have been experienced in economic systems during these years, the stability of the double-entry bookkeeping system is truly remarkable. A question that naturally arises from this fact is: Is it not possible to devise, say, a triple-entry bookkeeping system or is the present double-entry system unique?

The answer to the first part of the question is "yes." It has been shown that triple or quadruple or, in general, multiple-entry bookkeeping is possible.[18] However, these bookkeeping systems do not have the same power as a double-entry system for recording resource flows. The multiple-entry system developed there is merely classifica-

tional, in the sense that the multiplicity of entries is obtained by classifying the same set of assets based on three, four, or many classification schemes, such as physical properties of assets, claim on assets, responsibility of custody, location, age of assets, etc.

The answer to the latter part of the question is also "yes," insofar as we are interested in recording resource flows based on exchanges among them. It has been demonstrated that the essence of the double-entry system does *not* rest on the fact that the *same* set of assets are classified in two different ways (one based on types of assets and the other based on claims on assets). It rests on the fact that two *different* sets of resources are tied together as being a decrement (resources foregone) and an increment (resources obtained) in an exchange, and the equality of debit and credit is obtained because the value of the increment is set equal to the value of the decrement in a transaction.[19] Therefore, insofar as resource flows are perceived as transactions (namely exchanges), the bookkeeping system must be essentially based on double-entries. Thus, enormously complicated economic events of a firm are considered to be structured based on transactions which have increments and decrements, just as matter is constructed from atoms which have protons and electrons. However, not long ago, it was discovered that there is a third element in an atom which is called a neutron. This discovery teaches us that the way we are observing economic events by means of transactions may have a third element which we have neglected totally, and the introduction of the third element may develop the present double-entry system into a triple-entry system.

Thus, we have the following problem which is yet to be solved. Is it possible to perceive economic events of a firm to be a numerous collection of atomistic activities, each of which consists of three types of primitive factors (say, α, β, and γ) that can be combined with the same or different factors

---

[18] See Ijiri [18, Chapter 5], where this is elaborated in detail.

[19] For a discussion of this issue, see Ijiri [18, Chapter 5], which relates the double-entry bookkeeping system with the historical cost valuation method.

(α with α or α with β, etc.) in other activities? If this is possible, what is the way in which primitive factors (α, β, and γ) are mutually combined? Is a triple-entry bookkeeping system suitable for recording such atomistic activities, or is the uniqueness of double-entry still maintained there, too?

It is not clear whether a triple-entry system (excluding such a trivial system as classificational triple-entries, discussed above, or triple-entries obtained by combining two double-entries, namely, a → b and b → c combined to form a → b → c) is to be developed as an extension of a double-entry system[20] or whether such a system requires a totally new approach or even a totally new system of logic.[21]

In any case, would not a problem like this be just as challenging intellectually as the four-color problem?

6. Summary and Conclusion

In this paper, the nature of accounting research was analyzed by means of reviewing the processes involved in constructing descriptive models and those involved in constructing normative models. Then, as a means of making accounting research more intellectually challenging, it was proposed that a researcher who developed a descriptive model be required to state his conviction that under a certain set of conditions, observations contradictory to his findings would *not* be found, and that a researcher who developed a normative model be re-

quired to demonstrate that his model met detailed specifications of the goals to be served by the model. Finally, a suggestion was made that a list of unsolved problems in accounting be prepared to stimulate future accounting research. As an example, a problem of triple-entry bookkeeping was described, which was considered to be as challenging intellectually as the famous four-color problem in topology.

Whether research in any given field is more exciting or less exciting than those in other fields does not depend upon the field but only upon the researcher who engages in research. It is hoped that this view will be shared by many of those who engage in research in accounting.

---

[20] For example, in theory of numbers, the concept of integers is extended to consider $a + b\sqrt{m}$ to be integers, if a and b are integers and m is an integer ($\neq 0$, 1) whose square-root is not an integer. The mathematical structure of a quadratic field was created in this way. Here, we may ask: Would it be possible to develop a cubic field?

[21] In fact, it is possible to trace the root of the double-entry system to the two-valuedness of our logic. Thus, it is entirely possible that a triple-entry system requires a three-valued logic as its support. Furthermore, the present theories on many-valued logic are of first degree only. This means that the value of a statement A can be three (say, red, yellow and blue instead of just true or false) but a statement, "A is blue," is no longer valued as red, yellow or blue but as true or false. See, for example Rosser and Turquette [24]. A three-valued logic, in the true sense of the word, must have the property that no matter how a sentence is enlarged, its value can still take one of the three possibilities. It is, of course, not known whether such a three-valued logic is necessary to develop a triple-entry bookkeeping system, but this possibility definitely exists.

References

1. American Accounting Association, *A Statement of Basic Accounting Theory*, American Accounting Association, 1966.

2. American Accounting Association, "Report by Committee on Foundations of Accounting Measurement," *The Accounting Review* (Supplement, 1971), pp. 1–48.

3. Beaver, W. H., Kennelly, J. W., and Voss, W. M., "Predictive Ability as a Criterion for the Evaluation of Accounting Data," *The Accounting Review* (October, 1968), pp. 675–683.

4. Beveridge, W. I. B., *The Art of Scientific Investigation*, Vintage Books, 1961.

5. Buckley, J. W., Kircher, P., and Mathews, R. L. "Methodology in Accounting Theory," *The Accounting Review* (April, 1968), pp. 274–283.

6. Chambers, R. J., "Prospective Adventures in Accounting Ideas," *The Accounting Review* (April, 1967), pp. 241–253.

7. Cohen, K. J., and Cyert, R. M., *Theory of the Firm*, Prentice-Hall, 1965.

8. Cyert, R. M., and Grunberg, E., "Assumption, Prediction, and Explanation in Economics," in R. M. Cyert and J. G. March, *A Behavioral Theory of the Firm*, Prentice-Hall, 1963.

9. Devine, C. T., "Research Methodology and Accounting Theory Formation," *The Accounting Review* (July, 1960), pp. 387–399.

10. _____, *Essays in Accounting Theory*, Two Volumes, C. T. Devine, 1962.

11. _____, "Some Conceptual Problems in Accounting Measurements," in R. K. Jaedicke, Y. Ijiri and O. Nielsen (eds). *Research in Accounting Measurement*, American Accounting Association, 1966, pp. 13–27.

12. Friedman, M., *Essays in Positive Economics*, The University of Chicago Press, 1953.

13. Gardner, Martin, *New Mathematical Diversions from SCIENTIFIC AMERICAN*, Simon and Schuster, 1966.

13a. _____, *The SCIENTIFIC AMERICAN Book of Mathematical Puzzles & Diversions*, Simon and Schuster, 1959.

14. Grunberg, E., "Notes on the Verifiability of Economic Laws," *Philosophy of Science* (1957), pp. 337–348.

15. Hempel, C. G., *Fundamentals of Concept Formation in Empirical Science*, The University of Chicago Press, 1952..

16. Hempel, C. G., and Oppenheim, P., "Studies in the Logic of Explanation," *Philosophy of Science* (1948), pp. 135–175.

17. Hendriksen, E. S., *Accounting Theory*, Richard D. Irwin, 1965.

18. Ijiri, Y., *The Foundations of Accounting Measurement: A Mathematical, Economic, and Behavioral Inquiry*, Prentice-Hall, 1967.

19. _____, "Research and Its Processes," *Aoyama Business Review* (September, 1969), pp. 1–16.

20. _____, "Logic and Sanctions in Accounting," in R. R. Sterling and W. F. Bentz (eds.), *Accounting in Perspective*, South-Western, 1971, [1971a].

21. _____, "A Defense for Historical Cost Accounting," in R. R. Sterling (ed)., *Asset Valuation and Income Determination: A Consideration of the Alternatives*, Scholars Book, 1971 [1971b].

22. Kaplan, A., *The Conduct of Inquiry*, Chandler, 1964.

23. Ore, Oystein, *The Four-Color Problem*, Academic Press, 1967.

24. Rosser, J. B., and Turquette, A. R., *Many-Valued Logics*, North-Holland, 1958.

25. Sterling, R. R., "On Theory Construction and Verification," *The Accounting Review* (July, 1970), pp. 444–457.

26. Watson, J. C., *The Double Helix*, Signet Book, 1968.

27. Wheeler, J. T., "Accounting Theory and Research in Perspective," *The Accounting Review* (January, 1970), pp. 1–10.

28. Whyte, W. F., *Street Corner Society*, The University of Chicago Press, 1943.

chapter 7

Accounting Research—Science or Methodology?

PETER CAWS

City University of New York

It is a rare pleasure for somebody who works in philosophy of science to be presented with what is, to him, a new science, especially if it exhibits neatly the principles his philosophical work has led him to regard as paradigmatic of what a science ought to be. I had something of this pleasure on reading Professor Ijiri's fascinating text on "The Nature of Accounting Research." Without intending any slight to the accounting profession, I think it would be honest to say that few of us in philosophy of science would ordinarily be inclined to choose accounting as an illustrative example, yet Ijiri has convinced me that it has something to teach us as well as fitting into our preconceptions.

First as to this fitting. It may be, of course, that there is something pre-arranged about it—for I notice that even if philosophers have neglected accounting, the theorists of accounting have not neglected philosophy, as the bibliographies of the various papers presented at this symposium clearly show. This means that the standard language of scientific methodology occurs naturally in their discussions. But the applicability of this language seems genuine enough, and I find Ijiri's account of inductive and deductive methods, descriptive and

normative models, etc., relevant and enlightening in this new context. I wish to make one or two specific comments on the more or less standard points and then go on to something more general.

My first comment has to do with the novelty of research findings. While it is true, strictly speaking, that "there is no need for someone else to come up with the same idea once it has been developed," this conclusion presupposes a situation of perfect communication between scientists. It has been shown by some of the work of Robert Merton, among others, not only that almost every new idea is in fact discovered by more than one researcher at about the same time, but also—and correlatively—that a surprisingly high proportion of what passes for new research is, in fact, the repetition of old research, and that many results published as new could, with sufficient diligence, be found elsewhere in the literature. As abstracting services, computerized indices and the like become more common and more comprehensive this sort of thing is likely to decline, but this is possible only when a firm terminology has been established. Until a science reaches the level of stability that such a terminology represents it may have to resign itself to a certain amount of redundancy in research. There is nothing wrong with this—on the contrary it has been the standard pattern for years—but it does require some relaxation of the abstract standard of novelty.

My second comment has to do with the parallel, or lack of it, between descriptive/ normative on the one hand and inductive/ deductive on the other. As Ijiri represents it, a descriptive model is a special kind of inductive model, and a normative model is a special kind of deductive model. He goes on to say that the descriptive/normative boundary may be fuzzy, and I agree. What interests me is whether, given that the sets of categories do not exactly coincide, hybrid combinations are possible, e.g., inductive normative models or deductive descriptive models. I do not propose to answer my own query definitively, but I might suggest that people sometimes do things not because they feel they ought but because those things follow from other things that are done. I do not know whether, in seeking to account for what goes on in accounting (and I note parenthetically that in the language of scientific explanation and philosophical criticism the word "account" seems to crop up with surprising frequency once one's attention has been drawn to it) it might not happen sometimes that an adequate explanation of a given practice might be given in this way; if it did, the inductive base of the premises being left out (of account) for the moment, that might constitute deductive descriptive explanation. Also, people sometimes feel that they ought to do what everybody else is doing, and that might in turn be the basis of an inductive normative explanation.

My more general remarks take their point of departure from a kind of disappointment with Ijiri's text, which as I read on constituted something of an antidote to my initial euphoria about the new science. With one exception—to which I shall return in a moment, since it represents the most valuable lesson that I derived from the text—I did not feel, until I got to the triple entry bookkeeping at the end, that I had really confronted the specificity of *accounting* research at all. Now it is one thing to have

problematic categories and to look for names for them, and another to have interesting names and look for categories corresponding to them. "Observation," "theory," "model," and so on, as far as their technical uses are concerned, began as problematic categories encountered in scientific research, mainly in the physical sciences; the philosophy of science has tried to understand what is going on and to work critically on the language in which it is described—hence, the technical terms and the standard methodology (bearing in mind that "method" and "methodology" have quite different meanings). Is accounting, like physics a couple of hundred years ago, a science in search of a methodology, or is accounting research a methodology in search of a science? I do not attach moral weight to the answer to this question— either is a perfectly honorable condition. But I get the feeling that the second is closer to the truth. And this makes things interesting, since while the methodology of a given science is not likely to offer many surprises, the science of a given methodology may have unexpected features.

To have a science of anything is first to have recognized a domain and a set of phenomena in that domain, and second to have devised a theory whose inputs *and outputs* are phenomena in the domain (the first observations, the second predictions) and whose terms may describe the underlying reality of the domain.[1] The domain of accounting research (its "objects") is specified by Ijiri as a set of *relations* between "economic events of an entity and information recorded and reported about them." But relations, in turn, have their domains, namely the sets of things related by them, so that accounting research must presumably look at the events and at the reports and records as well. But when Ijiri comes to discuss the empirical aspects of accounting research, he goes outside these domains in two interesting ways: first to the uses for which the records and reports are intended,

[1]See R. R. Sterling, "On Theory Construction and Verification," *The Accounting Review*, 46 (July 1970), pp. 448 ff. for a discussion of some of the possible phenomena in the domain of accounting.

second to the interests of the people who put them to these uses. Earlier he speaks of accounting *procedures,* the aspect under which the layman becomes aware of the profession ("accepted accounting practice," and all that). Now while procedures are, in a way, relations between the events and reports—effective relations according to which the latter get generated out of the former—they are more obviously human activities, things people do with certain ends in mind, which are not just to be described and explained as physical or logical relations might be but which can also be justified, condemned, excused, and so on. The science that the methodology discovers turns out to contain essential ingredients of sociology, psychology, decision theory, the theory of utilities, semantics, and even for all I know criminology.

So after all, my disappointment was premature, since Ijiri now offers, not so much a new science, as a new way of looking at a lot of old sciences. For, generalizing from his own example, it seems to me obviously useful to apply the concepts of "hard" and "soft" figures to other cases. At first, the naive physical scientist, or his philosophical analyst, might be amazed to think that there could be any question about the *figures.* For them the paradigm of the numerical input to a scientific calculation would be a pointer reading, obtained by looking at a dial and following certain protocol rules ("if in doubt record the next higher number," and so on). It would seem extraordinary and shocking if the observer were to report a hard figure of 5, but under other circumstances report the same reading as a soft figure of 3. All such subjective factors, the positivistically inclined philosopher of science would be inclined to say, looking the observer sternly in the eye, must be in-

exorably eliminated from scientific practice. And, of course, in *that* context, falsifying the figures would be unthinkable, just as (I hope) it would be unthinkable for an accountant, looking in the petty cash box and seeing $20 there, to write down $5. The difference between physics and accounting may have something to do with the difference between petty cash (even if it is kept in an extremely elaborate and expensive box) and high finance. What the accountant gets to look at has already left the simplicity of the pointer reading far behind; his activity becomes, I take it, one of *interpreting* quite as much as *looking.*

This being the case, Ijiri's plea for his "contrapositive method"—a plea, in fact, for *specification* of the circumstances under which certain conclusions are drawn or interpretations made—makes excellent sense. I hope the profession will listen to him. But I am less worried about that than about the reflection that all this casts on the other sciences. For it is clear that every science leaves the pointer readings behind sooner or later, and it is what goes on at the higher and more complex levels that needs looking at. Every report of an experiment, every theoretical conclusion, can be looked upon as a bit of accounting—the giving of a report to the world of something that happened and what it meant. The profession of accounting, involved as it is with the world of business, has to face honestly (as Ijiri does) the utilitarian pressures placed upon research in it. But it is only that the pressures are more subtle elsewhere. Newton and men like him are above the battle; at other points in the establishment of the physical sciences, hard and soft figures may indeed come into play. And for this insight I am grateful to Ijiri.

On the Use of Surrogates
in Behavioral Experimentation

JOHN W. DICKHAUT

University of Chicago

JOHN LESLIE LIVINGSTONE AND DAVID J. H. WATSON

Ohio State University

When an artist wants to draw a recognizable scene—say a landscape—his intention is roughly as follows (although he does not phrase it this way): *to create a stimulus object to which people will respond in much the same way as they would respond to the countryside itself.* That is he intends to produce a *surrogate* of the countryside. He obviously cannot do this in its entirety. He cannot produce a surrogate with real bark, real trees, real clouds moving in real distance, so he must *abstract* only those aspects that are *necessary* to obtain the desired effect yet are reproducible by pigment spread on a flat surface of canvas or paper. (Hochberg [13, p. 36])

1. Introduction

A vigorous recent development in accounting research is the realization of the fundamental importance and relevance of the behavioral area. For example, according to the American Accounting Association Committee to Prepare a Statement of Basic Accounting Theory [30, p. 63]:

Because of technological changes and advances in knowledge of human behavior the scope and methods of accounting are changing and can be expected to continue to change. . . . Major areas in which changes are occurring which will influence accounting in the future are perceived as including:

1. Knowledge of decision processes.
2. Knowledge of human behavior.
3. Computer technology and systems design.
4. Measurement techniques and information theory.

In light of these developments accounting theory and practice will probably be broadened considerably in the future.

A number of studies have been published based on laboratory experiments. However, serious questions have been raised concerning the validity of the results of these experiments in the "real world." For instance, since most studies are laboratory experiments with student subjects, it has been asked if the laboratory can approximate complex reality and if student subjects can represent actual decision makers.[1] This compound question will be referred to as the

---

[1] See for instance, Bruns [7], Jensen [17], Birnberg and Nath [5], and Hofstedt and Kinard [14].

surrogation problem, a problem of crucial importance.[2]

In both the design of research and the interpretation of its results, it is desirable to know (or at least have some notion of) how much extrapolation can be made to nonexperimental situations. If reliably generalizable, such studies offer a relatively simple, speedy, and inexpensive means of expanding our knowledge. If no generalizations can reasonably be made from such work, all laboratory experimentation would be of little or no value. If any generalizations from laboratory experimentation are to be possible, criteria must be found for determining the extent to which the surrogation problem is resolved. The purpose of the present study is to explore the derivation of such criteria.

The paper is developed in four major sections. In Section 2, concepts and definitions related to the research process are introduced. In Section 3, surrogation is defined and some existing research related to surrogation is discussed. In Section 4, the relationships between the surrogation problem and the research process are discussed. The discussion incorporates an analysis of two types of surrogation included in the research process, the presentation of a major philosophical question related to the surrogation problem, and an examination of the existing claims of valid and invalid surrogations.

2. The Research Process

Several major concepts and definitions upon which this paper is built are found in Simon's "On Judging the Plausibility of Theories" [26] and Aronson and Carlsmith's "Experimentation in Social Psychology" [2].

Simon outlines five phases of the research process. In describing phase one he says: "The enterprise [research process] generally begins with empirical data, rather

than a hypothesis out of the blue" [26, pp. 457–58]. As an example of this phase, Simon describes the collecting of city population data consisting of the absolute size and rank of American city populations. In accounting, examples of this phase include the gathering of income numbers and securities prices on computer tapes, the building of a history of different accounting methods in *Accounting Trends and Techniques,* and the production of a stream of data from exploratory accounting studies, such as those by Bonini [6], Jensen [16], and Livingstone [20].

In the second phase of the research process, Simon says: "Striking features of the data (e.g., that they are linear on a log scale of minus one) provide for a simple generalization that summarizes them approximately" [26, pp. 457–58]. The Simon example of this phase is his linear plot of the rank and size data of city populations after this data has been transformed to logarithms. An example of this phase in accounting research is that the data in the Livingstone [20] study seem to suggest that a learning effect may alter the degree to which changes in accounting method may be incorporated by different public utility rate making bodies.

During phase three, Simon says: "We search for limiting conditions that will improve the approximation [that results from the simple generalization of phase two] by manipulating variables that will affect its goodness" [26, pp. 457–58]. With respect to his population, Simon considers the examination of cities in different countries, cities with similar and dissimilar rates of migration, etc. In accounting studies using the multiple regression technique (for example those by Benston [3] and Gonedes [10]) important variables, such as industry and market factors, are examined to determine whether these factors mediate any of the effects produced by the accounting variables.

In phase four, according to Simon, "We construct simple mechanisms to explain simple generalizations—showing that the latter can be deduced from the former" [26, pp. 457–58]. With respect to his population example, Simon described a simple explanatory model he built. The model consisted of

---

[2] Surrogation problems arise whenever a process of modeling or representation or abstraction takes place. Therefore, surrogation involves a greater range of problems than the present one alone, and hence, our choice of terminology is made only for the sake of convenience and implies no claim of wider generality for our discussion. In fact, we ignore many vital areas of surrogation, such as the nature of relations between surrogates and principals. For a useful discussion of surrogation, see Ijiri [15, pp. 4–19].

several assumptions about migration rates and the stability of populations which permit the deduction of the linear relationship between the logarithmic transformations of the rank and size data. In accounting, Stedry [27] employs an aspiration level mechanism to explain his experimental data.

In phase five, Simon says: "The explanatory theories generally make predictions that go beyond the simple generalizations in a number of respects and hence suggest new empirical observations and experiments that allow them to be tested further" [26, pp. 457–58]. With respect to Simon's population example, this phase can be characterized by the fact that his population model has implications for patterns of migration that may occur and that these implications can be tested.[3] In accounting, we have not found instances in which empirical observations have been procured to test the extended implications of an explanatory mechanism.

Related to Simon's description of the research process, and particularly relevant to the surrogation problem, is the fact that laboratory experimentation can be an integral part of any phase of the process. A laboratory experiment can produce original data or be used to reproduce another experiment's original data. Laboratory experiments can be used to re-establish the striking results of phase two and can certainly be the basis for discovering them. Laboratory experiments can be used to determine the improved approximations of phase three, since variables can be isolated and manipulated systematically to provide limiting conditions which might produce better approximations.

Laboratory experiments can also be used to test the simple explanatory mechanisms of phase four, since the experiments can provide an environment from which it can be deduced whether dependent variables respond to independent variables in a manner specified by the explanatory mechanism. Finally, the laboratory can be used to provide exactly those conditions that are necessary for testing alternate predictions of the explanatory mechanisms.

It should be emphasized that the previous statements do not indicate that laboratory experimentation has or will play its potential role in the accounting research process. The statements indicate only the possibility. To realize the possibility, some specific requirements in the design of an experiment must be met.

The work of Aronson and Carlsmith elaborates these requirements. They discuss four terms useful in relating the research process to the surrogation problem: experimental reality, internal validity, external validity, and mundane reality [2, pp. 22–26].

Experimental reality refers to the degree of involvement of the subject in the experiment, i.e., that the subject participating in the experiment is aroused and interested rather than bored and detached. As an example, the authors cite an experiment in which subjects were asked to read a newspaper. The subjects paid only scant attention to an article that was supposed to arouse their attention. Aronson and Carlsmith suggest that the experiment lacked experimental realism.

Internal validity is concerned with whether the experimental conditions, in fact, cause the observed outcomes. It is in the pursuit of internal validity that experimenters attempt to control or offset the extraneous variables so that these variables will not influence the outcome of the experiment. Procedures designed to meet the requirements of the statistical model (restrictions on subject-experimenter interaction, restrictions on subject-subject interaction, etc.) are also important elements in the establishment of internal validity.

External validity refers to the extent to which results of the experiment can be translated and extended to situations and conditions beyond the experiment. The problem of establishing external validity is a concern of this paper and is extensively discussed in Section 4.

Mundane reality refers to the attempt to

---

[3] Popper [23, p. 340] provides an alternative view to Simon's. "We can learn more about the heuristics and the methodology and even about the psychology of research by studying theories, and the arguments offered for or against them, than by any direct behavioristic or psychological or sociological approach. In general, we may learn a great deal about behavior and psychology from the study of the products."

include in an experiment any particular aspect of an environment on the presumption that the aspect makes the experimental environment more real. For instance, if one were to study executive decision behavior, the experiment possesses more mundane reality if, during the experiment, the executive has the same number of secretaries as he has at his office. If the executive has a leather chair at his office, the experiment which employs wood chairs has less mundane reality than the experiment which uses leather chairs.

3. Definition of Surrogation and Discussion of Relevant Literature

The word "surrogate" denotes an object which substitutes for or takes the place of a second object. An important aspect of this phenomenon is that it is dependent upon reference to particular functions or properties of the objects involved. For instance, Mrs. Henry, who has a teaching degree, is an appropriate substitute (i.e., surrogate) for Mrs. Jones, the teacher. However, Mrs. Henry, the 65 year old, is not an appropriate surrogate for Mrs. Jones, the 22 year old champion tennis player.

That surrogation is dependent upon certain properties of objects, as opposed to the object in toto, is seen when attempting to surrogate one set of objects for another set. For example, the Nixon daughters are appropriate surrogates for the Johnson daughters, if the property surrogated is that the objects in the set be related by being the daughters of Presidents. However, if the relationship between the objects in the set is that they be daughters of Democrats, then the Nixon daughters would not be appropriate surrogates of the Johnson daughters.

Often business and accounting researchers think only of experimental *subjects* as surrogates—usually students for businessmen. However, other possible surrogates are the research *setting* (whether inside or outside the laboratory) and the research *task*. In short, any factor which is used as a substitute for some other variable in the research is a surrogate.

In experimental research, the purpose of surrogation is to find an object or set of ob-

jects which can be substituted for another set of objects, because both sets possess the same property under investigation. Two important instances in which surrogation is used are (1) attempts by the experimenter to build "reality" into the research setting, i.e., to establish experimental reality, and (2) attempts by the experimenter to generalize the results from the experimental setting to another set of events, i.e., the attempt by the experimenter to establish external validity.

Some Comments on Existing Literature. The literature on the subject may be separated into comments concerning students as surrogates and comments concerning other experimental aspects as surrogates.

(a) *Student Surrogates*

Behavioral researchers often use student subjects in their laboratory experimentation. Bruns [7] notes that this raises a question about the external validity of the results of his study. Underlying reasons for this question are those given by Birnberg and Nath, who state [5, pp. 38–45]:

i) there is a lack of common skills and experience between students and businessmen, and

ii) there is a lack of comparable basic personality traits in both the subjects and the relevant non-experimental reference group.

One finds few criticisms of the experiments of Dyckman [9], Jensen [17], or Khemakhem [18] (all of whom used businessmen as subjects) because of improper use of surrogates. The usual criticisms of these experiments are based on the standard statistical questions, such as selection process bias or non-response bias.[4] A valid theoretical question, however, is whether businessmen in an experimental situation are good surrogates for businessmen in a non-experimental setting. This question, like the question of the use of student surrogates, cannot be answered by an appeal to classical statistics. For example, *two* conclusions may

[4]These are important questions, but they are a different kind of question from those being considered in this paper.

be drawn from the statistics in a study by Alpert [1]. One conclusion is that businessmen in a laboratory setting are poor surrogates for businessmen in a non-laboratory setting. Another conclusion is that students are poor surrogates for businessmen. Both inferences have unstated assumptions. The first inference assumes that students are good surrogates for businessmen in the laboratory; the second inference assumes businessmen in the laboratory are good surrogates for businessmen on the job. Alpert makes the second inference, but since there is no rationale provided, his choice can only be considered arbitrary.

(b) Other Experimental Surrogates

Similar questions can be asked with regard to the research setting and the research task. Birnberg and Nath [4, pp. 468–79] suggest that accountants can improve the usefulness of laboratory results if they bring portions of existing organizations into the laboratory, but the question of surrogation is not explicitly considered. Is the portion of the organization in the laboratory a good surrogate for the same portion of the organization outside the laboratory? Or, perhaps more importantly, is the portion of the organization in the laboratory a good surrogate for organizations, per se? Morris Zelditch in his article "Can You Really Study an Army in the Laboratory?" makes the following relevant statements [33, pp. 533–39]:

> An experiment aims only to reproduce that part of a concrete entity that is made relevant by some particular system of abstract variables. Therefore we do not even try to study armies in the laboratory, if by that is meant an army in the concrete sense of the word. We try only to create those aspects of armies relevant to some theory.
>
> Neither the organizational experiment, nor any other kind of experiment, attempt to create a completely 'real' instance of any concrete organization in the laboratory.

4. The Relationship between the Surrogation Problem and the Research Process

As was mentioned earlier, the attempt to establish experimental reality and the attempt to establish external validity are two important instances in which surrogation is used in the research process. The following analysis of the two instances provides the basis for a later discussion of (1) the philosophical implications of surrogation, and (2) current attacks and defenses of existing surrogation attempts.

The Analysis. We begin by assuming that the experimenter has designed an experiment to ask a specific question about the objects examined in the experiment. The question or questions may be ones that occur at any one of the five phases of the research process. For instance, at phase one, the experimenter may be asking what will be the resulting data if two variables are manipulated. Thus, an experimenter like Dyckman might ask: "What will happen when a person is asked to make the same decision on the basis of data prepared under the LIFO and FIFO inventory methods?" With respect to phase two, the experimenter may ask whether an experiment will produce a particularly striking result. For example, he may ask in a laboratory game if a company previously exposed to a change in accounting method is better able to adapt to further accounting method changes than a company which has not been exposed to a change. At phase three, it may be asked to what extent the manipulation of the additional variables may alter the original findings. At phases four and five, questions may be asked about the degree to which the simple explanatory mechanism is valid as a predictor when critical variables are manipulated.

At the time of the experiment, the experimenter could have chosen many objects to which the experimental question would be applicable. The set of all possible objects that the experimenter could use at the time the experiment was constructed would be called the domain of the question. For example, Dyckman could have constructed an infinite number of examples to ask his question concerning alternate inventory methods. All the possible examples would be in the domain of the question.

It is assumed that some mental mechanism allows the experimenter to establish whether a potential experimental object is in the domain of the question. This mental mechanism will be called the set of *specification rules*. The use of the words "mental mechanism" may indicate that it is assumed that this part of the experimental construction is programmable. Such an assumption is not being made; however, it is assumed that the experimental objects are of such a nature that they are capable of bearing on the question.

While it is clear that a set of specification rules exists, an important question remains unanswered: From where do specification rules come? It is relatively easy to say that an object is a company on LIFO or a company on FIFO, or to say that a particular company in a laboratory game has been subjected to a specific type of change in an accounting procedure. However, these examples represent only the objects in the lower or preliminary phases of Simon's description of the research process. Higher levels may demand what amounts to a creative leap in finding experimental objects to relate to experimental questions. For instance, Stedry used experiments with water jars to examine his aspiration level mechanism [27]. Weick [31] describes a number of inventive steps he takes to build organizations in the laboratory. These organizations are the ones to test simple explanatory mechanisms concerning critical relationships within organizations.

Hanson [12] provides a clue to the source of the set of specification rules in his examination of the idea that there may be a logic of discovery. He suggests that the logic of discovery is analogical, i.e., building analogies is part of the research process. Thus, Kepler upon finding that Mars had an elliptical orbit analogized that Jupiter had a non-circular orbit. Maxwell, Einstein, and Dirac similarly established analogies which gave direction to major scientific breakthroughs. Perhaps the notion of analogy is at work in the development of specification rules. For example, an initial data generating experiment is built on an analogy between some element of the experimenter's past experience and the potential experimental object. An experiment built to test a simple explanatory mechanism is an analogy

between the mechanism and the experimental objects.[5]

The derivation of specification rules is a subject which lends itself to future inquiry, especially with respect to concepts such as "creativity," "expertise," and "judgment." However, on the assumption that the importance of specification rules has been established, reconsider the construction of an experiment.

Preceding the experiment, the experimenter's store of knowledge contains a question which he considers significant and a set of specification rules. In addition, his store of knowledge probably contains a set of previous experiences with objects which meet the specification rules. This is shown in Diagram 1. Using his store of knowledge, the experimenter designs the experiment. The experiment is designed by choosing a particular combination of factors from a plethora of types of objects, types of experimental settings and types of measurements. Subject availability, the cost of the experimental apparatus, ease of measurement, and a variety of other criteria may influence the particular combination of factors chosen. However, at least two criteria must be satisfied: (1) the objects used must meet the set of specification rules, and (2) the measurements must allow determination of one answer to the experimental question. We can state:

  i) Experimental Reality is a necessary (but not sufficient) condition for Internal Validity,

  ii) Internal Validity is a necessary (but not sufficient) condition for External Validity.[6]

[5] For an example of research into the development of creative capacity, see Gordon [11]. Another very fine work related to both this and Hanson's [12] work is Kuhn [19].

[6] We may observe that mundane reality is purposely not included in our set of necessary conditions. See footnote 9. It may be asked what, if any, necessary conditions can be stated with respect to experimental reality. We consider a thorough treatment of this question beyond the scope of the present work, but have touched on related issues in our discussion of Specification Rules, and end our paper with some related comments.

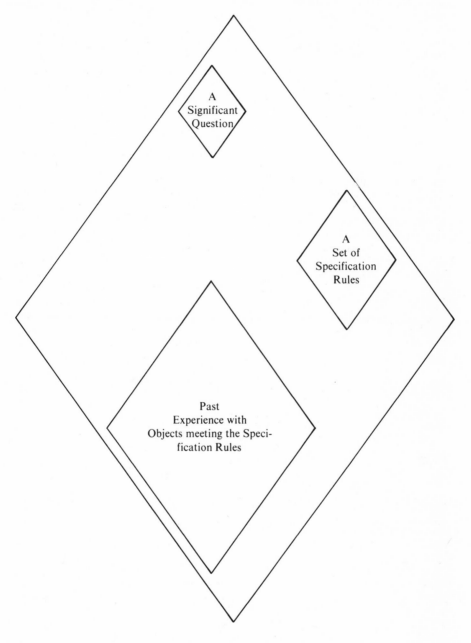

Diagram 1   Experimenter's Store of Knowledge Preceding the Experiment

When the objects used in the experiment meet the specification rules, there is a relationship between the experimental objects and the objects of past experience which meet the specification rules. The experimental objects are surrogates for the objects of previous experience which meet the set of specification rules. This is shown in Diagram 2. The arrow in Diagram 2 indicates the first type of surrogation to be examined, viz., experimental reality. The experimental objects are not necessarily substitutes for every aspect of the objects of the previous experience which meet the specification rules. Rather, the experimental objects are surrogates with respect to the particular properties established by the specification rules. Psychologists, for example, must establish experimental reality when they test theories which predict that a combination of a subject's particular psychological state and a particular environmental variable will evoke a particular type of subject reaction. Putting the subject in the correct state is an attempt to build reality into the experiment by making the experimental objects meet the specification rules.

It was noted earlier that Aronson and Carlsmith [2] say that experimental reality exists when the subject is involved in the experiment, and that "involved" means participation in an aroused and interested way rather than in a detached or bored fashion. If Aronson's and Carlsmith's examples of experiments which are claimed to lack experimental realism are examined, it is not simply lack of involvement which precludes experimental realism, but rather, it is lack of a particular type of involvement which permits an examination of the significant question.

The experiment which Aronson and Carlsmith say lacks experimental realism is one in which subjects read a newspaper. Subjects were supposed to become involved in the details of a particular article in the newspaper. When subjects paid only scant attention to the particular article, Aronson and Carlsmith concluded that the subjects were not involved in the experiment. However, the subjects may have been "involved" in the experiment; for instance, the subjects may have been involved in pleasing the experimenter or in hurriedly scanning the

CATEGORY	GENERAL CONTENT
1. Market potential	Supply and demand considerations for market areas of current or potential interest: e.g., capacity, consumption, imports, exports.
2. Structural change	Mergers, acquisitions, and joint ventures involving competitors; new entries into the industry.
3. Competitors and industry	General information about a competitor, industry policy, concerted actions in the industry, and so forth.
4. Pricing	Effective and proposed prices for products of current and potential interest.
5. Sales negotiations	Information relating to a specific current or potential sale or contract for the firm.
6. Customers	General information about current or near-potential customers, their markets, their problems.
7. Leads for mergers, joint ventures, or acquisitions	Information concerning possibilities for the manager's own company.
8. Suppliers and raw materials	Purchasing considerations for products of current or potential interest.
9. New products, processes, and technology	Technical information relatively new and unknown to the company.
10. Product problems	Problems involving existing products.
11. Costs	Costs for processing, operations, and so forth for current and potential competitors, suppliers and customers, and for proposed company activities.
12. Licensing and patents	Products and processes.
13. General conditions	Events of a general nature: political, demographic, national, and so forth.
14. Government actions and policies	Governmental decisions affecting the industry.
15. Resources available	Persons, land, and other resources possibly available for the company.
16. Miscellaneous	Items not elsewhere classified.

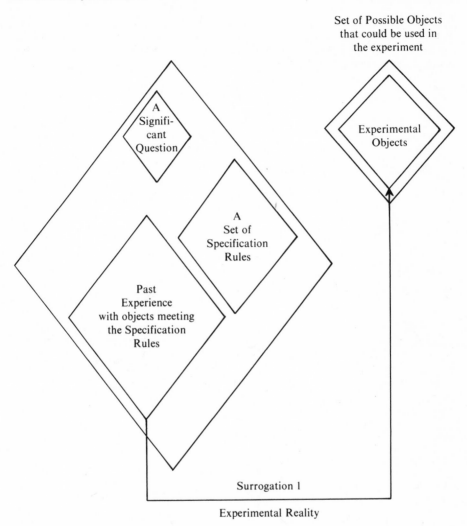

Diagram 2   Experimenter's Store of Knowledge Preceding the Experiment

newspaper. The difficulty in the experiment is not that the subjects were not involved, but rather that the type of subject involvement did not permit testing of the experimenter's hypothesis. In the terminology of this paper, it may be said that the experiment failed to meet the specification rules.

After the experiment is conducted, the experimenter's knowledge is augmented by the experimental results. The experimental results may lead to a striking new development or produce variables which can im-

prove "simple generalizations," or the results can confirm the predictions of some simple explanatory mechanism. In this case, it can be asked whether the significant question will be similarly answered with respect to future experiences with objects which meet the specification rules. Some of these possible experiences may be replications of the experiment which use different experimental objects, different measurements, or both.

If the experimental results yield a positive

answer to the significant experimental question, the experimental results are added to the previous experiences with objects which meet the specification rules. See Diagram 3.

If the results are positive, the experimenter will propose that possible future replications of the experiment are a subset of the possible future experiences with objects which

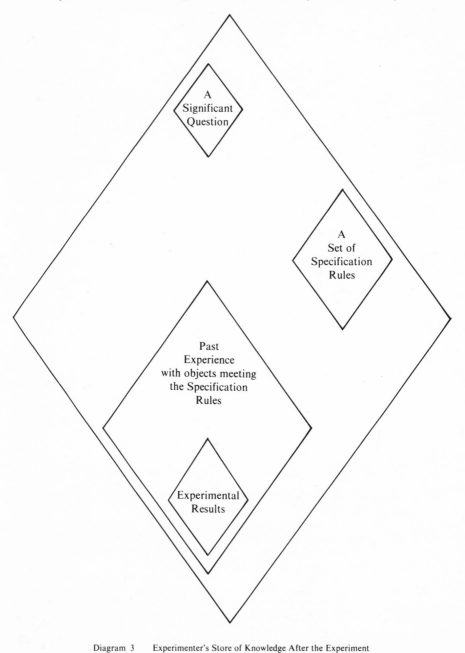

Diagram 3   Experimenter's Store of Knowledge After the Experiment

meet the specification rules. See Diagram 4. The arrow indicates a second type of surrogation involved in the research process, external validity. This type of surrogation involves the experimenter's attempt to generalize the results of his experiment to possible future replications of the experiment. A simple example is the following: A theory may be that *all ravens are black.* The experiment may involve the examination of 100,000 ravens, all of which are black. From this examination, the experimenter suggests that future ravens examined will be black. A more interesting example is the experimenter who, having examined college students, claims that the results of the experiment apply to the entire adult population. (See Peterson and Beach [22].)

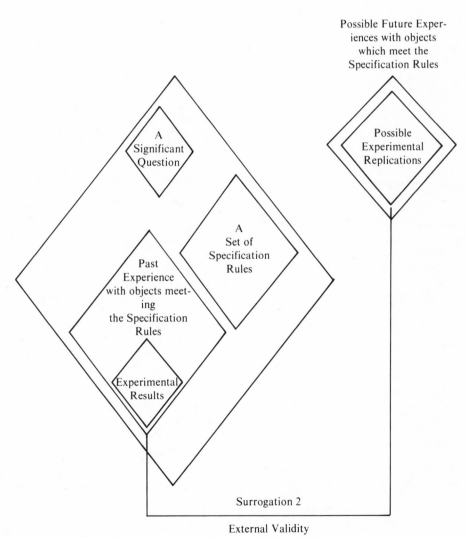

Diagram 4   The Experimenter's Store of Knowledge After the Experiment

Philosophical Implications of Surrogation. Underlying both forms of surrogation is a major philosophical issue. The issue, developed by Hume (see Salmon [25, Ch. 1]), can be applied to an inexhaustible set of questions. The most general form is: Is it possible to establish knowledge about unobserved objects on the basis of observed objects? A simple instance occurs after 60 marbles have been drawn from an urn known to contain 100 marbles, and all 60 marbles have been observed to be black. In this instance, the question is: Is it possible to say anything about the color of the unobserved marbles on the basis of the color of the observed marbles? A more important example of this type question is: Is it possible, on the basis of previously observed regularities in nature, to determine the continued existence of these regularities? Even the accountant must answer Hume's question. An illustration of the accountant grappling with the question occurs when he is trying to determine the useful life of a new asset. To determine the useful life of the asset, he may incorporate the life span of previous assets of the same type. In this case, he must answer the question: On the basis of the observed life span of assets of this particular type, is it possible to determine the unobserved life span of an asset of the same type?[7]

Hume's issue has not, to our knowledge, been resolved successfully, and any experimenter who claims to have a defensible surrogation technique must consider the issue. The experimenter who is trying to establish experimental reality must ask the question: From past experiences with objects which meet the specification rules, is it possible to say anything about the unobserved experimental phenomena: Will previously observed experiments with objects which met the set of specification rules enable the experimenter to say anything about the experimental objects? Or, more precisely, will previous experiences which produced objects which met the specification rules enable the experimenter to reproduce objects which will meet the specification rules? For instance, if the specification rule prescribes a specific psychological state (such as a level of motivation) for a subject, is there any guarantee that observed previous experiences that produced this state (for example, a monetary payment) will continue to produce the psychological state in the future?

With respect to external validity (the second type of surrogation), the experimenter who tries to extend his experimental results beyond the experiment must ask: With the observed experimental results, is it possible to say anything about the results of possible replications of the experiment? Is it possible to make statements about future replications on the basis of what has occurred?

Both types of surrogation—experimental reality and external validity—require an answer to Hume's question. Therefore it is not surprising that experimenters qualify their research with statements that their experimental question needs further study and that any reader attempting to generalize the research results must be cautious.

An Evaluation of Attacks upon and Defenses of Surrogations. It has been suggested above that Hume's question offers no consolation to the experimenter. However, is the question any less applicable to the experimenter's critics who assert that the experimenter's surrogations are in error? Can the person who criticizes the claim that the remaining 40 marbles are black establish that they are any other color? Can a person demonstrate today that the theory of relativity will not be applicable tomorrow? Is there observed evidence that unobserved asset life will be something different from the already observed life of the same type of asset? A conclusion that any generalizations of experimenters are false involves a jump from observed to unobserved phenomena. Such a jump involves an implicit answer to Hume's question, even if such a jump were that "students are not businessmen" and "the laboratory is not the 'real world.'" In addition, it may be argued that any surrogations which the experimenter's critics attempt or implicitly assume (be they generalizations of laboratory or other results) require that the critics solve Hume's problem. It should be

---

[7] Sterling [28] considers this very problem.

clear that until Hume's question is answered, sufficient conditions for valid surrogation techniques cannot be established. Thus, the experimenter and his critics alike are open to Hume's question.

Although there are insufficient conditions for establishing valid surrogations, there is a necessary condition which has been frequently ignored by both experimenters and critics. This condition is that the experimental objects, and the objects in possible future replications, must meet the set of specification rules of the experimental question. Since Hume's question is not yet answered, and since it seems impossible to answer, it may be wiser to try improving existing approaches to surrogation by stressing the necessary conditions rather than by attempting to answer Hume's question.

Another way to improve the understanding of surrogation is as follows. Most current experiments are related to phases one, two, or three of Simon's research process. While it is certainly possible to ask whether valid surrogation occurs at these levels, more abundant and precise questions about surrogation can occur once an explanatory mechanism has been developed. An explanatory mechanism permits the generation of multiple hypotheses, which means that a variety of properties that experimental objects must possess can be examined. Furthermore, since an explanatory model leads to more than one prediction, there are a variety of possibilities which may be extended and tested. Consideration of these possibilities would seem more advantageous than the consideration of just the "striking result" of Simon's phase two. With the possible exception of Stedry's work, very few explanatory mechanisms have been used in accounting experimental literature.[8]

The experimenter's critics often claim that the experiment is not "real" and, therefore, that the experimental results do not generalize. With respect to this claim, it is usually found that the critic desires that a type of reality different from experimental reality be included in the experiment. For this type of reality, every aspect of the experiment is required to conform to an aspect of previous experiences with objects in the domain of the experimental question. Aronson and Carlsmith, as we have stated before, have called this *mundane reality,* and they suggest that mere presence of mundane reality to a high degree does not guarantee that the experimental hypothesis will be validly tested.[9]

In addition, Campbell, Dunnette, Lawler, and Weick state [8]:

Undoubtedly the main objection to experimentation concerns its relevance to organizational problems. Experimental settings, after all, are not organizations, nor are they intended to be. Confusion about the issue of relevance is often collapsed into the simple assertion that 'experiments are artificial.' Before such an assertion is used to discount much of this chapter, some points should be considered. Zigler has described a prominent reason why experimental and natural settings differ and why this should not deter the use of experimentation. He observed that persons often regard experiments as irrelevant because they do not realize that one of the properties of an explanatory system

'. . . is that the processes suggested or the principles specified somehow transcend the world for which they were constructed and are applicable to other worlds as well. . . . What the experimenter is saying is that if such and such holds in the real world because of the principles expounded in the particular theory under investigation, then such and such should hold in the world which the experimenter has created. This translatability is what gives theoretical importance to experiments that involve phenomena which, taken in isolation, not only appear picayune but seem to have little relationship with what one observes in nature.'

In the language of this paper, it could be said that simply because the experimental objects are in many ways similar to objects in the set of previous experiences that meet the specification rules, it does not automatically follow that all the specification rules are met.

---

[8]However, for excellent works on the nature, construction and verification, in general, of theories in accounting, see Williams and Griffin [32] and Sterling [28].

[9]Aronson and Carlsmith [2, pp. 22–26] point out that mundane reality does not necessarily contribute to experimental realism: many real world events are boring and uninvolving. They cite as examples of experiments with high experimental realism and low mundane reality the well-known studies by Asch and by Milgram. See Aronson and Carlsmith.

5. Conclusion

We have discussed two types of surrogation processes which are concerned with experimental reality and external validity. With respect to both processes, several suggestions have been made. First, no sufficient conditions exist for establishing experimental reality or external validity. Conversely, sufficient conditions do not exist for establishing the *absence* of experimental reality and external validity. While this conclusion does not lead to any operational statements, it does seem to reinforce the feeling of futility of arguments in which one researcher claims he has captured the "real world" and others claim he has not.

Another suggestion that has been made is that experiments which are related to the establishment of explanatory mechanisms should produce more surrogation possibilities. As described by Simon, these mechanisms produce a number of interrelationships among their variables. Each interrelationship is a candidate for surrogation. The possibility of more interrelationships thus produces the possibility for more surrogations.[10] The possibility of more surrogations suggests the possibility of more varied testing procedures of the surrogations and of the explanatory mechanisms.

A third suggestion relies on the potentialities of additional research. For instance, is it possible at an individual level to develop a feeling about the quality of an analogy and, hence, a feeling about the quality of a surrogation? Possibly this feeling could be established in a probabilistic statement rather than a "yes-no" type statement.

The three suggestions discussed above relate to both of the surrogation processes: experimental reality and external validity. The following statements consider these processes individually.

With respect to experimental reality, one approach would be to use conditions which in earlier experiments produced a desired effect. Then, when the present experiment is performed, it can be examined to see if the previous desired effects do occur. Aronson and Carlsmith cite subject behavior (such as

sweating and trembling, symptoms of anxiety and fear) as evidence for experimental reality in the Milgram experiment [2].

With respect to external validity, a useful approach to future research may be to consider external validity from two points of view: (1) the individual experimenter's and (2) the research community's. The reason for such a consideration might be that the forces which lead an individual experimenter to decide to generalize may not be the same forces which lead the scientific community to generalize. In understanding the individual's establishment of external validity, a useful analogy may be the Bayesian decision framework extolled by such people as Raiffa [24] and embedded in the philosophical work of Salmon [25]. In understanding the research community's establishment of external validity a useful analogy may be that of Kuhn, who examines "scientific revolutions in which old paradigms are exchanged for new" [19, pp. 92–109 and 191–207].

References

1. Alpert, Bernard, "Non-Businessmen as Surrogates for Businessmen in Behavioral Experiments," *Journal of Business* (1967), pp. 203–07.

2. Aronson, Elliot, and Carlsmith, V. Merrill, "Experimentation in Social Psychology," in Gardner Lindzey and Elliot Aronson (eds.), *Handbook of Social Psychology,* 2nd ed., Addison-Wesley Publishing Co., 1968, pp. 22–26.

3. Benston, George J., "Published Corporate Accounting Data and Stock Prices," *Empirical Research in Accounting: Selected Studies, 1967,* Supplement to the *Journal of Accounting Research* (1967), pp. 1–54.

4. Birnberg, Jacob G., and Nath, Raghu, "Implications of Behavioral Science for Managerial Accounting," *The Accounting Review* (1967), pp. 468–79.

5. ———, "Laboratory Experimentation in Accounting Research," *The Accounting Review* (January, 1968), pp. 38–45.

6. Bonini, Charles P., *Simulation of Information and Decision Systems in the Firm,* Prentice Hall, Inc., 1963.

7. Bruns, William J., Jr., "The Accounting Period and Its Effect upon Management Decisions," *Empirical Research in Accounting: Selected Studies, 1966,* Supplement to the

---

[10] For a detailed treatment of a case in point, see [21].

Journal of Accounting Research (1966), pp. 1–14.

8. Campbell, John P., Dunnette, Marvin D., Lawler, Edward E., III, and Weick, Karl E., Jr., *Managerial Behavior, Performance and Effectiveness,* McGraw-Hill Book Co., 1970.

9. Dyckman, Thomas R., "The Effects of Alternative Accounting Techniques on Certain Management Decisions," *Journal of Accounting Research* (Spring, 1964), pp. 91–107.

10. Gonedes, Nicholas J., "The Significance of Selected Accounting Procedures: A Statistical Test," *Empirical Research in Accounting: Selected Studies, 1969,* Supplement to *Journal of Accounting Research* (1969), pp. 90–123.

11. Gordon, William J. J., *Synetics,* Collier-Macmillan Ltd., 1961.

12. Hanson, Norwood R., "Retroduction and the Logic of Discovery," in H. Geigl and G. Maxwell (eds.), *Current Issues in the Philosophy of Science,* Rinehart & Winston, 1969, pp. 20–35.

13. Hochberg, Julian E., *Perception,* Prentice-Hall, Inc., 1964.

14. Hofstedt, Thomas R., and Kinard, James C., "A Strategy for Behavioral Accounting Research," *The Accounting Review* (January, 1970), pp. 38–54.

15. Ijiri, Yuji, *Foundations of Accounting Measurement,* Prentice Hall, Inc., 1967.

16. Jensen, Robert E., "An Experimental Design for the Study of the Effects of Accounting Variation on Decision Making," *Journal of Accounting Research* (Autumn, 1966), pp. 224–38.

17. _____, "Discussion of Comparative Values of Information Structures," *Empirical Research in Accounting: Selected Studies, 1969,* Supplement to the *Journal of Accounting Research* (1969), pp. 180–81.

18. Khemakhem, Abdellatif, "A Simulation of Management Decision Behavior: 'Funds' and Income," *The Accounting Review* (July, 1968), pp. 522–34.

19. Kuhn, Thomas S., *Structure of Scientific Revolutions,* 2nd ed., The University of Chicago Press, 1970.

20. Livingstone, J. Leslie, "A Behavioral Study of Tax Allocation in Public Utility Regula-tion," *The Accounting Review* (July, 1967), pp. 544–52.

21. MacKenzie, Kenneth D., and Barron, F. Hutton, "Analysis of a Decision Making Investigation," *Management Science* (December, 1970), pp. 226–41.

22. Peterson, Cameron R., and Beach, Lee R., "Man as an Intuitive Statistician," *Psychological Bulletin* (1967), pp. 29–46.

23. Popper, K. R., "Epistemology Without a Knowing Subject," in B. Van Rootselaar and J. F. Staal (eds.), *Logic Methodology and Philosophy of Science III,* New Holland Publishing Company, 1968, pp. 439–57.

24. Raiffa, Howard, *Decision Analysis,* Addison-Wesley Publishing Co., 1968.

25. Salmon, Wesley C., *The Foundations of Scientific Inference,* University of Pittsburgh Press, 1966.

26. Simon, Herbert A., "On Judging the Plausibility of Theories," in B. Van Rootselaar and J. F. Staal (eds.), *Logic Methodology and Philosophy of Science III,* New Holland Publishing Company, 1968, pp. 439–58.

27. Stedry, Andrew C., *Budget Control and Cost Behavior,* Prentice Hall, Inc., 1960.

28. Sterling, Robert R., "The Going Concern: An Examination," *The Accounting Review* (July, 1968), pp. 493ff.

29. _____, "On Theory Construction and Verification," *The Accounting Review* (July, 1970), pp. 444–57.

30. Tracy, John A., "Nature and Function of Accounting," in Rufus Wixon, Walter G. Kell and Norton M. Bedford (editorial consultants), *Accountants' Handbook,* 5th ed., The Ronald Press Company, 1970.

31. Weick, Karl E., "Laboratory Experimentation with Organizations," in James G. March (ed.), *Handbook of Organizations,* Rand McNally and Co., 1965, pp. 194–260.

32. Williams, Thomas H., and Griffin, Charles H., "On the Nature of Empirical Verification in Accounting," *Abacus* (December, 1969), pp. 143–78.

33. Zelditch, Morris, "Can You Really Study an Army in the Laboratory," in A. Etzioni (ed.), *A Sociological Reader on Complex Organizations,* 2nd ed., Holt, Rinehart & Winston, Inc., 1969, pp. 533–39.

chapter 9

A Datum Are a System

KENNETH D. MACKENZIE

University of Kansas

Introduction

The paper by Dickhaut, Livingstone and Watson is a discussion of the use of surrogation in research and an evaluation of such research. Beginning with the primitive notion that a surrogate denotes an object which substitutes for or takes the place of a second object, they argue that surrogation is a necessity for conducting an inquiry. This view is supported by a description of research processes by H. A. Simon[1] and more specifically by the arguments of Aronson and Carlsmith[2] for conducting laboratory experiments. It is clear that there always exists an object for which any datum, variable, model, theory explanation and description is a surrogate. Laboratory experiments necessarily involve complex, interacting sequences or systems of surrogation. So do descriptions of the "real world" of one adult by another.

In general, there is always disagreement concerning the relevance of a system of sur-

rogation in one situation to a system of surrogation in another. When two systems of surrogation are inconsistent, there is a problem in judging the utility of the findings of one system to the other *for a specific purpose given stated conditions*. In particular, there are problems in comparing (1) laboratory findings from different experiments, (2) laboratory findings with the "real world" and (3) "real worlds" as seen by different observers and (4) the different "real worlds" seen by one observer. Given this state of confusion, critics of the "usefulness" of laboratory experimentation and proponents for conducting such research are always on solid ground. There is a lack of generally accepted criteria for judging the relevance of a laboratory finding to a "real world" phenomenon for a given purpose under given conditions. There is also a lack of measurement standards and widely accepted theories for describing or comparing situations. Thus, unless the purposes, conditions and methodology can be agreed upon in advance by a critic of experimentation and a proponent for conducting experiments, there will necessarily be conflicts when discussing a research finding.

The seemingly specific questions of (1) can complex environments identical with the "real world" be created in a laboratory

---

[1]H. A. Simon, "On Judging the Plausibility of Theories," in *Logic Methodology and Philosophy of Science III*, B. Van Rootselaar and J. F. Staal, editors (New Holland Publishing Co., 1968), pp. 439–457.

[2]Elliot Aronson and V. Merrill Carlsmith, "Experimentation in Social Psychology," in *Handbook of Social Psychology*, Vol. II, 2nd ed., Gardner Lindzey and Elliot Aronson, editors (Addison-Wesley Publishing Co., 1968), pp. 22–26.

setting? (2) are student subjects surrogates for a businessman in the "real world"? (3) is a businessman subject in an experiment a surrogate for a businessman in the "real world"? and (4) is it possible for businessmen to be surrogates for each other?, can always be answered both negatively and affirmatively. Given what is, to me, an almost pre-Copernican state of the social sciences of social psychology, organization theory and sociology, my sympathies lie with an intellectually honest businessman attempting to understand and apply these fields to practical problems.

Accepting such wide open issues mentioned above in comparing systems of surrogations, there is little justification for narrow mindedness and arrogance in a social scientist when discussing his relevance to the "real world." Of course, narrow mindedness and arrogance are not limited to the researcher side of the issues, and not all researchers are like this. However, as scientists, with some training in cumulative fields, it is up to us to set the higher standard. In cynical moments, I feel that many of the conflicts over surrogation problems are themselves surrogates for a long struggle for power and influence between scientific and industrial mandarins.

Despite many indirect reasons why problems of surrogation are discussed, the problems are genuine and merit close scrutiny. Dickhaut, Livingstone and Watson perform a needed service in focusing attention on these issues. I think, however, that if one strips their paper down to its fundamentals, their discussion on surrogation is actually a methodological exposition of a concept of data and the proper conduct of experiments. If we can accept the inevitability of surrogates, we can discuss systems of surrogations more generally in the context of laboratory experimentation. This will allow us to provide a conceptual framework for commenting on and extending the Dickhaut, Livingstone and Watson paper.

Experiments as Systems of Surrogates

Little is known about the origin of hunches, questions, problems, theories and hypotheses. A great deal is known about the relatively trivial and highly restricted question of how to examine a fixed set of data according to a fixed set of assumptions for the purpose of determining the degree of randomness at which these data will reject a particular hypothesis. To the extent that there exist an extant theory, systems of measurement and a methodology governing the generation of the data, techniques for simple hypothesis testing are usually sufficient for data analysis. In the social sciences, however, these prior conditions are seldom, if ever, met. But, the techniques of experimental design and analysis do depend upon the prior agreement of theory, systems of measurement and the methodology of collecting and processing of data wrested from an environment. This basic inconsistency between the actual and the ideal conditions for employing statistical procedures is often overlooked in the training of students and is undoubtedly a determinant in the conflict between "experimentalists" and practitioners and between substantive and technical theoretical issues. That the degree of disbelief in experimental findings is lower in the physical and engineering sciences than in the social sciences may indicate a much smaller inconsistency between actual and ideal conditions in the physical and engineering sciences. I think that the relatively greater attention paid to hypothesis testing procedures with the attending incorrect belief that these minor aspects of methodology can be separated from theory and measurement has been harmful.[3] It is like developing a species of crab with only one claw and no other legs. It may be a very powerful claw but such a creature is not likely to survive because it is overspecialized. That crab cannot help being malformed, but we should not be so forgiving of humans posing as social scientists. If they pretend to be scientists and methodologists rather than applied mathematicians, they probably should be barred from reproducing themselves in the form of graduates. There are other dire

[3]C. West Churchman, "The Systems Approach of Measurement in Business Firms," in *Accounting in Perspective: Contributions to Accounting Thought by Other Disciplines,* R. R. Sterling and W. F. Bentz, editors (South-Western Publishing Company, 1971), pp. 51–57.

remedies but the real problem is their incomplete and incorrect perception of an experiment. What is the concept of an experiment? This discussion of an experiment will parallel an analysis by Mackenzie and Barron.[4]

Ideally, the person occupying the social role as experimenter has a theory we shall denote by T. Given T, the experimenter perceives a problem he seeks to study by performing a ritual called an experiment, in order to compare implications derived from T with processed observations obtained by following strict procedures. He eventually obtains a set of results, denoted R. R is obtained from a special form of data, D_{HT}, which when transformed by a hypothesis testing technique, denoted τ_5, yields R. That is, $R = \tau_5 D_{HT}$. But, D_{HT} is obtained from a set of measures, M, applied to a set of raw data by a model, denoted τ_4. Or, $D_{HT} = \tau_4 M$. M, however, is a transformation, τ_3, applied to a prior set of raw data, D_R. Or, $M = \tau_3 D_R$. In turn, the raw data, D_R, are usually in the form of numbers or symbols derived by applying a system of coding, τ_2, on a set of recorded observations, D. That is, $D_R = \tau_2 D$. But D, the set of recorded observations depends upon a transformation, τ_1, which records D from a set of potential observations under the chosen experiment, Ω_E. Or, $D = \tau_1 \Omega_E$. Ω_E is the result of a transformation, τ_0, of a universe of potential observations (or class of experimental or real worlds), Ω. Thus $\Omega_E = \tau_0 \Omega$. Putting this together, we see that

$$R = \tau_5 \tau_4 \tau_3 \tau_2 \tau_1 \tau_0 \Omega.$$

Each of the τ_j's depends upon the theory T. It is clear that while the hypothesis testing technique, τ_5, is important, it is at the end of a longer chain of transformations any of which if altered could affect R. In fact, if τ_0, τ_1, τ_2, τ_3, and τ_4 are left to the control of others, for any given τ_5, R can be controlled by those controlling the other τ_j's. Hence, the emphasis placed on τ_5 is an overspecial-

ization like our one clawed crab.[5]

Practically, however, conventions and precedences of related studies contribute to a specification of τ_0, τ_1, τ_2, τ_3, and τ_4, in those fields[6] of inquiry where theory, measurement, and methodology are well defined. In new fields, for new theories, one has to be extremely cautious about the meaning of R. Suppose R is a number, a datum. This *datum represents a system* of a succession of transformations on plural objects. For this reason, to emphasize the nature of a datum, it is useful to summarize the above argument by stating that a datum *are* a system. Conceptually it makes little sense to differentiate a datum from data, since a datum is necessarily a plural object. It is singular only by convention, not by its nature.[7]

For example, a datum that the gross national product is XYZ summarizes separate amounts for sectors of an economy which in turn are summaries of subsectors according to a highly specialized set of transformations of definitions, accounting practices, sampling procedures, negotiations among agencies, legal conventions, etc., under a very special theory of economics. The number XYZ represents a hierarchy of systems of elements, structures and special relationships.

Given a theory, T, producing result R, an alternative theory T' producing result R', and a set of transformations $\{\tau_j\}$, j = 0, 1, . . ., 5, consistent with both T and T', then

[4]K. D. Mackenzie and F. H. Barron, "Analysis of a Decision Making Investigation," *Management Science,* 17 (December 1970), pp. B226–B241.

[5]This is analogous to a problem in linear programming where one person controls the objective function and another the constraints. Proper control of the constraints can so reduce a feasible solution set that the optimal solution is insensitive to the objective function. Further, if a certain solution is desired, it may be possible by controlling the constraints to achieve that solution.

[6]It must be noted that the set $\{\tau_j\}$, j = 0, 1, 2, . . ., 5 is usually much larger than six prototype τ_j represented here. For example, the same set of recorded observations, D, may be coded (τ_2) in different ways for different but related theoretical purposes.

[7]It is interesting to compare a datum with the light from a beacon on top of a tower on the top floor of a tall building. While it is certainly possible to examine the light separately, it does not make much sense from the point of view of air safety to have a light shining from a light bulb unless it is in a beacon on a tower at the top of a building. There are also the problems of maintaining a power source for the bulb, replacing burned out bulbs, repairing the tower and beacon and training pilots to heed the warning of the beacon. A datum is a surrogate for a whole system.

an *experiment* is the set

$$E = \langle \{\tau_j\}, j = 0, 1, \ldots, 5, (T, R), (T', R') \rangle.$$

The purpose of conducting E is to choose T or T' on the basis of whether R or R' obtains upon application of the transformation $\{\tau_j\}$, $j = 0, 1, \ldots, 5$ to Ω. If some (but not all) of the $\{\tau_j\}$ are known, then we have the conditions for an *investigation* rather than an experiment. If the theory is imprecise and none of the $\{\tau_j\}$ are known, the study is an *exploration*.

The purpose of exploration is an investigation and the purpose of investigation is an experiment. The purpose of experimentation is to develop theory. The main purpose of theory is to provide structure for what were before unstructured phenomena. These processes iterate and never really cease.[8] New facts, paradigms, conventions, measurement techniques, etc., can and do alter the iteration path. Techniques for conducting and analyzing experiments are relatively well developed. Techniques for conducting explorations and investigations are relatively undeveloped.

Each transformation, τ_0, τ_1, τ_2, τ_3, τ_4, or τ_5 is a procedure for surrogation. The composite of several transformations is another surrogation. The surrogation problem of Dickhaut, Livingstone and Watson decreases as one moves from an exploration towards an experiment. The results of an experiment should not be planned to apply to a "real world," since the purpose of experiments is to develop theory. It is the theory which must be applied to the "real world."

Explorers and investigators who want to apply the results of their labors directly to the "real world" are, in my opinion, premature, misguided and deserve strong criticism from any critical source. To claim un-

critical acceptance or influence in practical affairs because of sophisticated analyses of data from non-experiments is to clamor for undeserved credit. To *demand* influence on the basis of a theory having no *experimental* basis for support, is likewise premature. (The fact that this is successfully [in terms of income and power] done by many part-time academics and is the usual case in practical affairs, is certainly cause for envy but not emulation. Of course, criticism from those successfully employing the authority of poorly substantiated theories is particularly galling. The role of the social scientist is a humble one.) We should accept our humble status[9] and be arrogant about our humility. Our dominant predisposition should be that of doubt and criticism for our pet theories. Once a taste for it is acquired, humble pie can be delicious.

The Dickhaut, Livingstone and Watson paper was a small sliver of this much larger humble pie. Their argument lacked unity from paragraph to paragraph, the imposition of Simon and Aronson and Carlsmith is somewhat beside the point and their diagrams are confusing. Despite these minor problems the overall impact of the paper is clear. This critique is meant to augment and extend their basic argument and its implications. As a matter of fact both the paper and this critique are elaborations of C. W. Churchman[10] by way of E. A. Singer[11] and I. Kant.[12]

---

[8]See Mackenzie and Barron, *op. cit.*, for a heuristic for conducting an analysis of an investigation. They applied their heuristic to analyze a set of data which had been unsuccessfully analyzed by many by conventional methods. There is no claim that the heuristic is complete and there are sure to be many improvements. Their analysis does show how the iterations were made in a particular instance.

[9]Currently the various social sciences are exciting, vigorous but not too rigorous. There are no clear standards of measurements and basic concepts such as structure, change, norms, risk, attitude, task, incentive, motive, personality, boredom, leadership, power, hierarchy, conformity, etc., need more work. Stimulus-response causality is being replaced by notions of process; little is actually known about how to analyze process data. Mathematical and statistical procedures are just beginning to be developed for such problems. We are learning much; we are progressing slowly. The rate of progress may even be accelerating. There are many new ideas, theories abound, and on occasion we can even be useful. We quarrel a great deal and we tend to be committed to truth, but any appearance of rigor is more of an illusion than a fact. Our science is to be respected, but our results and theories must be taken with the proverbial grain of salt.
[10]Churchman, *op. cit.*
[11]E. A. Singer, Jr., *Experience and Reflection*, C. W. Churchman, editor (University of Pennsylvania Press, 1959).
[12]Immanuel Kant, *Critique of Pure Reason*, 1781.

chapter 10

Implications of Interactive Models for Accounting Research

MICHAEL S. SCOTT MORTON

Massachusetts Institute of Technology

1. Introduction

The widespread use of computers, beginning in the early 1960's, has led to a number of changes in the way accounting is practiced in the typical organization. Perhaps less apparent is the impact of computers on accounting research. The principal impact was on the ease with which models could be applied to accounting data to show us patterns that we had not hitherto suspected. The range of models and the kind of impact that it was possible for them to have, considerably widened the horizons of the researcher in the accounting field. Since the early 1960's we have watched the mushrooming of computational capabilities in organizations to the point where they are now commonplace. Coupled with this growth has been the parallel activity in the field of Management Science with its development of more complicated and often more useful models.

In particular, in the computer area we have seen the development of a whole new type of computational resource—that of multiple access computation. This has the desirable property of bringing computer power to the user no matter what his loca-

tion and at very low incremental costs. On the modeling side, we have had growing recognition of the concept of hierarchies of models [16], that is, sets of models that cover the range from very rough aggregate levels down to very detailed highly complex ones. In addition, of course, there has been the development of the Bayesian methodology and its application to business.

These forces and trends exist, and there is no way that they are likely to disappear—indeed quite the reverse seems to be true. Computational resources continue to drop in cost, and our understanding of models and how to apply them to managerial situations is increasing sharply. As a result of these trends, the use of interactive models in business organizations is on the increase [5, 11, 18]. These interactive, or conversational, models are of the type where the decision maker is involved in a dialogue with the system. The problem solving task is split between the man and the machine in an attempt to use the relative strengths of each. For certain classes of problem [13], this is much more effective than either the man or the system operating alone. As we will discuss below, these conversational systems are

95

appropriate for a different *class* of problems than the ones we have been used to dealing with in the past. Applicable though they are in business organizations, they are just as useful for performing certain kinds of research in the accounting area.

This general technology, that is, of models and flexible computational support, creates implications for accounting research in at least two major ways. The first of these major ways is that they create new research possibilities; new kinds of experiments are possible. We now have whole new ways of looking at the decision maker and his use of financial data. There is a wide spectrum of new research possibilities some of which are discussed later in this paper. They all have the characteristic, however, of expanding our researchable universe.

The second major set of implications for accounting research is concerned with methodology. Separate and distinct from the impact on the substantive areas of accounting discussed above is the impact on research methodology. The analytical tools available to the researcher change both in degree and in kind. Change in degree occurs with easy flexible access to a whole toolkit of analytical and model building techniques. (For example, see McIntosh and Griffel [12] and Eisner [7]). Changes in kind occur with the provision of altogether new analytical tools, such as the ones mentioned later in this paper as part of the Project Cambridge [6] research efforts.

The purpose of this paper is to raise some issues for accounting research that flow from the availability of conversational computer systems. It is *not* intended to be a rigorous treatment of the topic for computer specialists, but it is intended to identify some research horizons for the accounting profession. In the sections that follow, we will first discuss, very briefly, the outlines of the technological and conceptual changes that are underway. We will then return to the major implications raised above and expand these to provide a clearer view of the issues. This is followed by a summary of the implications that seem to flow from the discussion. In the Appendix is given a summary of an experiment using a conversational

system; this experiment provides an actual illustration of some of the points we have been raising.

2. The New Technology

It should, perhaps, be stressed at the outset that there has been no recent revolution in the computer business or in the modeling business that has suddenly made new things possible. Rather, what we have seen over the past ten years has been a steady and continuous advance in both of these areas. This advance has far outstripped our ability in organizations to apply it successfully, and so we have not yet seen very much of an impact. Nevertheless, large parts of this technology are quite straightforward and easy to implement in an organization. Now, once a company decides to do something, the costs of doing it have dropped sufficiently far that there is very little to stop rapid implementation. In short, we seem to have crossed a threshold, a threshold both in our understanding of what to do and in the costs of the technology necessary to do it. From the experience of organizations already active in this field, it is quite clear that these kinds of systems are going to be commonplace by the end of the next ten years. If the universities' research work is to continue to support the accounting profession, then it is important that they recognize these forces and the changes that they will bring about in organizations. For this reason, it is important to assess what this technology looks like and the directions in which it is taking us, so that we can understand these new fields of research and the payoff they have for the profession.

Conversational Systems Components. The use of the word "conversational" describes the essential feature of the new computer technology. It implies a system (see Figure 1) that has the human user, the computer terminal (ranging in type from teletype to interactive display system), the communications line from the terminal to the central computer, some form of multiple access computer and the data base and models that go with it.

From experimental work in company situations, it has become clear that there are certain features of such conversational systems (see Morton and Gorry [17]) that ought to exist if the system is to provide adequate support for problem-solving [19]. It should be stressed that such systems are only applicable to a *limited* (but interesting) *set of problems.* For these problems, a conversational system should have:

—Terminals. Terminals that can communicate fast enough not to hinder the decision process, preferably with the ability to draw vectors. To help interaction, a light-pen, touch-sensitive screen or some similar device is required. Such terminals cost between $13,000 and $60,000 as recently as three years ago. A variety of similar terminals are now available in the range of $3,000 to $12,000. Similar reductions in cost have taken place with the computers required to drive such systems.

—Communications Link. To provide true remote capability the terminal should be capable of being driven over regular telephone lines or a micro-wave link.

—Multiple Access Computer. The central computer involved need *not be time-shared,* but it should be able to support several remote users with adequate response time and data-base [15].

—Model-Bank. The system will typically require a set of models to support the decision process. These may be simple, such as a budget model, or complex, such as a large simulation model.

—Data-Base. The data-base should consist only of the data required for a particular decision. It is not necessary to have a "complete" operational control data-base.

Conversational Models. The models that are appropriate for use in an interactive environment are generally "delivered" to the user in a way that makes them appear quite different from those we are familiar with under a batch processing mode. They range from the simple kinds of budgeting models to elaborate and complex simulation models, and they are used, as with any model, to turn raw data into useful information for the decision maker. Their distinguishing characteristics are that they allow the decision-maker to control his progress through the solution, and they permit him to insert his judgments about variables cheaply and effectively. The first characteristic allows the decision maker to move toward a solution using his insights about the problem solution process. For example, at one stage in the process, he might decide to do a variance analysis on the manufacturing budget, the next time he is faced with a similar problem, he might feel it was more appropriate to look at the standard costs that are involved. It is his judgment about the best way to proceed that is dominant. In yet other situations, he might call for an optimizing model, such as linear programming, to solve one piece of his overall problem. In all cases, however, such a conversational system is appropriate when the model alone or the decision maker alone cannot make as good a decision as the two in combination.

The other major characteristics of conversational models is the ability that can be built in to collect and use judgmental data from the decision maker. He can insert his judgment easily, flexibly and economically about uncertain events, and the model will incorporate these in the analysis. Two features—the user's control of the process and the ability to incorporate judgments—are the major characteristics of the models available in interactive systems. These types of models allow us to support new classes of problems [17], and hence, they have interesting ramifications for accounting research. One such example is given in the Appendix. To provide illustrations for the material that follows, it will be useful to summarize here some of the main points from the Appendix. The following example illustrates the research methodology implications as well as those connected with the substance of the research findings.

3. Interactive Models—An Example[1]

Model Description. In the project, an interactive system was built and then used in a

[1]The material in this section has been taken from Benille, Wagner and Zannetos [3], [4].

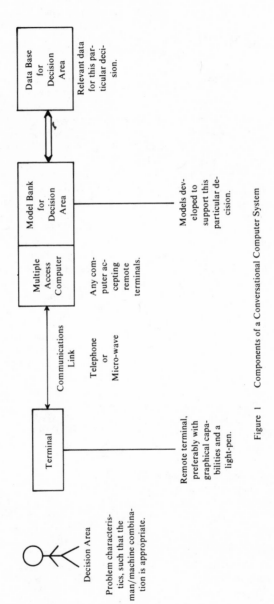

Figure 1 Components of a Conversational Computer System

series of experiments with senior line managers. The problem area was that of a capital investment decision [2]. Two basic courses of action were open to the decision makers. The first was to discontinue producing a textile product, which was part of a firm's entire line of textiles, sell off the associated equipment and inventory, and collect the associated accounts receivables. The second major class of alternatives was to continue producing the product for the next four years (the equipment would be worn out at that time) and, given that decision, further decide upon the best pricing strategy to follow. The problem is represented in the tree structure in Figure 2. There are varying degrees of uncertainty about the revenues to be generated if the firm does go out of business, and these have to be estimated by the decision maker. Similarly, if the firm stays in business, there are a series of alternatives. Both the revenue and expenditure side have considerable uncertainty attached to their major components. The pricing decision obviously will affect the market share and the revenues. There is also uncertainty about the scrap value of the equipment and the sort of inventory and accounts receivable experience that the company will have. Similarly, on the expenditure side, both the labor and material costs can vary quite sharply. All inputs to the elements on the end points of the tree are in the form of cumulative subjective probability distributions. Given these subjective probability distributions, the system then computes the expected value of the various alternatives.

In general, the objective of risk analysis models is to provide structure to the problem environment by identifying the basic components of risk and having the manager assign to each of these components probability measures for possible outcomes. In this particular setting, the problem structure has been laid out in tree form for the decision maker. Thus, the basic elements of revenues and expenditures which can vary in this particular setting have been laid out on the tree. The decision maker is then able to specify quickly and simply through the terminal the possible ranges of outcomes and their associated probabilities of occurrence.

Clearly, if more variables are of concern, then they can be added to the tree, until such time as the decision maker is satisfied that he has all the components he wishes.

Once all of the outcome states for each of the elements of risk have been described in the form of probability distributions, these distributions can be aggregated by means of a Monte Carlo type of process to develop a probability distribution describing the expected net return for the alternative being modeled. After examining one alternative, other possibilities can be immediately tested and compared. Thus, models of this type provide both a framework for structuring decision alternatives through the identification of the elements of risk in a hierarchical manner, and they also provide a methodology for analytically dealing with risk, through the use of probability distributions and the Monte Carlo simulation.

The Experiment. In this instance, the general goal was to assess the impact of such interactive decision systems on managerial decision making behavior. In particular, we wanted to find out how executives would deal with capital investment and competitive pricing decisions under conditions of uncertainty. This sort of planning problem is more difficult than the normal operational problems in the company because of the absence of structure, the absence of many of the required factual elements, and the presence of uncontrolled environmental factors. The risk analysis technique which we have discussed above was chosen as the basis for the model, because it incorporates a facility for structuring problems, a methodology for utilizing subjective estimates of the elements for which no factual information exists, and a technique for introducing risk and uncertainty through the use of subjective probability distributions.

Two groups of executives were run in the initial experiment, and a summary of some of the main points is given in the Appendix. (For details, see Beville, Wagner and Zannetos [3], [4]). For purposes of illustration, we can draw out two points from the experimental use of the system.

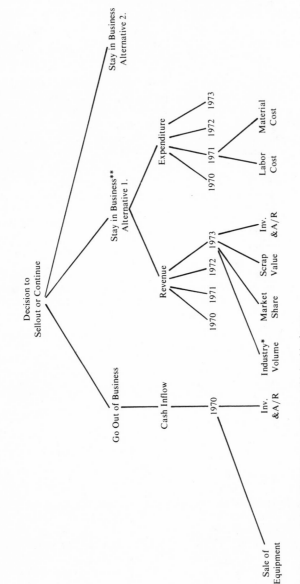

*Subjective probability distributions are entered at this level in the tree.
**Prices for each year and the cost of capital are entered at this level in the tree.

Figure 2   Structure of the Problem Tree Implemented on the IGRAM System

—The first is that the models and decision processes available to the decision maker affect the number of alternatives the decision maker considers, the numbers he uses in these alternatives and the kinds of data he uses.

—The second is that the executives trusted the system and assumed that the model was "good," and therefore, they looked at fewer alternatives. It should be stressed that both of these two points have merely been suggested by the data in the experiment and are in no sense proven facts. Further research and experimentation will be required to establish if they are generally true. However, for our purposes here, they serve to illustrate the kinds of issues that can be explored with the use of interactive models.

This experiment has been quoted to give a feel for both the kinds of issues that can be explored and one way in which the exploration can be done. The specific sorts of research areas that this one example suggests are many. For example, looking at the implications of the first suggestion above, namely, that the models and decision processes that are available affect the number and kinds of alternatives considered, the types of data used and the values attributed to those. There are, of course, a number of *general* research issues that are raised by this suggestion. These go beyond our interests in accounting research, but they include such things as categorization of kinds of models and decision processes and the effects these have on the specific alternatives considered by the managers. From an accounting standpoint, however, the greatest impact is likely to be on the data base questions. Questions, such as the types of accounting data that we should make available to managers through such models, the means by which we collect this, the methods by which we make it available·and a whole series of similar questions that will have to be answered if such models are to be used effectively by decision makers. The mere fact that some managers will use such decision support systems, whereas others in the

same company continue with the old process, means that we may be in a position of maintaining two data bases, and more importantly perhaps, have different managers using completely different kinds of information on which to base their decision.

Similarly, with the second suggestion from the experiment above, namely, that the executives trusted the system and assumed that there was, in fact, a "good" model and, therefore, looked at fewer alternatives. This "suggestion," raised by the use of this interactive model in an experimental setting, poses at least three other questions for accounting research. The first of these is, that if such models are to be used by decision makers, then what is the role that ought to be played by the accountants in the process of such model building. Models take on a new significance in settings of this sort, and in a sense, they become part of the information itself. This point has been made by others before, for example:

"[Accountants] as a group must become involved in the evaluation, refinement, and construction of the appropriate decision theories." (Sterling [21, p. 63]).

With the advent of useful conversational technology, these issues become even more important for the profession to face. If accountants are responsible for the accuracy of information that is collected in the company, then perhaps some questions will be raised about whether or not accountants should be responsible for the models and their use. Put in other words, this point could be stated in the following way. Under old decision making methods, managers would take the accounting data, examine these and use internalized, intuitive kinds of models to process these data and arrive at a decision. Under the system that is described in this experiment, the manager does not "see" much of the data (indeed, some of it does not even exist in explicit form), but rather, he inputs some judgments in between himself and the data base, and what he sees is the outcome of applying these judgments to the basic data. In short, it is possible in systems of this type for the decision maker to never see the underlying data base but only to see the results of the application of his judgment to this data base. This raises a whole series of issues of "accountability" for the decision support systems and the models involved, and the role that accountants in an organization should play in such systems.

The points we have made above are merely to illustrate the kinds of research issues that are raised with the use of interactive models. These examples should provide some context for the general implications discussed in the following section.

4. Implications for Accounting Research

It was argued in the Introduction that interactive models had two major types of implications for accounting research. The first of these was that there would be new research possibilities opened up by the availability of interactive models; the second was that the available research methodology would change. Having discussed the technology and introduced an example of a research experiment using an interactive model, this section of the paper now returns to the original theme and elaborates on the two major topics.

a. Implications of Interactive Models— New Research Areas.

(1). Access to the Decision Process.

From the description of the use of the interactive model that we have seen above, it is clear that it allows new kinds of research to be undertaken. First, and perhaps foremost, is the fact that these systems allow access to the decision process itself. The decision maker uses the terminal to make his decision, and the computer system can be made to track what he is doing. Having saved this trace of the steps in the decision process we can, at the conclusion of the experiment, analyze this protocol of the subject and pull out the information we require. There is no other experimental vehicle which has quite this same capability of monitoring a human engaged in complex problem solving. Ready access to the decision process has tremendous power in helping us look for cause and effect relationships between what the user sees in his accounting information and the actions he takes with that informa-

tion. Discovery of such cause and effect relationships would allow us to examine the kinds of accounting information that prove to be most useful for given decisions.

In addition, with the protocol, we are able to test the impact of models that process accounting information, to see whether we have been able to improve the quality of the decision. By having a detailed step by step trace of which information the decision maker has used in which sequence, the kinds of questions he has asked and the alternatives he has tested, we can examine the "inside" of the decision process. This kind of detailed examination does not get directly at what is going on inside the decision maker's head, but it is a considerable improvement over our present means of access to the decision process. By understanding the process at a lower level of aggregation than we do now, it is possible to find methods of improving the decision process. In short, the construction of models to improve the decision process is considerably enhanced by the insights we gain with this access to the decision process [14]. Research into all of these topics is possible with interactive systems, and it is an area with promise of substantial payoff.

(2). "Objective" Accounting Data and Judgment.

A second characteristic of this technology is that we are, for the first time, marrying accounting information with judgment in an explicit fashion. The decision maker can ask for the accounting data that he feels are relevant, and when he can do so in a simple yet powerful fashion, it does not hinder his thoughts. By exploring and rearranging the data, he is able to develop a basis upon which he can formally apply his judgment and intuition. This ability, coupled with the traceability mentioned above, provides us with insights that we have not had in the past. For example, in the model in the Appendix, the system allowed the manager to apply his best judgments to a well structured statement of the problem. The system could be used to develop this structuring of the variables, and then, on top of this relatively clear, well organized base of facts, he could apply his judgment.

To combine managerial judgment with facts effectively in this way requires a great deal of further research. Our use of this model suggests ways of providing the user, be he manager or researcher, with tools to aid him in structuring his problem, whether it be in tree form or some other form. Similarly, there is a lot of work to be done in developing models that can successfully take the structure the user develops, accept his judgments where required, and then compute an answer.

(3). Decision Support Systems.

The third characteristic of interactive models that offers us an interesting difference from previous research work is that of involving the decision maker so closely with his decision process that it becomes possible for the models to be sequentially adaptive. In developing a model appropriate for the decision at hand, virtually all of the decision makers we have worked with have made suggestions about changes that they recommended in both the data and the model. This degree of involvement results in a great deal of learning and much more useful models than has heretofore occurred [1]. In addition, of course, the original model builders and the analysts involved find changes that they wish to make as they watch the use of their model, and as they watch the ways in which it is applied by the decision maker. Having the manager be this close to such an adaptive, evolving type of model is not something that we have been able to do in the past, and it, therefore, raises a host of interesting research possibilities in assessing managerial use of accounting information.

Finally, by providing access to relevant facts in a simple and powerful fashion, it becomes possible for the user to impose his criteria as to what is relevant and his preferences on the ordering and level of aggregation of the data with which he. is dealing. This means that instead of having to accept a large mass of accounting information in the form in which the accounting department has chosen to present it, the user now has the possibility of structuring this information to suit his changing decision making needs. The implications of this for the structuring of the data base and the fashion in which information is maintained are far reaching. Instead of the simple hierarchical arrangement with which we are familiar, we may, in fact, be forced into the position of having to provide the managers with an associative data base. As can be seen in the use of the IGRAS model shown in the Appendix, it is simple to request information. Such flexible access combined with some simple filtering [18] can result in the removal of almost all standard "status" reports involving accounting information. However, there has yet to be research on good methods for coding the basic data so it can be aggregated and organized in the form appropriate for most users. The research possibilities in assessing the improved efficiency of using such systems, the impact on the organization of having relevant accounting information readily available, and so forth, are enormous.

(4). Operational Problems.

As a result of organizations adopting this new technology and installing systems of this general nature, we are certain to find a significant increase in the types of accounting issues which the profession will be *asked* to solve [8]. The new areas of accounting research that will arise as a result of the applications of this interactive technology are hard to predict precisely. In fact, a primary research activity might well be to assess the likely types of problems that are going to arise in an effort to predict the areas in which we will require further accounting research work. In this way, we might be able to anticipate some of the issues that will arise and be better prepared to deal with them when they do occur.

There are several major areas in on-going organizations which have been impacted to some degree or other by the use of interactive models. One example is the question of interactive models in cost accounting. Systems have been built and used in which interactive terminals and related models have been employed to derive product costs. In at least one situation, these costs were a direct input to the bid decision in the sales of products [18]. In such systems, the manager inputs his judgment about the appropriate assumptions, such as volume at the time the order will be manufactured, special costs in relation to this item, and so forth. The data base and the cost system is then modified in light of these assumptions and a relevant cost is generated. Such a system allows the manager to move back and forth between a direct or marginal cost all the way through to a full cost, as he sees fit. Clearly, the use of such systems poses a number of operational problems for the cost accountant, not the least of which is the data base problem and the problem of defining cost center boundaries when the manager changes those boundaries.

There are other areas in which interactive models have been in operational use, areas of use which will eventually create research questions. These include decisions involving capital investments where conversational systems allow the manager to look at the impact on the financial statements, evaluate competing alternatives, and so forth. Similarly, in the budgeting area, we have systems that support the setting up of the initial budget as well as the negotiation that is involved in controlling organizations through the budgets. Negotiation sessions, with the various parties all present in the same room at the same time, result in a significantly different budgeting process and one that uses accounting information in a different way than the classical process. In all of these areas, research on the types of models to be used as well as their implications for the organization is greatly needed.

*b. Implications of Interactive Models—
Research Methodology.*

All of the above material suggests many ways in which interactive models will have an impact on research methodology in accounting. We can summarize these impacts by splitting the problem in two—the implications for the tools available to the researcher and the implications for the researcher's research design. In the latter case, interactive models provide a new challenge in accounting research design. We have a new set of tools and can, therefore, explore some new areas. In general, the research design that is used will have to pay more attention to the kinds of issues and method-

ology raised by Rhode [20]. An example would be in doing the research discussed above, where we gain access to a decision process in which accounting data is important. Here, the measurements and methodology that we have available to us when we explore human decision making are meager, and much pioneering remains to be done.

The second methodological implication affects the researcher as he is provided with a set of tools that are both different in degree and different in kind from his current tools. The difference in degree is provided when the researcher uses the conversational system as a working tool for analysis of his experimental results. This can make available to him a powerful range of analytical languages. When well designed (see McIntosh and and Griffel [12] and Eisner [7]), these are easy to use in a conversational mode and provide access to an immense range of statistical, econometric and other model building tools. Experimenters in the social sciences have been able to build a series of tests quickly and conveniently that allow them to explore their data for possible results.

The difference in kind occurs when the researcher is using new measurement methods and needs a different form of research support. Monitoring a "slave" terminal and watching the manager use accounting data in "real-time" on his own terminal is one such example. Others occur in protocol analysis or when applying a series of standard statistical tests quickly and easily on a terminal and probing with these to find patterns in the data. This quick probing mode is only possible on a powerful conversational system, but when available, it seems to provide real assistance to researchers in the social sciences (See "The Cambridge Project" [6]).

5. Conclusions

In conclusion, there are some general points which are extremely important if the accounting profession is to take advantage of the kind of power that is now available. The first point is, that we can be certain that such interactive models will be in widespread use in the coming years. The technology is currently available and rapidly becoming inexpensive. Since this technology offers significant support for certain aspects of management decision making, it is quite clear that it will be used in organizations. Our experience at MIT has demonstrated that the technology forms a powerful tool for research work. It is a safe assumption that researchers in universities will be able to build interactive models, then apply them to whatever area is of interest.

There is no avoiding the fact that interactive models will be with us in the university and will become widespread in organizations. As a result, we are going to have a whole new field in which the accounting profession can conduct research. It may not be an exaggeration to say that because of the rapid change of pace that we have seen over the last few years, the accounting profession will have to organize itself to deal with this new area in a way different from any change in the past. Accounting has managed, by and large, to absorb the impact of traditional batch processing, but it is less clear that we will be so successful in dealing with the problems that will arise because of the interactive technology. At the very least, we need to be clear about what forces are at work and we must recognize the kinds of changes that are likely to occur.

The second conclusion that I think can be drawn from the material we have discussed above is, that the accounting field in universities is going to have to think about some change in organizational form. On the basis of performance so far, it seems unlikely that many accounting departments can remain isolated and still deal with this new phenomena of interactive models. Even if it were possible, it would not be desirable. The ideal organizational structure for research in this area is one in which academicians who are interested in accounting issues can mix freely with those interested in different kinds of models as well as those who are interested in computer problems. It is only if these three classes of people are generously intermixed, are we going to see good research results from the general field of interactive models. This field requires a mix of skills which no one person is likely to possess. Thus, if we are to use interactive models in accounting research, we must find some organizational design that will allow these three groups to function together. Many universities find organizational change difficult, and this is often doubly true in accounting departments, so we are faced with a significant problem if we are to make progress in this area.

Finally, there is the need to develop new methodology and research strategies if we are to succeed in doing the kind of research that will allow us to make much progress in this new field. Classical experimental design, traditional field research and the usual form of laboratory experiment, all have their place, but unfortunately, we are in a position in this area where industry is ahead of many universities. If the research profession is to begin to tackle the problems and challenges that are inherent in this field, then we will have to find creative mixes of our previous methodologies and strategies in order to make the progress required. The fundamental difficulty is that a lot of the research involved deals with improvements in decision making. This is an unstructured, complex task, and it is extremely hard to assess the impact of a particular model on the decisions made by managers [9]. There is a fundamental lack of information about the way human beings make decisions and about the kind of models that can support this. Despite these difficulties, the potential is enormous and the field is exciting. The challenge is there, the only question that remains is whether we can organize effectively to accept it.

Appendix

*1. Interactive Models in Accounting—
An Example**

Experimental Goals. This section of the paper discusses the use of an interactive model in a series of experiments that have been conducted at the Sloan School at MIT.

*The material in this Appendix summarizes a small portion of some experimental work done by Professor Zannetos and Messrs. Beville and Wagner. The complete write up is contained in [3] and [4].

The experiment involved building an interactive system and then using it in a series of experiments with senior line managers. The system was termed "An Interactive Graphical Risk Analysis System" (IGRAS). A number of features of the experiments with this particular model are not relevant for our purposes in this paper, so what is described in this Appendix is only a subset of the work, and it is intended to be illustrative, only.

The goals for the use of this model were several. The first and most general of the goals was to continue the experiments conducted at the Sloan School regarding the impact of interactive decision systems on the managerial decision making process. We have an on-going interest in how a manager's actual decision processes will be changed by the provision of more powerful, analytical support. In particular, within this experiment, we were expecting to examine the impact of the system on the "design" and "choice" phases of the decision process.

We expected that the system would help the decision maker in the design phase by:

(1) Facilitating the structuring of the alternative courses of action.
(2) Bringing to bear on the problem the decision maker's subjective estimates of the values of uncertain variables.
(3) Performing the complex computations required to accomplish (2) above.
(4) Facilitating sensitivity testing.

As for "choice" activity, the system was expected to have an impact in aiding the decision maker in his evaluation of the alternatives by:

(1) Providing more information than the manual methods. The system accomplishes this mainly by providing a graph of the probabilistic distribution of the net present values rather than just the expected values which were normally provided by manual methods.
(2) Displaying information in a format which is easy to understand. The system, for example, provides graphs rather than tables of values or mathematical descriptions of the various probability curves.
(3) Allowing the decision maker to comprehend the impact which his subjective estimates of risk and uncertainty have on computed expected outcomes.

(4) Making it easy for the subjects to change the values of the planning and decision variables and thus easily evaluate and choose among alternatives." (Beville, Wagner and Zannetos [4, p. 10])

One of the major hypotheses which we were anxious to explore was whether or not the decision makers would tend to have more confidence in their computer-aided decisions than they did in their manual ones. This proposition appeared *a priori* to be reasonable for the following reasons:

(a) The system allows the subjects to bring to bear all of their knowledge—objective, subjective and risk estimates—on the evaluation of the future consequences of each alternative course of action. Thus the results will tend to appear to them as more dependable and "scientific."
(b) The system gives the subjects better knowledge of the structure of the problem, and through sensitivity testing, an idea of the relative impact exerted by the key variables on expected outcomes. They will feel therefore that they have a firmer grasp of the problem and that the computer-aided decision rests on a firmer foundation.
(c) The system carries out the calculations and gives the decision maker additional quantitative information concerning the degree of risk and uncertainty associated with a proposed course of action. The additional information in this case consists of the graphs of the various terminal probability distributions, which is normally not available under manual methods.
(d) The system displays probabilistic information in formats, namely graphs, which are easier to understand than alternative formats, such as tables or listings of distribution parameters.
(e) Psychologically the subjects may feel insecure and tend to accept the results of manipulations they do not very well understand. Furthermore, the feeling that systems are designed by "experts" who undoubtedly store in the computer the best decision making models known to them tends to encourage too much faith in the results of such models.

A second hypothesis is that the decisions made with the aid of the computer, that is, the courses of action recommended, will differ from those suggested by manual methods. This was felt to be true because:

(a) The system provides the subjects with more

information concerning risk and uncertainty than they will be able to generate by using manual methods.

(b) When using the computerized system, the subjects will tend to rank the risk and uncertainty inherent in an alternative higher as a factor influencing their decision than they will when using manual methods. This appears logical since measures of risk even in their simplest form, e.g., variance, and general shape of the distribution of net present values, will be nearly impossible for the subjects to generate by using manual methods. They, therefore, will not tend to appreciate the significance of risk in decision making. If this hypothesis is proven then certain aspects of the educational value of the computerized system are proven also. (Beville, Wagner and Zannetos [4, p. 11])

The Model Structure. The problem which was implemented under the IGRAS system was a capital investment decision [2]. Two basic alternative courses of action were open to the decision makers, the first being to discontinue producing a textile product which was part of a firm's entire line of textiles, sell off the associated equipment and inventory, and collect the associated accounts receivables. The second major class of alternatives was to continue producing the product for the next four years (the equipment would be worn out at that time) and, given that decision, further decide upon the best pricing strategy to follow. The problem is represented in tree structure in Figure 1. As can be seen from this figure, there are two basic alternatives—to go out of business or to stay in business. There are varying degrees of uncertainty about the revenues to be generated if the firm does go out of business, and these have to be estimated by the decision maker. Similarly, if the firm stays in business, there are a series of alternatives. Both the revenue and expenditure side have considerable uncertainty attached to their major components. The pricing decision obviously will affect the market share and the revenues, and there is also uncertainty attached to the scrap value of the equipment and the sorts of inventories and accounts receivable experience that the company will have. Similarly, on the expenditure side, both the labor and

material costs can vary quite sharply. All inputs to the elements on the end points of the tree are in the form of cumulative subjective probability distributions. Given these subjective probability distributions, the system then computes the expected value of the various alternatives.

In general, the objective of risk analysis models is to provide structure to the problem environment by identifying the basic components of risk and assigning to each of these components probability measures for all possible outcomes. In this particular setting, the problem structure has been laid out in tree form for the decision maker. Thus, the basic elements of revenues and expenditures, which can vary in this particular setting, have been laid out on the tree. The decision maker is then able to specify possible ranges of outcomes and their associated probabilities of occurrence. Clearly, if more variables are of concern, then they can be added to the tree, until such time as the decision maker is satisfied he has all the components he wishes.

Once all of the outcome states for each of the elements of risk have been described in the form of probability distributions, these distributions can be aggregated by means of a Monte Carlo type of process to develop a probability distribution describing the expected net return for the alternative being modeled. Thus, such models provide both a framework for structuring decision alternatives through the identification of the elements of risk in a hierarchical manner, and also, they provide a methodology for analytically dealing with risk through the use of probability distributions and the Monte Carlo simulation.

The Experimental Setting. In this instance, then, the general goal was to assess the impact of such interactive decision systems on managerial decision making behavior. In particular, we wanted to find out how executives could deal with capital investment and competitive pricing decisions under conditions of uncertainty. This sort of planning problem is more difficult than the normal operational problems in the company because of the absence of structure, the

Michael S. Scott Morton

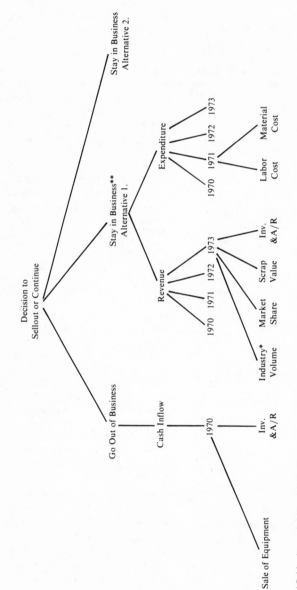

Figure 1   Structure of the Problem Tree Implemented on the IGRAM System

* Subjective probability distributions are entered at this level in the tree.
** Prices for each year and the cost of capital are entered at this level in the tree.

absence of many of the required factual elements, and the presence of uncontrolled environmental decisions. The risk analysis technique, which we have discussed above, was chosen as the basis for the model, because it incorporates a facility for structuring problems, a methodology for utilizing subjective estimates of the elements for which no factual information exists, and because it is a technique for introducing risk and uncertainty through the use of subjective probability distributions.

The experimental design involved two sets of subjects and was therefore replicated twice. One group of subjects were from the Sloan School's Senior Executive Program and the second group of subjects from a program, known as the Greater Boston Executives, which contained executives from local Boston companies with slightly less experience. Each group of subjects had to solve the problem twice, the first time using manual solution techniques and the second time using the IGRAS system. In each replication of the experiment, the subjects were assigned to two two-man teams at random. Members of the odd numbered teams solved the problem with manual methods first and then solved it with the aid of the computerized IGRAS system. Members of the even numbered teams solved the problem with the aid of the IGRAS system first and then solved it with manual methods. This order-

ing scheme was intended to neutralize the learning effect of having to solve the problem twice. Figure 2 illustrates the sequence of steps taken by the teams during the conduct of the experiment.

At the end of this Appendix, there are a series of figures which show the kinds of interaction and the types of displays that the managers had available to them when using the interactive system. Complete details on the way the system was built, the amount of effort it took and other details of the design and use of interactive models is given in the paper previously referenced [4]. The exhibitis are largely self-explanatory, and it is clear from looking at them that the system is easy to use and contains a great deal of information in an easily understandable form.

General Results. The purpose here is not to discuss the content of the results of this particular experiment but rather to identify this class of experiment and the methodology that is involved with this type of technology. In other words, for our purposes, we are interested in the methodological issues raised by this kind of experiment and in clearly delineating the forms of technology and the kind of research that can be done with these sorts of tools. Specific results of this particular experiment can be found in the references already cited. For our purpos-

Order of Events

Odd Numbered Teams	All Teams	Even Numbered Teams
	Answer Questionnaire # 1. Receive Copy of Case Receive Hertz [10] Article	
Solve Case Manually Answer Questionnaire # 2		
	Receive Copies of IGRAM Users' Manual	
	Briefing on and Demonstration of IGRAM System.	
	Solve problem with IGRAM System	
Answer Questionnaire # 3		Answer Quesionnaire # 4 Solve Case Manually Answer Questionnaire # 5
	Class Discussion of Problem and IGRAM System	

Figure 2   Experimental Procedure

es, it will be useful for us to pick up one of these results and describe it.

The results in both replications only weakly supported the hypothesis that decision makers would examine more alternative courses of action when using the system than when using manual methods. Table 1 contains the results of the experiments.

As can be seen in Table 1, the only case where a set of teams reported examining fewer alternatives when using the computer system than when using manual methods (3.67 versus 3.70) was the odd numbered GBE teams. All other teams reported an increase, although in no case were their mean differences statistically significant. The startling result revealed by these data is that the odd numbered team members in every instance examined significantly more alternatives than did the even numbered team members. In the case of the Senior Executives, the odd numbered teams examined 5.56 computer-aided alternatives versus 5.00 manual alternatives, while the even numbered teams examined 3.43 and 2.86 alternatives, respectively. The overall average number of alternatives was 5.34 for the odd numbered teams versus 3.14 for the even numbered. These data are statistically significant at the 0.1% level. Similar results are revealed by the Greater Boston Executives' experiments, although not as strongly.

Another startling observation is the difference in the variances between the odd and the even numbered teams, which differences are again statistically significant at the 0.1% level. The fact that the odd numbered teams solved the problem manually first seems to have had an important influence upon their decision on how many alternatives to examine.

A possible explanation of the results of Table 1 is that the method initially used by a decision maker sets the style he will use in subsequent decision making, including the general number of alternatives he will examine before arriving at a decision. When the odd numbered teams first approached the problem manually, they were possibly not very confident in their manual methods of considering risk and uncertainty. Therefore, they examined many different alternative courses of action before they made their final decisions. The even numbered teams, however, first solved the case with the aid of the computerized system. They possibly had a high degree of confidence in the way the computer system handled risk, so they did not feel the need to examine many alternatives. The high level of confidence of the even numbered teams, therefore, may have led them to a strange sense of security, which resulted in their examining fewer alternatives, on average, than did the odd

Table 1.   Number of Alternative Courses of Action Examined

SE Computer-aided		Manual		Both	
Odd	Even	Odd	Even	Odd	Even
m = 5.56[1]	m = 3.43[1]	m = 5.00[2]	m = 2.86[2]	m = 5.34[4]	m = 3.14[4]
v = 2.25	v = 0.858	v = 6.29[3]	v = 0.8[3]	v = 4.00[5]	v = 0.508[5]
n = 9	n = 7	n = 8	n = 7	n = 17	n = 14

GBE Computer-aided		Manual		Both	
Odd	Even	Odd	Even	Odd	Even
m = 3.67[6]	m = 2.66[6]	m = 3.70[6]	m = 2.50[8]	m = 3.68[10]	m = 2.58[10]
v = 6.00[7.]	v = 0.427[7]	v = 5.34[9]	v = 0.455[9]	v = 5.34[11]	v = 0.417[11]
n = 9	n = 12	n = 9	n = 12	n = 18	n = 24

Where m = mean of the sample; v = variance of the sample; and n = sample size

[1]T-test on difference means is significant at 0.1% level.
[2]T-test on difference between means is significant at 5% level.
[3]F-test on ratio of variances is significant at 2.5% level.
[4]T-test on the differences between the means is significant at the 0.1% level.
[5]F-test on the ratio of the variances is significant at the 1% level.
[6+8]Difference is significant at the 10% level.
[7+9+11]Ratio of variances is significant at the 1% level.
[10]Difference is significant at the 5% level.

numbered teams. The results were presented to the participants without the experimentor's views as to the cause being expressed, and the participants provided the same explanation.

Hence, the method first used by the decision maker sets the style he will use in subsequent decision making. *Given their respective styles,* as reflected by the number of alternatives they considered, three of the four-groups did, however, examine more alternatives when they used the system than when they used manual methods. We must stress again, however, that *for each group,* the mean differences between the number of alternatives examined (computer-aided versus manual) were not statistically significant, contrary to our expectations.

For our purposes here in considering the use of interactive models in accounting research, there are perhaps two general points we can make from the description of one part of the results of the use of this model. The first point is that the models and decision processes available to the decision maker affect the number of alternatives he considers, the numbers he uses in those alternatives, and the kind of data he uses. The second is that the executives trusted the system and assumed that the model was "good" and therefore looked at fewer alternatives. It should be stressed again that both of these two points have merely been suggested by the data we have given here and are in no sense proven facts. Further research and experimentation will be required to establish if they are generally true. However, for our purposes here, they serve to illustrate the kinds of issues that can be explored with the use of interactive models.

2. System Description

The pages that follow provide a quick overview of the kinds of displays the system generates in the course of the problem solving process. The sequence of problem solving and the variables involved are under the control of the decision maker. He is able to move back and forth using a simple command language. The executives found the system easy and comfortable to use with little time spent on learning.

The system is programmed in PL/1 on MIT's time-sharing facility and uses a low cost graphical display for output. Response time to a user's request is only a few seconds, and the display is written in less than two seconds so that interaction is not impeded by the hardware.

Functional Commands. The functional commands which are available for interaction with elements are:

1. *Re-enter data.* This command is used to enter new data or to alter previously entered data. When at the independent elements, this command causes the coordinates for the cumulative probability distribution which are required to specify the distribution to be displayed. (See Figure 1). If for each probability level no value has been previously entered, the system will pause and wait for the user to type one in. If a value already exists, it will be displayed. The user has the option of either typing in a new value or keeping the old value by typing "new line."

2. *Examine level parameters.* This command is also a data-entering command and is used for entering model parameters, i.e., non-probabilistic model values. Figure 2 shows an example of this type of data-entering capability for the price and cost of capital parameters for a model alternative.

3. *Take data from another alternative.* This command allows transferring to an element data which have been previously entered at another element without having to re-type the data.

4. *Graph data.* This command graphs the output of the element at which the system is located. If one has previously requested the system to save a graph (this command will be described next), then the saved graph will also be displayed in addition to the graph for the element at which the system was located when the command was given. Figure 3 gives an example of the graph of

A) Re-enter a graph
B) Move to next sequential position
C) Other

Type desired option:

You are at: Sale of equipment.   Go out of business

The parameters involved are

$$x \text{ if } y = 0.05$$
$$x \text{ if } y = 0.10$$
$$x \text{ if } y = 0.25$$
$$x \text{ if } y = 0.50$$
$$x \text{ if } y = 0.75$$
$$x \text{ if } y = 0.90$$
$$x \underline{\text{ if } y} = 0.95$$

Parameter Name	Normal Value	Current Value	New Value
x if y = 0.05	NONE	NONE	80000
x if y = 0.10	NONE	NONE	83000
x if y = 0.25	NONE	NONE	87000
x if y = 0.50	NONE	NONE	90000
x if y = 0.75	NONE	NONE	94000
x if y = 0.90	NONE	NONE	98000
x if y = 0.95	NONE	NONE	

Figure 1   Entering Probability Distribution

A) Revenue
B) Expenditure
C) Graph data
D) Move to next sequential position
E) Examine level parameters
F) Other

Type desired option: e

You are at: Model Alternative

The parameters invoved are

              Price 1970
              Price 1971
              Price 1972
              Price 1973
              Cost of capital

  3 decimal digits will be retained.

Parameter Name	Normal Value	Current Value	New Value (if desired)
Price 1970	NONE	1.750	1.80
Price 1971	NONE	1.850	1.80
Price 1972	NONE	1.950	2.00
Price 1973	NONE	2.050	2.10
Cost of capital	NONE	0.100	.12

A) Revenue
B) Expenditure
C) Graph data
D) Move to next sequential position
E) Other

Type desired option:

Figure 2   Entering Data for Model Parameters

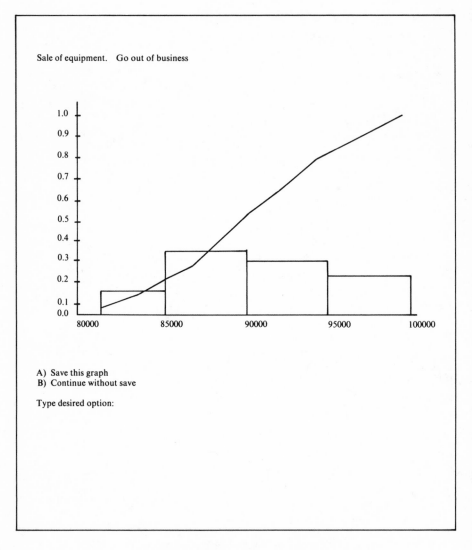

Figure 3   Graph of Distribution Entered for the Sale of Equipment Element

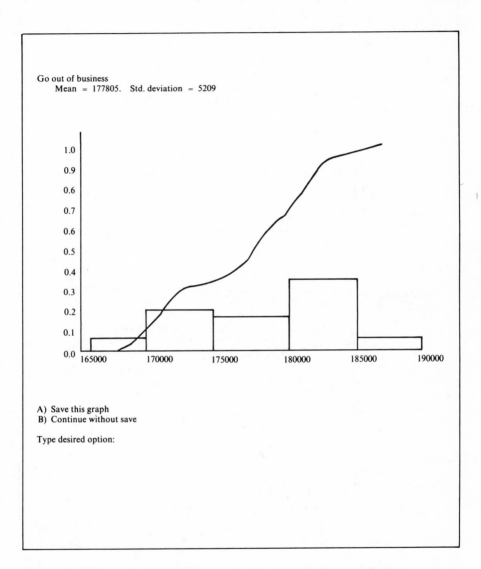

Figure 4   Graph of Expected Return from the Alternative of Leaving the Business

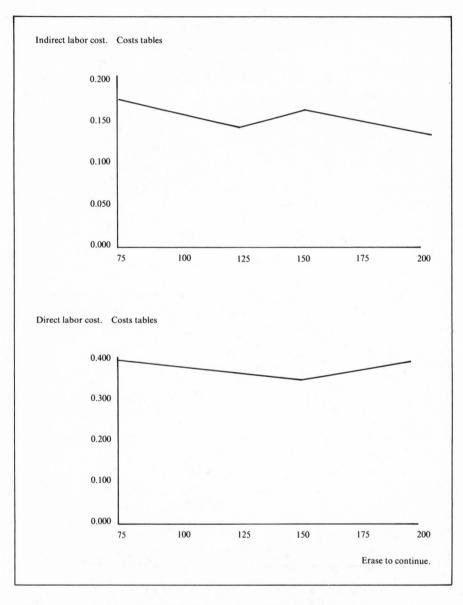

Figure 5   Graphs of Functional Data for Indirect Labor and Direct Labor Costs as a Function of Volume

an input distribution, Figure 4 shows a typical model output graph for the distribution of the expected return after taxes, and Figure 5 shows the graphs for functional data for labor costs.

5. *Save top, or bottom graph.* This command causes the system to save either the top or bottom graph which is currently being displayed and to redisplay it on the bottom half of the screen the next time the "graph data" command is given.

References

1. Ackoff, R. L., "Management Misinformation Systems," *Management Science* (December, 1967), pp. B147–B156.

2. "Atherton Company" in R. N. Anthony, *Management Accounting: Text and Cases,* Irwin, 1970.

3. Beville, J., Wagner, J. H., and Zannetos, Z. S., "The Development of an Interactive Graphical Risk Analysis System," Working Paper No. 502–70, Sloan School of Management, MIT, 1970.

4. _____, "An Experiment with Interactive Planning Models," Working Paper No. 503–70, Sloan School of Management, MIT, 1970.

5. Boulden, J. B., and Buffa, E. S., "Corporate Models: On-Line, Real-time Systems," *Harvard Business Review* (July-August, 1970), pp. 65–84.

6. "The Cambridge Project, Annual Report," MIT, June 1969–June 1970.

7. Eisner, M., "Manual for the TROLL System," Econometrics Project, MIT, 1969.

8. Gerrity, T. P., "The Design of Man-Machine Decision Systems," unpublished Ph.D. dissertation, Sloan School of Management, MIT, June 1970.

9. Gorry, G. A. "The Development of Managerial Models," *Sloan Management Review* (Winter, 1971), pp. 1–16.

10. Hertz, D. B., "Risk Analysis in Capital Investment," *Harvard Business Review* (January-February, 1964), pp. 95–106.

11. Jones, C. H., "At Last: Real Computer Power for Decision Makers," *Harvard Business Review* (September-October, 1970), pp. 75–89.

12. McIntosh, S. D., and Griffel, D. M., "Admins Mark III," Center for International Studies, MIT, 1970.

13. Morton, M. S. S., "Interactive Visual Display Systems and Management Problem Solving," *Sloan Management Review* (Fall, 1967), pp. 69–81.

14. _____, *Management Decision Systems: Computer-Based Support for Decision Making,* Harvard Business School, Division of Research, 1971.

15. _____, "Spectrum of Computer Systems," Working Paper No. 477–70, Sloan School of Management, MIT, 1970.

16. _____, and Crowston, W. B. S., "The Design of Hierachical Decision Systems, Working Paper No. 547–71, Sloan School of Management, MIT, 1971.

17. Morton, M. S. S. and Gorry, G. A., "A Framework for Management Information Systems," *Sloan Management Review.*

18. Morton, M. S. S. and McCosh, A. M., "Terminal Costing for Better Decisions," *Harvard Business Review* (May-June, 1968), pp. 147–56.

19. Morton, M. S. S., and Stephens, J., "The Impact of Interactive Visual Display Systems on the Management Planning Process," *Proceedings of the IFIP Congress 68,* Edinburgh, Scotland, August, 1968. (Also Working Paper No. 356–68, Sloan School of Management, MIT, 1968.)

20. Rhode, J. G., "Behavioral Science Methodologies with Application for Accounting Research," Arthur Young Accounting Colloquium II, University of Kansas, 1971.

21. Sterling, Robert R., *Theory of the Measurement of Enterprise Income,* University Press of Kansas, 1970.

chapter 11

Interactive Processing in Accounting Research

Robert S. Kaplan

Carnegie-Mellon University

Reviewing this paper proved to be a difficult task. It is written in a very confusing style and it exhibits a general lack of substance and knowledge of the relevant literature. My criticisms can be directed at the use of the following words in the title: "Interactive Models," "Accounting" and "Research." Each will be discussed in turn.

Professor Morton claims that the availability of interactive processing opens new dimensions and challenges for management. I agree wholeheartedly with this opinion, but it is unfortunate that such a weak case has been made for this position in the paper. For example, the author claims that interactive models are "quite different from those we are familiar with under a batch processing mode." But this statement is clearly contradicted by the author's own example of an interactive model. The model described is the well-known Hertz simulation technique for risk analysis which has been applied for ten years now and can be run in either a batch processing mode or in an interactive one. While there are obviously certain advantages for using time-sharing here, the model is essentially the same, independent of the computational resource used.

Most of the other statements made about the virtues of interactive models are also true about all decision models no matter how they are implemented. For example, all decision models turn raw data into useful information for the decision maker, not just interactive ones. The author further claims that interactive models enable the decision maker to insert his judgment about events and variables. Yet this is clearly not a unique characteristic of interactive models. When I run a linear or dynamic programming model on a batch processing system, I must insert my best knowledge of the relevant variables. If I am unsure about particular values, I can either run a stochastic version of the model after specifying a probability distribution or do parametric and sensitivity analysis by running a number of deterministic models. It is also claimed that interactive models facilitate dialogues between decision makers and analysts in the evolution of decision models. This dialogue, though, is likely to occur in the development of all decision models not just ones to be implemented on an interactive system.

Thus, this paper (with one exception to be discussed below) is really talking about decision models in general, not interactive models in particular. It does not pass the contrapositive test suggested by Ijiri at this conference. The use of the word "interactive" in the title of this paper is superfluous and misleading. This is unfortunate because I share the author's belief in the importance of time-sharing systems in management practices. But the significance of time-sharing is not that it enables us to solve entirely new kinds of models, but rather that it provides a difference of degree in reaction time and flexibility.

The difference between time-sharing and batch processing is a quantitative difference in reaction time, not a qualitative one. Therefore, we should focus our attention on the aspects of decision models for which this reduction in turn-around time can truly be beneficial. The case for interactive processing is not helped by claiming that it is all things to all people. It should rest on a serious analysis of the specific advantages that it does offer over other forms of processing and the costs of providing this level of service. Loose and unsupported statements such as "This degree of involvement results in a great deal of learning and much more useful models . . ." provide little insight into the relative usefulness of interactive models.

The one unique feature of interactive processing discussed in this paper is the description of how the decision maker can control his progress through a solution procedure. This process is retarded in a batch processing mode because of the significant delays between successive runs. In addition, the author makes the point that the record of the decision maker's protocol in a complex, problem solving situation provides a unique vehicle for understanding executive thought processes. I shall have more to say about this point when talking about research, but the above points were the only ones in which the author was truly talking about interactive models, as opposed to models in general.

The author is also not precise in his use of the word "accounting." Since this is an accounting colloquium, I recognize that the word "accounting" should appear somewhere in the title of a paper and as frequently as possible in the text. However, I had a hard time finding what on this paper was unique to the accounting area. As a test,

therefore, I re-read the paper and any time that I encountered the word "accounting," I substituted "production" or "marketing" or "finance" or, more generally, "management." (Try this with the first paragraph.) In only one case could I find a passage where these substituted words were out of context. Thus, with this one exception, we find that this paper is not about accounting in particular but about decision making or management in general. This is not necessarily bad since decision models are useful in many disciplines but it is confusing if one is looking for specific accounting applications as promised in the title. There is a burden of proof on the author to demonstrate how his general remarks specifically affect the practice of accounting.

In fact, the impact of decision models and computers on the accounting process has been extensively investigated in a much more comprehensive and systematic manner than this paper suggests. Rather than attempt to summarize these efforts, I refer the interested reader to the American Accounting Association committee reports on Management Decision Models (1969) and Accounting and Information Systems (1971) which both contain extensive discussions and references on the issues hinted at in the present paper.

The one place in the paper that does focus on specific accounting issues is the discussion of the accountant's responsibility for the data base and collection of relevant information for the firm. The impact of decision models and computerized information systems on the information generating process is indeed profound. But this is a well-known and accepted idea (see the two AAA committee reports cited previously) and does not constitute a startling revelation at this time. The author does raise an issue as to whether accountants having generated certain types of information should be "responsible" for the models that use this information. He claims that there are a whole series of issues of "accountability," but I could not quite figure out what the author had in mind here. Accountable to whom or for what? Are accountants responsible for auditing the decision maker's judgment in using the data accountants present? The author would have done well to be more specific on this point since it was the only issue he raised that was specifically addressed to accountants.

There are some important questions that interactive computers do raise about the accounting process which the author has not discussed. One is the question of security and access to the data base. It is entirely conceivable that high level executives should not have access to very detailed and instantaneous data about the company. You don't want vice-presidents monitoring the consumption of pencils in an office and you probably don't want them to see the short-run daily fluctuations that occur in the normal course of operations. On the other hand, a department manager should not be able to see the operations of a completely independent department in another division. A central data base, easily accessible from remote terminals, could easily lead to too much information being available for good management practices. This implies that we have to think very carefully about what information we want to make available to managers at all levels and to properly secure information systems so that illegal access to unauthorized data is not possible.

Another problem arises in the audit trail of a time-shared system. As more of the transactions of a firm are entered remotely from terminals and processed in the central data computer, the difficulty of reconstructing the transaction's history is increased. Changes in the data base may be made from a remote location and, if we are not careful, no permanent record of the source and nature of such transactions will be maintained. Therefore, the use of an interactive system must be coordinated with the firm's auditors to be sure that an objective and easily traceable record is always available. The existence of a central data file of the corporation also introduces new possibilities for auditing, e.g., surprise audits from remote terminals or more frequent monitoring of operations. Of course, other questions such as loss of records through theft, fire, power shutdowns, system failures or even malicious destruction of magnetically coded files must be carefully considered as we perform more of the traditional accounting processes on electronic computers.

My final comments have to do with the type of research efforts the author is advocating. We are told throughout the paper about the great amount of research that needs to be done but these urgings are usually at a superficial level and do not give much insight into the detailed types of research efforts that need to be done (e.g., "We have a new set of tools and can, therefore, explore some new areas." "Experimenters in the social sciences have been able to build a series of tests quickly and conveniently that allow them to explore their data for possible results.")

Ijiri has stated at this conference that "In many parts of accounting, present research processes are so loosely constructed that nobody seems to be able to prove or disprove anything scientifically." The overwhelming feeling I get in reading the present paper is a lack of a rigorous and formal approach to studying interactive processing models. I fear that the research emerging from such an approach will be of little value unless we can be much more precise in the questions that we should be studying.

One place where the author has given a specific indication of research methodology is the discussion of the power of interactive computers to monitor the informational requirements and thought processes of decision makers. Research in this area is potentially very fruitful to guide us in organizing the data base and indicating directions for the development of new objectives for normative decision models. However, the author is again guilty of overlooking the literature describing this feature. For example, in a paper written three years ago we can find the following sentences, "The computer effectively amounts to a built-in laboratory capable of recording its own operations completely and playing them back for *ex post facto* reruns whenever desired for further manipulation and analysis. This capability for regenerative recording is a great leap forward in experimental method because. . . . the experimenter . . . can study man-computer communication the way it is, in the raw."[1] The author has similarly omitted references to the research on the characteristics, advantages, and disadvantages of interactive processing. These efforts have been concentrated at the RAND Corporation[2] and Systems Development Corporation,[3] as well as M.I.T.[4]

In summary, this paper contained very little that was new. Even more, it failed to adequately recognize the existing literature in the areas that it purported to discuss. And further, the author confounds whatever points he wished to make by not emphasizing the unique features of interactive processing (vis a vis computers in general), by not distinguishing between accounting and decision making or management in general, and finally by not being explicit in the type of research effort he was advocating. I find these failures especially unfortunate because the area is an important one and we need to have good directions for formal research on the important questions that exist here.

[1]H. Sackman, "Experimental Analysis of Human Behavior in Time-Sharing and Batch-Processing Information Systems," Conference for Research on Management Information Systems, Graduate School of Industrial Administration, Carnegie-Mellon University, June 17–19, 1968.

[2]J. W. Shaw, "JOSS: Experience with an Experimental Computing Service for Users at Remote Typewriter Consoles, P-3149, The RAND Corporation, Santa Monica, California, May 1965; G. E. Bryan, "JOSS: 20,000 Hours at a Console—A Statistical Summary," AFIPS Conference Proceedings, Vol. 31, 1967 Fall Joint Computer Conference, pp. 769–777.

[3]Robert A. Totschek, "An Empirical Investigation into the Behavior of the SDC Time-Sharing System," SP-2191, System Development Corporation, Santa Monica, California, July 6, 1966; Paul V. McIsaac, "Job Descriptions and Scheduling in the SDC Q-32 Time-Sharing System," TM-2996, System Development Corporation, Santa Monica, California, June 10, 1966.

[4]Allan L. Scherr, "An Analysis of Time-Shared Computer Systems," Research Monograph No. 36 (The M.I.T. Press, 1967); Thierry G. Raynaud, "Operational Analysis of a Computation Center," Technical Report No. 32, Operations Research Center, Massachusetts Institute of Technology, July 1967.

chapter 12

Behavioral Science Methodologies with Application for Accounting Research: References and Source Materials

JOHN GRANT RHODE

University of Washington

The difference between the deliberate research activities of the behavioral scientist and the casual observations and conclusions of the sophisticated layman are mainly matters of procedure or method (American Accounting Association [3, p. 7]).

1. Introduction

Accounting has developed with some assistance from other disciplines, such as economics, law and statistical methods. Reliance on these disciplines provided part of the structure surrounding current accounting practice and theory. A realistic examination of the validity surrounding this practice and theory may best be made by reliance on yet another academic discipline—that of behavioral science.

Hypotheses concerning the activities of individuals must eventually be tested by analyzing the behavior of real-life subjects. This is necessary since the most rigorous logical speculation may break down when empirical evidence indicates results opposed to the stated logic. Moreover, sophisticated simulation techniques, which are essentially no different than logical argument, simply cannot completely capture all of the factors that encompass the decision process of actual decision makers. Because the simulator, or researcher, may overlook some factors, the simulations must also be tested against the actions of real decision makers. Consequently, the ultimate test of hypothesized behavior is observed behavior.

Because behavioral scientists have established methods for analyzing, explaining and predicting selected behavior, it seems reasonable that accountants should utilize these methods to better understand accounting and its effects. Further, since Hofstedt and Kinard [50] noted some of the interest which academic accountants have developed in the behavioral effects of accounting's technical functions (Bruns [10], Livingstone [62]), the personal characteristics of accountants (Sorter and Becker [81]), and the impact of accounting information systems (Argyris [6], Stedry [82], DeCoster and Fertakis [21]), it seems appropriate to catalog several of the popular methodological tools developed by behavioral scientists which may have application to accounting research.

Some of the better background materials for the design of experiments on behavioral inquiry are found, not surprisingly, within the literature of psychology and sociology. This literature may be classified as: (1) representing philosophical pre-experimental considerations (Bakan [7], Kaplan [55], Webb, Campbell, Schwartz and Secrest [89]), (2) essential design constructs (Campbell and Stanely [14], Cox [19], Edwards [29], Festinger and Katz [33], Goode and Hatt [38], Kerlinger [57], Riley [73] and Simon [77]), and (3) structured approaches to data analysis and interpretation (Hays [48], Siegel [76], and Snedecor and Cochran [78]).

While these sources provide accounting researchers with a thorough introduction to a *general* knowledge of research design, it is the purpose of this discussion to catalog *specific* behavioral research techniques available for accountants interested in research of a behavioral nature. Techniques used for the design of experiments, such as pre-test and post-test control groups, and means of analyzing data, such as factor analysis, will not be discussed. Rather, specific tools, such as the use of personality measures, and research methods, such as a field study, will be emphasized.

The behavioral science data collection methodologies, not the accounting problems suitable for these methodologies, will be discussed, since different accounting researchers would likely place different value judgments on the importance of researchable problems. Once the accounting problem to be investigated has been defined, the means of gathering data may be determined.

2. Data Collection Methods—Tests, Interviews, & Questionnaires

Although data collection may take various forms, its primary concern is with the analysis of subject responses from a sample group to discover attributes of a population. Correspondingly, standardized psychological tests and interviews and questionnaires, because they deal with the sampled response

from a larger population, are all considered data collection techniques.

Standardized Psychological Tests. Data from standardized psychological tests allow behavioral accounting researchers to examine the personal characteristics of not only accountants but also individuals exposed to accountants and their work. It is not sufficient to note that different people will interpret the same financial information in different ways—especially if it is possible to obtain psychological test scores on the subjects within the experiment. Standardized personality tests like the California Psychological Inventory (CPI) (Gough [40]) can reveal personality scores on eighteen scales grouped into four basic trait descriptions: (1) measures of poise, ascendency and self assurance: (2) measures of socialization, maturity and responsibility; (3) measures of achievement potential and intellectual efficiency; and (4) measures of intellectual and interest modes. Using this type of test, one may, for example, partially explain why subjects, who receive the same financial accounting information, make consistently different investment portfolio decisions. Because the CPI can be administered in approximately thirty minutes, and since the test does not contain potentially embarrassing questions, it may be used with most sample groups. The CPI has recently been used by accounting researchers (DeCoster and Rhode [22]) to examine the validity of the accountant's stereotype.

Other suitable tests for categorizing subjects on the basis of personality traits are the Minnesota Multiphasic Personality Inventory (Hathaway & McKinley [47]), the Guilford-Zimmerman Temperament Survey (Guilford and Zimmerman [43]), the Allport-Vernon Lindzey Study of Values (Allport and Vernon [2]), the Gordon Personal Inventory (Gordon [39]), and the Edwards Personal Preference Schedule (EPPS) (Edwards [28]). An extensive analysis of the reliability and validity statistics surrounding each of these tests may be found in the sixth edition of the *Mental Measurement Yearbook* (Buros, [11]). A brief but comprehensive description of these tests is also noted by Guion [44].

As an indication of insightful uses for standardized psychological tests, consider the following examples. The Guilford-Zimmerman survey was used to explore the personality variables of persons interested in art (Roubertoux [74]), the influence of sex roles on leadership was analyzed using the CPI (Megargee [64]), and personality differences between heavy and light drinkers was reported with EPPS scores (Reiter [72]). The use of these tests for behavioral accounting research, particularly on the characteristics of accountants, is limited only by the imagination of accounting researchers.

In addition to classifying individuals on the basis of a range of personality characteristics, it is possible to use tests like the California F-scale (Adorno, et al. [1]) to label subjects on the basis of specific authoritarian tendencies. This scale was used by behavioral accounting researchers in the study of corporate personality (Sorter and Becker [81]).

Another useful method of classifying personal characteristics is by vocational interests. The two dominant tests in this area are the Strong Vocational Interest Blank (SVIB) (Strong, et al. [84]) and the Kuder Preference Record (Guion [44]). A final type of test suitable for use by behavioral accounting researchers is one which classifies leaders on the basis of tendencies to act in a considerate manner versus being task oriented. One of the established tests which describes leaders on the basis of these traits is the Ohio State Leadership Behavioral Description Questionnaire (Fleishman, et al. [36], Fleishman [35]). A shortened version of this test was used to assist in analyzing the characteristics of subjects exposed to budget-induced pressure (DeCoster and Fertakis [21]).

Another established instrument of leadership effectiveness investigates the relationship between leadership variables, group-task situations and group productivity (Fiedler [34]). This instrument was used to examine how the esteem for one's least-preferred co-worker is related to an individual cognitive complexity (Mitchell [66]) and can easily be extended, for instance, to an analysis of productivity for audit teams in public accounting.

Some attention should be paid to two considerations surrounding the use of psychological tests. First, the tests were both developed and validated by psychologists. Consequently, behavioral accounting researchers have the advantage of using tests already established without having to expend energy to develop test items and norms. At the same time, the accounting researcher is not likely to be very sophisticated in the use of these tests. As a result, he would be well advised to enlist the assistance or advice of a behavioral scientist skilled in administering psychological inventories.

Secondly, it may not be necessary for the behavioral accounting researcher to use psychological tests when structuring his experiments. If one holds to the theory that a large enough sample group will contain a mixture of subject personality, vocational interest, and leadership characteristics representative of the population studied, the detailed individual classifications may be unwarranted. By this reasoning, for instance, the influence of risk-avoider subjects are effectively cancelled by the risk-taker subjects. Or, if an experimenter is able to use both a control and experimental group in his study, it may not be necessary to test for individual differences when experimental differences do not result between two groups.

It is, of course, difficult to determine when a sample group is large enough so that the individual personality differences of subjects can be ignored because of their insignificant effect on experimental bias. While sample size level is, at best, a matter of personal judgment, researchers should feel uncomfortable when ignoring the effect of individual differences in sample groups of ten or fewer subjects—particularly if there is no control group.

A final caution concerns the use of psychological tests. Since serious moral and technical criticisms have been leveled at psychological testing, particularly personality tests (Baritz [8], Whyte [90], Gross [41]), it is incumbent upon the behavioral accounting researcher to be familiar with the ethical pronouncements of the American Psychological Association (APA [4], [5].) Moreover, since most of the tests cited can be obtained only by APA members, it is often mandatory that behavioral accounting researchers (who want to use psychological tests) work closely with professional psychologists.

In sum, the standardized psychological tests may be useful as a methodological tool for accountants—especially if situations develop where it is desirable to analyze personality characteristics of subjects when determining the results of the experiment. A careful reading of select psychological test references (Dunnette [24], Cronbach and Gleser [20], Guion [44], Buros [11], Dunnette & Kirchner [25], Edwards [27], Ellis [30], Ferguson [32] and Guilford [42] will reveal that some psychological tests have been validated, while others have not. Information on the reliability and validity of standardized tests is succinctly summarized by Buros [11]. Close association with a behavioral scientist is essential for accountants interested in using tests, no less than accountants are necessary advisors to financially-naive individuals.

Interviews and Questionnaires. Probably the most extensively used data collection techniques are interviews and interview schedules or questionnaires. The primary advantage of a face-to-face interview is that the researcher can interpret the interview questions for his subject, so as to elicit the most valid response. In this manner, the researcher is able to assure himself that the subject understands the question posed before moving on to other questions. While the researcher may be certain that his questions are properly interpreted, there is a trade-off, in that this process can be rather costly in interviewer time. This makes personal interviews somewhat expensive when large samples are used. Moreover, if it is necessary to use several interviewers to gather the data within a short time period, the researcher runs the risk of incorporating interviewer bias in the study. Because of disparate styles for asking questions, the use of different inter-

viewers may elicit different types of responses from subjects.

Two of the most successful uses of personal interviews reported in the accounting literature were concerned with budgets and control. Argyris [6] used interviews in his study of the impact of budgets on people, and Hofstede [49] used a combination of personal interviews and structured questionnaires in his work on the game of budget control. Hofstede's book is especially recommended for the accounting researcher interested in using interview techniques, because it contains an appendix listing the actual questions asked throughout his interviews together with the distribution statistics resulting from the interview data.

Some of the better references on interviewing techniques are found in the Institute for Social Research [53], Trull [88], Maccoby and Maccoby [63, Vol. 1], Parten [69, pp. 162–3] and Goode and Hatt [38].

To overcome the personal interview problems of interviewer bias and cost of interviewer time for data gathering, the use of printed questionnaires has evolved. Problems still arise, because one question may have different meanings for different individuals and a confused respondent cannot ask the questionnaire for additional clarification. In addition, the response rate may be less than desired—responses from mailed questionnaires seldom average over sixty percent (Kerlinger [57]). For both these reasons, the response to questionnaires may not be as valid as the response to personal interviews.

Nonetheless, when it is necessary to sample a large group, say in excess of one hundred subjects, and the interview schedule is somewhat lengthy, a researcher will often use questionnaires rather than interviews for reasons of consistent application and economy.

References, primarily from psychology, concerned with the construction of proper items in questionnaires include Dillehay and Jernigan [23], Torgerson [87], Hofman [51], Institute for Social Research [53], Kornhauser and Sheatsley [58, Appendix C], Hyman [52], Cantril [16], Payne [70] and Ferber and Verdoorn [31]. It is again important for behavioral accounting researchers to seek the aid of behavioral scientists when designing questionnaires. To ignore this assistance is to invite the type of challenge which Cook [18] experienced when her study on the effect of frequency of feedback on performance was criticized by Becker [9] for having uninterpretable questionnaire items. One of the accounting examples describing the development of a lengthy questionnaire is Sorensen's [79], [80] study of bureaucratic and professional tendencies in public accounting firms.

Each of the primary data collection techniques, standardized psychological tests, interviews and questionnaires, offers two types of information: factual and opinion. The factual response allows for categorization, whereas the opinion response indicates a subject's position on an issue or question. Accounting researchers may be more interested, however, in using survey research techniques for purposes of classification, since the accounting activity examined is likely to be one of observable behavior (e.g., investment decisions) subject to experimental manipulation. Classification of subjects based on personal characteristics is especially helpful when researchers conduct laboratory experiments, field experiments and field studies—particularly with small samples.

3. Data Collection Methods—Laboratory, Field and Sociometry

Laboratory Experiments. Laboratory experiments are characterized by their control of potential influence factors or independent variables which might affect the problem under investigation. This condition is accomplished by conducting the research in a setting which bears only minimal resemblance to an everyday work or living situation. By eliminating extraneous variables so that they cannot affect the dependent variable, the strict control which can be exercised over laboratory studies also makes them suitable for replication by other researchers.

The same rigor of control which is so beneficial for purposes of isolating experimental effects and providing a basis for replication, augurs against extrapolating laboratory findings to the real world. An example of this effect is found in the work of Stedry. While conducting a laboratory experiment to examine the effect of budget levels on performance, Stedry [82] affirmed hypotheses related to aspiration levels. In a following field experiment conducted in a large engineering plant, Stedry and Kay [83] attempted to test some of Stedry's earlier laboratory results using on-the-job foremen. The findings were inclusive. Moderator variables, such as individual personality differences and age added to a small sample size, accounted for as much of the explainable variance as did the experimental controls. Accordingly, the results of the laboratory experiment, partially for lack of realism, could not be generalized to the real world.

Two additional accounting researchers reported laboratory studies of decision making and investment analysis. Jensen's [54] study, which entailed a computer simulation and responses from professional security analysts investigated relationships between security evaluation and portfolio selection and alternative methods of financial reporting. In a later study, Dyckman [26] investigated the relationship between investment analysis and general price level adjustments. Dyckman's study would be particularly helpful to someone interested in laboratory experiments, because the appendices list in detail the data supplied to participants—such an extensive listing of procedural forms not only serves well as a guideline for other behavioral researchers, but also facilitates the replication of Dyckman's study. Although Dyckman's work has already passed substantial review (Caplan [17]), it is useful to further highlight some of its features. The experiment is preceded by a thorough literature review, the model for the experiment is well detailed, the hypotheses are clearly stated, the statistical tests are explicit and the analysis is rather complete. In short, the study is methodologically sound and should serve as a guide for future experiments on accounting problems. One of its strengths is the series of caveats identifying possible sources of biased responses. Such disclosure is both academically honest and educational. Subsequent behavioral researchers and replicators are well advised of experimental difficulties to avoid.

When behavioral research originates in a laboratory setting, it has the possibility of developing a strongly defensible theoretical structure, since the predictive variables under examination can be closely controlled. Assuming this is a desirable achievement, behavioral researchers would do well to consult some of the classical literature on laboratory experimentation, as provided by Festinger and Katz [33], Sherif [75] and Newcomb [68, pp. 345-357]. Useful reference on effective laboratory studies with application to accounting researchers may be found in Milgram's [65] behavioral study of obedience and Tilker's [86] work on socially responsible behavior as a function of observer responsibility and feedback.

It is important to note that questionnaires and standardized psychological tests are often used in another setting. As a result, behavioral methodologies and tools are not limited to any one purpose and may be used within different classifications, as were the questionnaires utilized by Dyckman in his laboratory experiment.

Field Experiments. A field experiment is often the next form of inquiry following a laboratory experiment. Field experiments utilize less direct control over experimental variables than do laboratory experiments. Field experiments more closely resemble real-world situations, and it is possible to examine behavior in a setting where subjects are exposed to the interaction of complex stimuli.

As a consequence of a realistic experimental setting, the researcher is better able to generalize his findings beyond the experimental setting. But, the somewhat relaxed control of a field experiment means that it is also more difficult to manipulate and isolate all of the variables affecting the outcome of the study. Correspondingly, because of its lack of control, the field experiment may not be as generalizable as the researcher intended. This will occur if the researcher has doubts about what variables, controlled or uncontrolled, are most responsible for affecting the results of the experiment. For

this reason, it is especially important for field research studies to incorporate a control group. Otherwise, with relaxed experimental conditions, it is difficult for a researcher to determine if his critical variables really had an effect on the environment he attempted to change.

Accounting researchers interested in conducting a behavioral study using field research methods would do well to examine French [37] and Katz [56], two of the standard references.

Two recent field experiments with application to accounting research are reported in the behavioral literature. One is a study of communication and acquaintance networks (Korte and Milgram [59]) and the other is an analysis of the accuracy of employment interviewers, students and Certified Public Accountants in identifying the interests of accountants (Hakel, Hollmann and Dunnette [45]). Both of these studies are suitable for extension or replication by behavioral accountants.

Field Studies. The basic difference between field studies and field experiments is the use of non-participant observers in field studies to *record* behavior, whereas field experiments entail the use of an experimenter and other independent variables to *manipulate* behavior. Thus, the researcher simply observes the results of behavior in a field study.

Because the behavioral researcher in a field study is non-reactive, there is a considerable drop in precision from a field experiment to a field study. There is, however, an increase in realism and potential extrapolation to other settings in the real world. Indeed, there is both an increase in realism and decrease in control over the study as one moves along a continuum from, say, computer simulations to laboratory experiments to field experiments to field studies.

It is also necessary to have highly-skilled observers in a field study to insure that valid observations are being made. A recent study, (Bryne, Ervin and Lamberth [12]) on the continuity between the experimental study of attractions and real-life computer dating, is a good example of the field study technique and also references arguments contrasting the choice between laboratory experiments and field studies.

One of the most extensive collections of referenced research and field study techniques is given by Webb, et al. [89] in their work on unobtrusive measures. After arguing that the presence of an experimenter, coupled with the subjects' knowledge that they are part of an experiment, will sufficiently contaminate an experiment so as to affect its validity, Webb and his associates urge that experimenters pay more attention to analyzing behavior on the basis of examining the residue once the behavior has taken place. Using this technique, the researcher becomes an auditor much like archeologists who attempt to explain behavior solely on the basis of its remains.

Sociometry. Psychology's behavioral science sister discipline—sociology—may also provide assistance to accounting researchers. As defined in a text on the foundations of behavioral research (Kerlinger [57]), sociometry is a method of ". . . gathering and analyzing data on the choice, communication, and interaction patterns of people in groups." Because accountants are concerned with the communication of their information, as well as the communication path, sociometry is a methodological tool with possible application to accounting research. One form of sociometry, that of plotting sociograms, which indicates patterns of communication was utilized by two accounting researchers (Swieringa and Carmichael [85]) to contrast formal versus informal interaction patterns during a study of internal control in a parts depot.

Some of the standard reference works on sociometry are Lindzey and Borgatta [61, Vol. 1, Ch. 11], Proctor and Loomis [71, Ch. 17] and Moreno, et al. [67]. Current use of sociometry is also noted by Leik and Nagasawa [60] in their study of social status and social structure, a work which has application for analysis of public accounting positional hierarchies. Again, accounting researchers who apply sociometric analysis to their behavioral studies should enlist the assistance of an established behavioral scientist. Sociometry is likely to have more application to managerial, as opposed to financial, accounting research problems, because the communication paths and processes are more constrained by the physical boundaries of an organization. Conversely, published financial information which reaches the investing public and interested outsiders often travels paths too circuitous and varied for maintenance of adequate experimental control.

4. Summary

In sum, the presentation of any partial listing of source materials on behavioral science research tools and methodologies requires two cautionary statements. First, any listing of this nature is highly subjective and based on personal reading habits and tastes. Second, it is repetitiously urged that researchers interested in behavioral experiments which explain accounting-related problems consult a behavioral scientist along with the reference sources of his choice. The absence of such consultation can be overcome only by extensive personal study of behavioral science literature. Perhaps the most valuable contribution of the behavioral sciences to accounting research is access to behavioral scientists. It is difficult enough to maintain research skills without having to newly acquire them. This listing is, hopefully, a first step toward maintenance or acquisition of those skills.

References

1. Adorno, T. W., et al., *The Authoritarian Personality: Studies in Prejudice,* Harper & Row, 1950.

2. Allport, G. W., and Vernon, P. E., *Study of Values: A Scale for Measuring the Dominant Interests in Personality,* Houghton Mifflin, Co., 1931.

3. American Accounting Association, *Report of the Committee on Behavioral Science Content of the Accounting Curriculum,* 1970.

4. American Psychological Association, American Educational Research Association & National Council on Measurements Used in Education (joint committee), "Technical Recommendations for Psychological Tests

and Diagnostic Techniques," *Psychological Bulletin* (1954), pp. 201–238.

5. American Psychological Association, "Ethical Standards of Psychologists," *American Psychologist* (1963), pp. 56–60.

6. Argyris, Chris, *The Impact of Budgets on People,* School of Business and Public Administration, Cornell University, 1952.

7. Bakan, David, *On Method: Toward a Reconstruction of Psychological Investigation,* Jossey-Bass, Inc., 1969.

8. Baritz, L., *The Servants of Power,* Wesleyan University Press, 1960.

9. Becker, S. W., "Discussion of the Effect of Frequency of Feedback on Attitudes and Performance," *Empirical Research in Accounting: Selected Studies, 1968* Supplement to the *Journal of Accounting Research* (1968), pp. 225–228.

10. Bruns, W. J., Jr., "Inventory Valuation and Management Decisions," *The Accounting Review* (April, 1965), pp. 345–357.

11. Buros, O. K. (ed.), *The Sixth Mental Measurements Yearbook,* Gryphon Press, 1964.

12. Byrne, Donn, Ervin, Charles R., and Lamberth, John, "Continuity Between the Experimental Study of Attraction and Real-Life Computer Dating," *Journal of Personality and Social Psychology* (1970), pp. 157–165.

13. Campbell, David P., "Changing Patterns of Interests Within the American Society," *Measurement & Evaluation in Guidance* (1968), pp. 36–49.

14. Campbell, D. T., and Stanley, J. C., *Experimental and Quasi-Experimental Designs for Research,* Rand McNally, 1966.

15. Cannell, C., and Kahn, R., "The Collection of Data by Interviewing," in L. Festinger and D. Katz (eds.), *Research Methods in the Behavioral Sciences,* Holt, Rinehart and Winston, Inc., 1953.

16. Cantril, Hadley, *Gauging Public Opinion,* Princeton University Press, 1947.

17. Caplan, E. H., Book Review of T. R. Dyckman, *Investment Analysis and General Price-Level Adjustments, The Accounting Review* (October, 1970), pp. 808–810.

18. Cook, D. M., "The Effect of Frequency of Feedback on Attitudes and Performance," *Empirical Research in Accounting: Selected Studies, 1968* Supplement to the *Journal of Accounting Research* (1968), pp. 213–224.

19. Cox, D. R., *Planning Experiments,* Wiley, 1958.

20. Cronbach, L. J., and Gleser, G. C., *Psychological Tests and Personnel Decisions,* University of Illinois Press, 1965.

21. DeCoster, D. T., and Fertakis, J. P., "Budget-Induced Pressure and Its Relationship to Supervisory Behavior," *Journal of Accounting Research* (1968), pp. 237–246.

22. _____, and Rhode, J. G., "The Accountant's Stereotype: Real or Imagined, Deserved or Unwarranted," *The Accounting Review,* (October, 1971), pp. 651–664.

23. Dillehay, Ronald C., and Jernigan, Larry R., "The Biased Questionnaire as an Instrument of Opinion Change," *Journal of Personality and Social Psychology* (1970), pp. 144–150.

24. Dunnette, M. D., *Personnel Selection and Placement,* Wadsworth Publishing Company, Inc., 1966.

25. _____, and Kirchner, W. K., *Psychology Applied to Industry,* Merideth Publishing Company, 1965.

26. Dyckman, T. R., *Investment Analysis and General Price-Level Adjustments: A Behavioral Study,* American Accounting Association, 1969.

27. Edwards, A., *Techniques of Attitude Scale Construction,* Appleton-Century-Crofts, 1957.

28. Edwards, A. L., *The Social Desirability Variable in Personality Assessment and Research,* Dryden, 1957.

29. Edwards, A. L., *Experimental Design in Psychological Research,* 3rd ed., Rinehart and Winston, 1968.

30. Ellis, A., "The Validity of Personality Questionnaires," *Psychological Bulletin* (1946).

31. Ferber, Robert, and Verdoorn, P. J., *Research Methods in Economics and Business,* Macmillan, 1962.

32. Ferguson, L., *Personality Measurement,* McGraw-Hill, 1952.

33. Festinger, Leon, and Katz, Daniel (eds.), *Research Methods in the Behavioral Sciences,* Holt, Rinehart and Winston, Inc., 1953.

34. Fiedler, F. E., *A Theory of Leadership Effectiveness,* McGraw-Hill, 1967.

35. Fleishman, E. A., "A Leader Behavior Description for Industry," in Ralph M. Stogdill and Alvin E. Coons (eds.), *Leader Behavior: Its Description and Measurement,* Research Monograph No. 88, Bureau of Business Research, The Ohio State University, 1957.

36. _____, Harris, E. F., and Burtt, H. E., *Leadership and Supervision in Industry, Research Monograph No. 33,* Bureau of Educational Research, The Ohio State University Press, 1955.

37. French, J., "Experiments in Field Settings," in L. Festinger and D. Katz (eds.), *Research Methods in the Behavioral Sciences,* Holt, Rinehart and Winston, Inc., 1953, pp. 118–129.

38. Goode, W. J., and Hatt, P. K., *Methods in Social Research,* McGraw-Hill, 1952.

39. Gordon, L. V., "Research Briefs on Survey of Interpersonal Values," Science Research Associates, Chicago, (mimeograph).

40. Gough, H. G., *Manual for the California Psychological Inventory,* Consulting Psychologists Press, 1957.

41. Gross, M. L., *The Brain Watchers,* Random House, 1962.

42. Guilford, J., *Personality,* McGraw-Hill, 1959.

43. _____, and Zimmerman, W. S., "Fourteen Dimensions of Temperament," *Psychological Monographs* (1956).

44. Guion, R. M., *Personnel Testing,* McGraw-Hill, 1965.

45. Hakel, Milton D., Hollmann, Thomas D., and Dunnette, M. D., "Accuracy of Interviewers, Certified Public Accountants and Students in Identifying the Interests of Accountants," *Journal of Applied Psychology* (1970), pp. 115–119.

46. Halpin, A. W., *Manual for the Leader Behavior Description Questionnaire,* Bureau of Business Research, The Ohio State University Press, 1957.

47. Hathaway, S. R., and McKinley, J. C., "A Multiphasic Personality Schedule (Minnesota): I. Construction of the Schedule," *Journal of Psychology* (1940), pp. 249–254.

48. Hays, W. L., *Statistics for Psychologists,* Holt, Rinehart and Winston, Inc., 1963.

49. Hofstede, G. H., *The Game of Budget Control,* Van Gorcum and Comp., 1967.

50. Hofstedt, T. R., and Kinard, James C., "A Strategy for Behavioral Accounting Research," *The Accounting Review* (January, 1970), pp. 38–54.

51. Hofman, John E., "The Meaning of Being a Jew in Israel: An Analysis of Ethnic Identify," *Journal of Personality and Social Psychology* (1970), pp. 196–202.

52. Hyman, Herbert, *Interviewing in Social Research,* University of Chicago Press, 1954.

53. I.S.R. (Institute for Social Research of the University of Michigan), *Manual for Interviewers,* Survey Research Center, Ann Arbor, 1960.

54. Jensen, Robert E., "An Experimental Design for Study of Effects of Accounting Variations in Decision Making," *Journal of Accounting Research* (1966), pp. 224–238.

55. Kaplan, Abraham, *The Conduct of Inquiry: Methodology for Behavioral Science,* Chandler Publishing Company, 1964.

56. Katz, Daniel, "Field Studies", in L. Festinger and D. Katz (eds.), *Research Methods in the Behavioral Sciences,* Holt, Rinehart and Winston, Inc., 1953.

57. Kerlinger, F. N., *Foundations of Behavioral Research: Educational and Psychological Inquiry,* 1964.

58. Kornhauser, A., and Sheatsley, P., in Selltiz, C., et al., "Questionnaire Construction and Interview Procedure," *Research Methods in Social Relations,* rev. ed., Holt, Rinehart and Winston, Inc., 1959.

59. Korte, Charles, and Milgram, Stanley, "Acquaintance Networks Between Racial Groups Application of the Small World Method," *Journal of Personality and Social Psychology,* (1970), pp. 101–108.

60. Leik, Robert K., and Nagasawa, Richard, "A Sociometric Basis for Measuring Social Status and Social Structure," *Sociometry* (March, 1970).

61. Lindzey, G., and Borgatta, E., "Sociometric Measurement," in G. Lindzey (ed.) *Handbook of Social Psychology,* Addison-Wesley, 1954.

62. Livingstone, J. L., "A Behavioral Study of Tax Allocation in Electric Utility Regulation," *The Accounting Review* (July, 1967), pp. 544–552.

63. Maccoby, E., and Maccoby, N., "The Interview: A Tool of Social Science, in G. Lindzey (ed.), *Handbook of Social Psychology,* Addison-Wesley, 1954, pp. 449–487.

64. Megargee, Edwin I., "Influence of Sex Roles on the Manifestation of Leadership," *Journal of Applied Psychology* (1969), pp. 3-7–382.

65. Milgram, S., "Behavioral Study of Obedience," *Journal of Abnormal & Social Psychology* (1963), pp. 371–378.

66. Mitchell, Terence, R., "Leader Complexity and Leadership Style," *Journal of Personal-*

ity and Social Psychology (1970), pp. 166–174.

67. Moreno, J., et al., *The Sociometry Reader,* Free Press, 1960.

68. Newcomb, T. and Hartley, E. (eds.), *Readings in Social Psychology,* Holt, Rinehart and Winston, Inc., 1947.

69. Parten, J., *Surveys, Polls and Samples,* Harper & Row, 1950.

70. Payne, Stanley, L., *The Art of Asking Questions,* Princeton University Press, 1951.

71. Proctor, E., and Loomis, C., "Analysis of Sociometric Data," in S. Cook, M. Deutsch and M. Jahoda (eds.), *Research Methods in Social Relations, Part Two,* Holt, Rinehart and Winston, Inc., 1951.

72. Reiter, Henry H., "Note on Some Personality Differences Between Heavy and Light Drinkers," *Perceptual & Motor Skills* (1970), p. 762.

73. Riley, M. W., *Sociological Research I. A Case Approach, II Exercises and Manual,* Harcourt, Brace & World, Inc., 1963.

74. Roubertoux, Pierre, "Personality Variables and Interest in Art," *Journal of Personality and Social Psychology* (1970), pp. 665–668.

75. Sherif, M., "Group Influences Upon the Formation of Norms and Attitudes," *Readings in Social Psychology,* 3rd ed., Holt, Rinehart and Winston, Inc. 1958, pp. 219–232.

76. Seigel, Sidney, *Nonparametric Methods for the Behavioral Sciences,* McGraw-Hill, 1956.

77. Simon, J. L., *Basic Research Methods in Social Science: The Art of Empirical Investigation,* Random House, 1969.

78. Snedecor, G. W., and Cochran, W. G., *Statistical Methods,* 6th ed., The Iowa State University Press, 1967.

79. Sorensen, J. E., *Professional and Bureaucratic Organization in Large Public Accounting Firms,* unpublished Ph.D. dissertation, The Ohio State University 1965.

80. _____, "Professional and Bureaucratic Organization in Large Public Accounting Firms," *The Accounting Review* (July, 1967), pp. 553–565.

81. Sorter, G. H., and Becker, S. W., "Corporate Personality as Reflected in Accounting Decisions: Some Preliminary Findings," *Journal of Accounting Research* (1964), pp. 183–196.

82. Stedry, Andrew, C., *Budget Control and Cost Behavior,* Ford Foundation doctoral dissertation series 1959 award winner, Prentice-Hall, 1960.

83. Stedry, Andrew C. and Kay, E., *The Effects of Goal Difficulty on Performance: A Field Experiment,* M.I.T., Sloan School of Management, 1964.

84. Strong, E. K., Jr., Campbell, D. P., Berdie, R. F., and Clark, K. E., *Strong Vocational Interest Blank for Men, Form T399R,* Stanford University Press, 1966.

85. Swieringa, R. J., and Carmichael, D. R., "A Positional Analysis of Internal Control," *The Journal of Accountancy* (1971), pp. 34–43.

86. Tilker, Harvey A., "Socially Responsible Behavior as a Function of Observer Responsibility and Victim Feedback," *Journal of Personality and Social Psychology* (1970), pp. 95–100.

87. Torgerson, W. S., *Theory and Methods of Scaling,* John Wiley & Sons/Chapman & Hall, 1958.

88. Trull, S. G., "Strategies of Effective Interviewing," *Harvard Business Review* (1964), pp. 89–94.

89. Webb, E. J., Campbell, D. T., Schwartz, R. D., and Sechrest, L., *Unobtrusive Measures: Nonreactive Research in the Social Sciences,* Rand, 1961.

90. Whyte, W. H., Jr., *The Organization Man,* Doubleday Anchor, 1956.

chapter 13

Problems in Behavioral Research Design

LYMAN W. PORTER

University of California, Irvine

Professor Rhode has given accountants interested in conducting behavioral research a concise and relatively thorough guide to the location of basic references concerning data collection instruments and techniques. In virtually no instances can the quality of his references be challenged from the perspective of the behavioral scientist. That is, most of the specific instruments he cites (e.g., California Psychological Inventory, Strong Vocational Interest Blank, Ohio State Leadership Behavioral Description Questionnaire, etc.) are among the better ones currently available, and the methodological source books and articles (e.g., those by Guion, Buros, Dunnette, Kerlinger,[1] etc.) represent the work of some of our leading authorities. So, although some additional or substitute items might be added to the bibliography, all in all it is hard to argue with the essence of Rhode's paper.

However, if we are to carry out good research in the behavioral science area, we need more than just valid and tested instruments and techniques. We need, in addition, to use them effectively in research designs that permit us to draw valid and warranted conclusions and that allow for sound generalizations. Therefore, I would like to address myself to some methodological issues not directly dealt with in Rhode's paper but which relate to his general topic and which can be considered as an extension of some of his basic points. My comments will focus on some cautionary problems associated with the design of studies and on the need for more extensive utilization of certain categories or types of studies.

There is one major advantage that present-day accountants moving into behavioral research will have compared to past—and, to an extent, present—generations of behavioral scientists: they will, or should, be able to avoid many of the methodological pitfalls that have repeatedly ensnared psychologists and sociologists over the years. They will be able to profit from some of the lessons that the social scientists have learned through painful trial and error. Thus, since accountants are just now beginning to move into behavioral research, we can reasonably expect right from the start that the relative quality of their investigations will be high!

[1] R. M. Guion, *Personnel Testing* (McGraw-Hill, 1965); O. K. Buros, editor, *The Sixth Mental Measurements Yearbook* (Gryphon, 1964); M. D. Dunnette, *Personnel Selection and Placement* (Wadsworth, 1966); and F. N. Kerlinger, *Foundations of Behavioral Research: Educational and Psychological Inquiry* (Holt, Rinehart, & Winston, 1964).

Despite this seeming advantage, accountants, like the rest of us, may still fall prey to some of the more alluring traps that abound along the research trail. Perhaps it will be useful to mention a few for illustrative purposes. Recently, I had occasion to review some research design proposals by accountants on topics dealing with behavioral phenomena. One of the characteristics that appeared in the discussion sections of some of the design proposals was a tendency to confuse—or at least not distinctly separate—the notion of correlation from causality. It is easy, particularly in field studies, for any researcher to stumble unwittingly into the causality phraseology when his design only permits statements about correlations or relationships. This is particularly so if he is not on the alert for this slip. We frequently get involved, often very involved, in a design in which we measure subjects on two variables (e.g., attitudes toward a certain type of accounting procedure and behavior in a specified situation), one of which we have reason to believe in advance should cause or determine the values of the other variable. Then, when our research data show the two variables are, as we hoped, fairly highly correlated, we proceed to talk about the relationship *as if* they were causally related. Such statements, of course, are not permissible if they are based on the results of the typically-designed field studies where the variables have not been specifically manipulated by the researcher to rule out confounding factors. While the necessity for the avoidance of such "causal leaps" may seem obvious, the relative frequency with which they crop up in articles submitted to (and sometimes published in) reputable behavioral science journals attests to the ease with which they can slip by the unwary researcher. Eternal vigilence . . .

Another pitfall—particularly common, but not limited, to Ph.D. thesis proposals—is well described in the words of Underwood: this is the "danger . . . that the investigator will fall into the trap of thinking that because he went from an artistic or literary conception [of a variable] . . . to the construction of items for a scale to

measure it, he has validated his artistic conception."[2] This, of course, is particularly a danger when one is constructing one's own measuring instrument—usually a test or questionnaire—instead of relying on a so-called standard instrument already in the literature (of the type mentioned in Rhode's paper) whose validity has presumably been demonstrated. Since there will be many occasions on which the researcher will have good reasons to use a newly-constructed instrument (because it is, hopefully, more precisely designed for his particular purposes), it behooves him to consider possible antidotes to this potential hazard. Perhaps the best is that proposed by Campbell and Fiske[3] who advocate a "multi-trait, multi-method" approach in which two or more traits (variables to be researched) are measured by at least two distinct methods. Violations of this proposed solution to the situation described by Underwood occur most often when a single research method is used to gather data on several different variables. In such an instance it is impossible to tell whether the variables are related only because they share a common method of measurement. Essentially, the Campbell-Fiske approach (and the article should be consulted in its entirety for a complete understanding of the approach) involves attempting to obtain convergency between two different methods measuring the same trait, and discrimination for the same method measuring supposedly different traits (e.g., so that a set of questions designed to measure "status" correlates higher with other measures of status than the same set of questions correlates with measures of, say, "power").

A variant of the mono-method problem occurs when the researcher obtains measures of several "different" variables from the same sources and concludes that the variables are, "in nature," highly related. An example would be where a given sample of respondents completes a self report meas-

[2]B. J. Underwood, *Psychological Research* (Appleton-Century-Crofts, 1957), p. 55.
[3]D. T. Campbell and D. W. Fiske, "Convergent and Discriminant Validation by the Multitrait-Multimethod Matrix," *Psychological Bulletin,* 56 (1959), pp. 81–105.

ure (e.g., self ratings of job performance) and also a measure about their attitudes towards some external object or person (e.g., company practices). At the very least, an *independent* source should provide the data for one of the variables if an obtained relationship of this sort is to be regarded as more than merely spurious. Again, one finds this requirement frequently violated in behavioral research, particularly in studies utilizing long questionnaires supposedly designed to measure "a number of variables."

Let me turn briefly from some of the possible contaminating influences on research results to a discussion of what I think are important methodological approaches that should be pursued with greater frequency. The first is somewhat related to the previously-mentioned multi-trait, multimethod approach. This is the need for construct validation research in behavioral science in general and thus in the accounting/behavioral area in particular. While the notion of construct validity has been around for some 15 years,[4] it still does not permeate very greatly the research dealing with organizations. The idea of construct validation refers to attempts to demonstrate that a given construct *is* related to other constructs to which it logically should be related, and is *not* related to those constructs or variables with which it logically should not be associated. Basically, the plea for construct validation is a plea for substantiating fragmentary or one-study findings by showing that variables supposedly being measured operate in a variety of circumstances in the way that available theory says they should operate. Construct validation is a goal that is never completely reached, but at least it should be one which is more often approached than is presently the case.

A second type of research design that needs to be implemented more frequently is that of longitudinal studies. Too often in research dealing with behavior in organizations we base broad generalizations, sometimes bordering on cause-effect interpretations, on strictly cross-sectional (one

point in time) data that do not permit such sweeping inferences. Longitudinal studies have a number of problems—e.g., cost in time and money, subject attrition, etc.—but they can provide a sounder basis for arriving at causal conclusions than the typical cross-sectional investigation. Knowing when certain phenomena emerge in time in relation to each other can rule out some, but not all, of the alternative causal hypotheses relating to a given relationship between variables. This advantage would seem to indicate the desirability of increasing the usage of this type of study in behavioral research relevant to accounting.

Another category of needed research is that of a comparative nature—particularly where specific relationships are being compared across a sample of different organizations or among different units of the same organization. The literature of organization behavior is littered with a multitude of findings obtained from a single sample of subjects in a single organization. The dreary conclusion that many of these findings appear to be utterly non-cumulative attests to the fact that most researchers, when they begin their investigations, do not take into account sufficiently the necessity of demonstrating the range and breadth of their findings by the mechanism of explicit comparative studies. The greater use of comparative-designed research will go a long way in aiding us in interpreting the meaning of the data that are obtained in organizational behavior studies. Without comparative-type studies, even the best measuring instruments are not very useful for helping to formulate reasonably robust generalizations.

Finally, I think it is fair to say that the accumulated organizational research has taught those of us in the behavioral sciences at least two lessons that ought to be passed on to accountants embarking on these kinds of endeavors: (1) laboratory and field research, and researchers, should not be so separate and on such relatively non-speaking terms as they have in the past and still are in many instances; and (2) there ought to be relatively equal emphasis on both empirical data *and* theory as a field is being developed—too much empiricism unleav-

[4] See L. J. Cronbach and P. E. Meehl, "Construct Validity in Psychological Tests," *Psychological Bulletin,* 52 (1955), pp. 281–302.

ened by some theoretical structuring leads to confusion, and too much dominance of empirical research by certain powerful and popular theories often leads to narrow perspectives and a failure to appreciate the richness of the behavioral world about us.

In conclusion, let me just remind both those of you who are skeptical about what a behavioral approach can do for accounting and those of you who are enthusiastic about it that someone some years ago made a comparison between progress in the physical sciences and progress in the behavioral sciences: the former he likened to climbing a mountain—each step built directly on those constructed below and demonstrated clear progress towards the top; in the social sciences, progress was likened to finding one's way through a forest in a fog—often we lose our way and may even circle back on ourselves but every once in a while the fog lifts and we can see our way through a little more clearly. To this I might only add that we can hope that our research efforts do not turn the fog into something worse (such as smog), and that the specific research problem "trees" that we encounter do not obscure our vision that we are indeed in a "forest" of interrelated problems.

chapter 14

An Inquiry into the Conditions Favoring Research by Members of an Accounting Faculty

Edward L. Summers

University of Texas

1. The Subject of This Inquiry

The subject of this inquiry is the environment in which careful, systematic investigation and evaluation of original propositions regarding accounting are most likely to occur. Our model approximates research as a multistage process whose stages are probable outcomes during a given time interval in any environment. These probabilities can be regarded as a function of environmental parameters, some of which may be controllable by accounting faculty and administrators. This paper tentatively identifies some of these factors (without actually delving into their fundamental nature) and suggests qualitatively how they may affect the probability of the research "outcome." It does not fix the value of any factor for all accounting faculties. It does not appraise the significance of environmental factors relative to all other factors.

Accounting research occurs in situations in and out of the accounting subculture. We here ignore all of the latter (without thereby implying that they are unimportant). Of the former, the ones immediately in mind are:

1) Publicly supported universities

2) Privately supported universities
3) Firms whose members or employees engage in accounting
4) Government and other public agencies
5) Accounting professional organizations

Only entries in (4) have an obligation, other than social, to perform accounting research. (5) may perform research to support or discover positions on questions of practical accounting. Research by (3) is done directly to benefit clients. (1) and (2) do not provide facilities or even discrete funds of any consequence for research, yet accounting research is done there, and it is on that research that we concentrate now. We particularly want to consider accounting research done in publicly supported universities, because this paper is encouraged by an organization consisting mostly of professors of accounting in publicly supported universities. (The author, himself, is among the latter.) The environmental factors we shall develop are not controllable by some accounting faculties. These faculties probably should not engage in the research process, since they cannot control conditions strongly affecting the success of the research.

The typical accounting professor at such a school teaches two to four preparations per week and is partly responsible thereby for the education of 50 to 300 young men and women. He is charged with numerous important and trivial administrative tasks. His first profession is teaching; but his "other" profession is accounting, and many accounting faculty members participate in the activities of practical accountants—joining the NAA, AICPA, FEI, or other organizations, attending meetings, and even holding office therein. Why should such a person be interested in research?

A few men and women are naturally, energetically and articulately curious. For the rest of us, a variety of factors influence our answer to that question. A reward structure may tend to favor the professor who shows evidence that he engages in research. We are then interested in knowing what conditions favor productive research by the typical accounting professor whose underlying motivation may be nothing more exciting than job security.

2. The Social Significance of Accounting Research

This section states the assumptions that justify an environmental structure favoring research. We assume that the problems of information collection and communication are a matter of interest to a society faced with allocating scarce resources using imperfect information. We assume that the net effect of all accounting research is to alleviate such problems. We assume that accounting will not be an exception to the present public policy of encouraging research in universities. We assume that the typical accounting professor is capable of performing research. We assume that he is capable of transferring his knowledge gained from research to other individuals or groups in usable form.

3. The Research Process

Our research process description is adapted from Simon's "On Judging the Plausibility of Theories" [34], and it has the following stages or phases. (This enumeration should not be accepted as defining only discrete projects as research or implying that coexisting research efforts at the same or different stages are not related):

Problem. A matter of explanation, allocation or prediction which is not resolved. When it is resolved, there will be less uncertainty than before about the environment of the researching entity (or its principal). As a result, that entity's welfare will be increased.

Inspiration. The most difficult part of the process is to conceive the "trick" or insight that leads eventually to an explanatory model incorporating the problem. Some persons seem to be more adept at conceiving than others. One's native ability may be encouraged or repressed by external factors in work and environment.

Model Elaboration. The model is enriched and enlarged, though never at the expense of explanatory simplicity. The result is an engine that resolves the original problem and produces concrete assertions about aspects of the real world that can be directly observed. These assertions are deductively related to the same structure of the model which resolved the original problem.

Validation. In order to validate the model, it is necessary to observe that the model's assertions about the real world are true. The design, execution and interpretation of experiments for this purpose are the best described and understood parts of the research process.

Application. The researcher is usually not in a position to compel resolution of the original problem in terms of the results of his research. Therefore, he must put his results into such form that interested parties will not be in doubt as to what the researcher has concluded and why. It is also his obligation to communicate his results by placing them on the public record through publication.

4. Conditions for Accounting Research To Occur

These conditions are:

1) A curiosity about accounting theory and practice. Accounting is practical but not entirely lacking in formal structure. One who seeks to extend or modify that structure must understand it. He must maintain an organized interest in accounting practice.

2) Access to economic resources, tools of statistical evaluation, logical analysis, empirical observation and other com-

ponents or building blocks of the research process.

3) Contact with other parties who share the same or similar curiosity and who will provide constructive analytical criticism continuously throughout the research process and after it is completed.

If these conditions exist, then no step in the research *process* previously outlined may be prevented from occurring. (Of course, these conditions are not *compelling*.)

Relation of Conditions to Research Stages. Some conditions above apply more to one stage of the research process than to others. Accordingly, we have indicated in Table 1 on a 0-1-2 scale the conditions in the order of their importance to each stage of the research process. A low ranking does not mean that the condition is unnecessary, nor does high ranking mean that the condition is sufficient. The research process' stages have, in the opinion of the author, a higher probability of occurence when a highly-ranked condition exists than when only lower-ranked conditions occur.

lend itself to administration of tables (similar to Table 1) as experimental instruments designed to elicit the preferences of accounting researchers for environmental components they believe would increase their research productivity. Lack of such a scale does not prevent us from proposing and illustrating the relationships, however.

5. The Elements of Academic Environment

A history professor is attracted primarily to a tradition of search for causal relationships which explain a set of past events. An accounting professor is similarly, and primarily, attracted to an academic tradition and also to a profession whose short-term interests require a substantial pragmatic judgmental element in practice. We will examine these elements to understand how they may contribute to the existence of conditions for research to occur. The elements considered are:

teaching
administration
personal development
associates

Table 1.   Relation of Conditions to Research Stages

Conditions	(1) Problem Formulation	(2) Inspiration	Steps (3) Model Elaboration	(4) Model Validation	(5) Model Application
1) Curiosity about (and knowledge of) accounting practice	2	1	1	1	2
2) Access to problem solving tools	0	0	2	2	0
3) Mutually constructive critical analysis	1	2	1	2	2

2 = highly important
1 = moderately important
0 = slightly important

The purposes of the ranking will become apparent as we enumerate components of the accounting professor's environment. For some of our purposes, e.g., relating conditions for occurence of research to stages in the research process itself, the rankings should be on a ratio scale. Such a scale might have numbers from 0–5 instead of 0–2, which would also permit representation of relative importance between components of the environment. This type scale would also

community
reward structure
accounting profession
computers
accounting organizations

Teaching. A professor's first job is to educate. He attracts students by his reputation for adding to *their* appreciation and enjoyment of life (and possibly also their earning power). The public suffers him to remain on its payroll because he has this reputation or may quickly develop it. To educate, the professor relies primarily on his lectures and assigned readings. He utilizes visual effects, computer programs, assigned problems, library readings, field trips, group projects, internships, guest lecturers, student presentations, exhortation and threats, grades, and so on. No two professors are alike in utilizing these devices. One's effective tool is another's useless gimmick. The professor employs them to develop one or more of five processes:

1) Concept Originating
2) Concept Communicating
3) Concept Reinforcing
4) Concept Applying
5) Motivating

It would be absurd to advocate one weighted mix of these methods as the optimal strategy for teaching. All except (5) above are eligible to satisfy one or more of the three conditions which must exist in order for research to take place. In larger classes of students, (5) probably receives increasing attention at the expense of the other processes. If true, this would indicate that research is favored by smaller class sizes—even at the expense of an increased teaching load in terms of contact hours.

Administration. This includes devising a grading system, applying it, and reporting the results to the registrar. Other tasks include serving on departmental, college, and university committees, as chairman or dean, and in professional organization offices. "Administration" here (see Table 3) means making resource allocation decisions that will affect other faculty members. The opportunities in administration for doing good are substantial and attractive; on the other

Table 2.   Contribution of Teaching Processes to Research-Enabling Conditions

Conditions for Research	Teaching Processes				
	(1) Concept Originating	(2) Concept Communicating	(3) Concept Reinforcing	(4) Concept Applying	(5) Motivating
1) Curiosity and knowledge about accounting practice	2	2	1	1	0
2) Access to problem solving tools	0	0	0	1	0
3) Reciprocal criticism of publicized research results	2	2	1	2	0

2 = highly important
1 = moderately important
0 = slightly important

Table 3.   Contribution of Administrative Functions to Research-Enabling Conditions

Conditions for Research	Administrative Committees	Professional Organizational Officer	Departmental Administrator	Fund Raising & Budget Growth	Recruiting Faculty	Recruiting Students	Curriculum Management
1) Curiosity and knowledge about accounting practice	1	2	0	1	0	0	1
2) Access to problem solving tools	0	0	1	2	2	2	1
3) Mutually constructive critical analysis	1	0	1	0	2	1	0

2 = highly important
1 = moderately important
0 = slightly important

hand, there is little about the administrative *process* that encourages the best in anyone; it seems to be the *aqua regia* of teaching by its ability to disrupt, absorb, and dissolve an administrator's academic personality.

It is the administrator's responsibility not only to make resources required by research available, but also to sustain the conditions permitting performance of research and even to encourage participation in research by individual faculty.

Personal Development. The educator must maintain competent specialized knowledge of developments in accounting. Knowledge becomes obsolete in deceptive and insidious ways. There are fads and styles among those who labor in any body of knowledge. But one who dismisses all change as attributable to these causes will eventually be unable to understand the literature, much less grasp the current problems of his discipline or perceive new problems. He is blocked at the first step of the research process. We list a few representative activities and diversions which provide opportunities for personal development in Table 4 and relate them to research conditions.

4) Doctoral candidates
5) Students professionally interested in accounting
6) Other students
7) Administrators
8) Accounting practitioners

No class of associates has a uniform influence on each part of the research process. For example, practitioners are sources for descriptions of current accounting problems and the limits within which problem solutions may fall in order to be acceptable, but they are not much help in testing hypotheses or model building.

Professors at other universities are friendly but difficult associates because of the limited time for joint collaboration. There is not enough common time to develop common understandings and to agree on the concept descriptions which constitute the specialized jargon used to work on the problem. Time, common understanding and common jargon are the foundations on which constructive extended interaction may take place, especially at the stage of model elaboration. Professors at other universities

Table 4.   Contribution of Personal Development Activities to Research-Enabling Conditions

Conditions for Research	Instructing in PD Courses	Discussant at Professional Meetings	Publication of Papers/Monographs	Reading Professional Literature	Keeping a Consulting Practice	Writing Textbooks	Leave of Absence at Another University
1) Curiosity and knowledge about accounting practice	2	1	2	1	1	0	1
2) Access to problem solving tools	0	0	0	1	0	0	1
3) Mutually constructive critical analysis	0	2	1	2	1	1	2

2 = highly important
1 = moderately important
0 = slightly important

Associates. These are arbitrarily considered to be drawn from eight classes—

1) Professors at other universities
2) Professors at same university in non-accounting disciplines
3) Professors at same university in accounting

serve most usefully as references, e.g., for prospective new faculty members, with whom one may create opportunities for closer contact and to whose ideas one may later give closer attention.

Non-accounting professors contribute enrichment of models of recognized problems. The opportunities for productive communication are limited, however, by time and incentive. Consequently, such men serve best as evaluators of results.

Accounting professors at one's own university are the persons one sees most often (after students). They vary widely in age, academic rank and interests.

Doctoral candidates are younger than faculty associates; their interests in teaching are probably less active than their research interests, since the latter are required for completion of their doctoral programs. Nearly all doctoral programs in accounting also include specific research requirements. Many dissertation supervisors, however, have looked forward to working with a candidate on a dissertation only to realize the candidate is taking the attitude, "Give me a topic so I can write on it."

Students working for a degree in professional accounting should not be discounted as associates. They are young, highly motivated and independently critical. They are in a hurry. Their criticism, if encouraged, can be lively and relevant. However, they are immature, inexperienced and narrowly prepared. Their participation is limited to faultfinding rather than to inspiration or elaboration, but they offer through enthusiasm an intangible benefit—motivation to undertake the research process.

A professor seeks intuitively to draw asso-

ciates from as many of these classes as possible. He need not limit the number of associates from any one class. Table 5 relates associate classes to the conditions for research to occur.

Community. Relatively few universities are located in major metropolitan areas. The benefits of freedom from urban pressure for the process of inquiry have been described by others. The disadvantages are that the professor does not always have access to a balanced societal experience; that is, his environment may not provide opportunity for him to become aware of problems in society requiring research. The professor's impression of commerce may be through the mass-circulation slick-paper magazines, the newspapers, and the personnel directors of firms recruiting at the universities. It is not firsthand. Smaller communities, in which many universities are situated, occasionally support modest consulting practices by accounting professors. These local businesses tend to be smaller than their big-city equivalents. It is not unfair to say that their very real and challenging problems are not representative of the problems faced by managers of the majority of the country's resources.

At the political level, elected officials may strongly interfere with the activities of facul-

Table 5.   Contribution of Associates to Research-Enabling Conditions

Conditions for Research \ Associate Classes	Professors at Other Universities	Professors at Same Univ. in Non-Acctg. Disciplines	Doctoral Candidates	Students Professionally Interested in Accounting	Other Students	Administrators	Accounting Practitioners	Professors at Same Univ. in Accounting
1) Curiosity and knowledge about accounting practice	0	0	1	1	0	0	2	1
2) Access to problem solving tools	0	1	1	0	0	2	0	2
3) Mutually constructive critical analysis	1	0	1	0	0	1	1	2

2 = highly important
1 = moderately important
0 = slightly important

ty. The resulting intra-community tension may have repressive overtones, with unpredictable effects on the future pattern of faculty activities. The energy normally used to sustain self-imposed intellectual discipline and concentrated assaults on research-prone problems is consumed in defense of academic "territory" and status quo.

Table 6 indicates the community contribution to a favorable research environment.

every reward structure. A complication is that any single reward structure encourages different behavior in different personalities. Reward structures may be altered to reward most the already-existing behavior of a few individuals whose work has impressed the incumbent administrators, or who *are* the administrators. Other individuals may adjust to the structure or change it. If the reward structure does not imply preconceived

Table 6.   Contribution of Community Attributes to Research-Enabling Conditions

Conditions for Research	Large and Diverse Community	Established Business	Established Accounting Practices	Consulting Opportunities
1) Curiosity and knowledge about accounting practice	1	1	2	2
2) Access to problem solving tools	0	1	2	0
3) Mutually constructive critical analysis	1	0	1	1

2 = highly important
1 = moderately important
0 = slightly important

Table 7.   Contribution of Reward Structure Incentives to Research-Enabling Conditions

Conditions for Research	Regular Advancement	Publication Incentives	Teaching Incentives	Community Service Incentives	Research Incentives	Consulting Incentives
1) Curiosity and knowledge about accounting practice	1	0	1	0	1	1
2) Access to problem solving tools	1	0	1	1	1	0
3) Mutually constructive critical analysis	1	1	2	0	1	1

2 = highly important
1 = moderately important
0 = slightly important

Reward Structure. An accounting professor, like everyone else, has goals, norms and taboos which are influenced by his environment, including the extant reward structure. The reward structure interacts with the professor's own personality to produce, among others, these dynamic effects:

1) Encouragement of certain behavior
2) Discouragement of certain behavior
3) Indifference to certain behavior
4) Ambivalence (simultaneous encouragement and discouragement) toward certain behavior.

Of these, the last is least desirable. All effects are likely to exist to some extent in

preferred behavioral patterns, small groups may attempt to take over and revise it. Such groups form, disband, exhibit little or no internal discipline, and show uneven results in terms of tangible projects completed—books, papers, and so on. The energy consumed in attempts to change the reward structure is not available for research.

We favor a reward structure flexible enough to recognize activities other than research yet rigid enough to encourage sustained participation in a few activities instead of association with the largest possible number of activities. The reward structure should accommodate a broad range of personalities with different mixes of goals, norms and taboos, yet it should be so firmly immune to other than deliberate change that anyone would think seriously before attempting to overthrow it. Table 7 lists incentives considered to be conducive to research.

The Accounting Profession. The accounting profession is certainly the most important one serving business. Perhaps accountants themselves have not fully grasped the reality and responsibility of their prominence; one still reads of practitioners publicly denying that *they* wear green eyeshades —as if this ancient visual aid constituted the only possible manifestation of professional obsolescence.

If the accountant proudly recognizes the position of accountancy today, he may not regard that place as necessarily permanent. He may also be defensive about the speed with which the rise to the top takes place. Yet, he fears only unfair advantage, exercised by those to whom accounting independence and influence are anathema.

Professional accountants are most often found in the practice of taxation, independent auditing, bookkeeping and systems design. They are less often found in industrial or governmental enterprises. Further, public accounting professionals take more direct interest in accounting education than do other accountants. The accounting professor who seldom leaves his campus obtains his firsthand impression of practicing accountants from visiting public accountants. These visits usually occur as part of a staff recruiting program. Staff recruiters are part of the profession, but they *do not* provide an adequate basis for a professor's contact with the profession his students will enter. These men have an overriding responsibility for personnel which means that they are not the men in direct and intimate contact with the problems of interest to educators.

The accounting profession goes to modest lengths to provide assistance to accounting professors. Summer employment may usually be had for the asking. Money for scholarships, travel and attendance at professional meetings is sometimes available. Subscriptions to periodicals, certain intra-firm educational materials and filmstrips are furnished. Occasionally, enough money materializes to permit establishment of a chair or professorship, to finance publication of a journal, or to support a research center. Even so, it is probably true that accounting professors have not approached the limits of practitioner generosity.

To approach these limits would require changes in the outputs of accounting professors. The additional money might come out of firm profits, but more likely, it must be diverted from internal education and research efforts. The only reason to divert it would be because the firm's educational purpose could be better accomplished by universities. The purpose for intra-firm education and research is to improve the quality of professional services the firm can render. The firm's method is to provide education-indoctrination in subjects such as practice management, professional ethics, client relations, practice growth, audit methodology, SEC practice, and so on. None of these are very popular subjects in university accounting curricula, nor are they currently attractive as research topics. To attract more private sector support, accounting professors will have to show that they can teach these things better than accounting practitioners. Table 8 shows the contribution of practitioner support to research-enabling conditions.

In terms of research, the accounting firm seeks answers to questions that arise in the course of client relations. It seeks the proper interpretation or application of already developed rules. The accounting professor seeks to develop new rules; practicing accountants may generally prefer this to be done on a profession-wide scale.

Computers. A computer may provide essentially the same interactive functions as libraries and associates. A large competent computer utility with its program library, conversational ability and publications can be as valuable and stimulating as a library, as critical and objective as a competent associate.

Computer utilities may provide these kinds of services:

Batch processing—for education purposes as well as statistical evaluation of numerical

Table 8.   Contribution of Professional Support to Research-Enabling Conditions

Conditions for Research	Campus Visits by CPAs	Faculty Fellowships in Accounting Practice	Financial Assistance	Educational Materials	Professorships, Centers, Journals	Continuing Education Support
1) Curiosity and knowledge about accounting practice	1	2	1	0	0	0
2) Access to problem solving tools	0	0	2	0	0	0
3) Mutually constructive critical analysis	0	2	2	0	1	1

2 = highly important
1 = moderately important
0 = slightly important

Table 9.   Contribution of Computers to Research-Enabling Conditions

Conditions for Research	Batch Processing	Conversational Capability	Statistical and Other Program Libraries	Programming Consultants
1) Curiosity and knowledge about accounting practice	0	0	0	0
2) Access to problem-solving tools	2	2	2	2
3) Mutually constructive critical analysis	0	0	1	1

2 = highly important
1 = moderately important
0 = slightly important

arrays, such as might be the result of some sort of behavioral experiment.

Conversational processing—for education purposes as well as for personal or non-teaching calculations.

Programming—a variety of language compilers, information storage devices, and programming consultants for use in developing information systems or constructing special-purpose programs not found in the existing library.

Interpretation—to help in using already existing programs, including those which produce statistical analysis of observed data.

Table 9 shows the contribution of computers to a favorable research environment.

Accounting Organizations. The national practitioners' organizations are well known and make a significant contribution to the practice of accounting. Activity in them as an officer (as opposed to collecting copies of or publishing in the periodical) can help provide contact with practitioners. But what about the AAA and other professor-oriented organizations?

The AAA provides opportunities to work with colleagues at other universities. It offers extra-university recognition for quality teaching or research activity. It offers classroom-useful materials which enrich one's knowledge of the theoretical structure of accounting. TIMS and other organizations composed of specialists whose work sometimes overlaps accounting offer comparable advantages without the same emphasis on the accounting discipline. Participation in their activities may not be recognized by one's associates as improving *accounting* competence.

Summary. We have identified and briefly discussed these elements of the accounting professor's environment:

Teaching (Education)
Administration
Personal Development

Associates
Community
Reward Structure
Accounting Profession
Computers
Accounting Organizations

The first three of these may be controllable by the professor, himself. The last six are not controllable by the professor but he can take advantage of considerable latitude in interacting with them. The reader should bear in mind that the tables which summarized the relation of each factor to the conditions enabling research were not empirically derived, but they represent the hypotheses of the writer.

To improve and generalize these tables, the interval scale of measurement used should be converted into a ratio scale and should be expanded to include a unique range for each table. Thus, the range might be 0–3 for personal development factors but 0–12 for associates factors. Within the range, any magnitude would be assignable to any factor to show its contribution to research-enabling conditions. The revised scale and ranges should be used to establish the opinions of a sampling of accounting professors at public universities where research is appropriate. Only then might conclusions generalizable to substantial numbers of accounting faculty be within our grasp.

The sections that follow are based on the preceding development and are representative of the kinds of conclusions that should be possible.

6. Strategies for the Administrator

An administrator has little opportunity to engage in research himself. However, he can provide or contribute to the research-enabling conditions, for many of which he is the administrator. Our initial statement was that research is a multistage process. Each stage is an outcome of time period. The probability of that stage occurring depends on, of course, previous occurrence of earlier stages, and also on environmental variables.

In planning for any one period, the administrator has the advantage over the individual of being able to depend on the law of averages; if he establishes the proper conditions, some research will occur. He need not concern himself with who will do it. The individual, of course, must do without the law of averages in a single period and discipline himself to execute research. Over the long run, he perhaps has the law of averages on his side, too.

The administrator has the problem that a particular policy he may adopt will cause some persons to have a higher probability of performing research than others. Another policy may penalize the former and benefit the latter. Then, too, research topics may not all be equally significant. The administrator may be tempted to make decisions that favor one variety of research or one topic over others. Research stages are different in the conditions that favor them. The resources and conditions that favor problem perception differ from those that favor critical evaluation of results, and so on. An abrupt change in environment may cause termination of projects underway. Refusal to change an environment favoring problem perception may also prevent the natural progress of research to completion.

The table on the following page shows the activities or factors whose total scores in the previous tables relating variables to research-enabling conditions were *more* than three. A score higher than three is an "above average" score in the sense that there are three conditions and the expected score on each condition should be *one*.

If the table showing variables contributing significantly to conditions enabling research is regarded as a 12×3 matrix "A" and the table relating conditions to specific research stages is regarded as a 3×5 matrix "B," the result of multiplying $A \times B$ will be a 12×5 matrix showing the significance of each variable to each research stage. We again caution that the subjective character and interval scale of both matrices render their product extremely tentative. The matrix product is displayed in Table 11, Significance of Variables to Research Stages.

Table 10.   Table Showing Variables Contributing Significantly to Conditions Enabling Research

	Contributing to Condition		
	1	2	3
Teaching Processes			
Concept Originating	2	0	2
Concept Communication	2	0	2
Concept Applying	1	1	2
Administrative Functions			
Recruiting Faculty	0	2	2
Personal Development			
Read Professional Literature	1	1	2
Leave of Absence at Another University	1	1	2
Associates			
Professors at Same University in Accounting	1	2	2
Community			
Established Accounting Practices	2	2	1
Reward Structure			
Teaching Incentives	1	1	2
Professional Support			
Faculty Fellowships in Accounting Practice	2	0	2
Financial Assistance	1	2	2
Computers			
Programming Consultants	0	2	1
Accounting Organizations			
(not analyzed			

Table 11.   Significance of Variables to Research Stages

	Research Stages					
	(1)	(2)	(3)	(4)	(5)	
	Problem Formulation	Inspiration	Model Elaboration	Model Validation	Model Application	Total
(1) Concept Originating	6	6	4	6	8	30
(2) Concept Communicating	6	6	4	6	8	30
(3) Concept Applying	4	5	5	7	6	27
(4) Recruiting Faculty	2	4	6	8	4	24
(5) Read Literature	4	5	5	7	6	27
(6) Leave of Absence at Another University	4	5	5	7	6	27
(7) Professors at Same University in Accounting	4	5	7	9	6	31
(8) Established Accounting Practices	5	4	7	8	6	30
(9) Teaching Incentives	4	5	5	7	6	27
(10) Faculty Fellowships in Accounting Practice	6	6	4	6	8	30
(11) Financial Assistance	4	5	7	9	6	31
(12) Programming Consultants	1	2	5	6	2	16

Six of the variables in this table show up as contributing especially strongly to the research process itself. These are (1) Concept Originating and (2) Concept Communicating, two of the processes of teaching; (7) Professors in Accounting at the same university, one group of associates; (8) Established Accounting Practices, one community aspect; (10) Faculty Fellowships in Accounting Practice and (11) Financial Assistance, two means of professional support for research.

An administrator also has to take a "systems" approach to his job of managing an organization paid by the public primarily to teach. He must consider organizational activities other than research and allocate organization resources to them. He cannot excuse more than a small percentage of his faculty to go on leave (for of the six variables listed above, one will absent the professor from his home faculty) when there are classes to be taught. He cannot let the research-related aspects of personality be a major consideration in faculty recruiting if he must have a man in, say, tax and there are only two or three available.

Perhaps one project that would be worthwhile to an administrator would be analyses of all activities occurring within his organization. Utilities on a ratio scale may be assigned to these activities according to their significance and also to the variables which affect their intensity. Review of such analyses might produce a list of variables important to balanced pursuit of all of the organization's activities. It might also indicate the overall importance of environment relative to other factors influencing organization behavior. An interesting possibility is that a method of doing this can be devised that is generally applicable in any reasonably stable and narrow-purposed organization, such as an accounting faculty.

7. Strategies for the Professor

Not many professors are hired to do research. The notion persists that published results of research manifest the intellectual vigor of their authors. This inquiry has not investigated that proposition. It does appear, as an independent observation, that the teaching professor who expects to do research must either be content with very little research or he must make his time spent teaching count twice—that is, his teaching must furnish material for research or otherwise be a part of the research process.

There is a trend in teaching now to increase academic "productivity" by inserting electromechanical devices, such as computers and television sets, between the instructor and the student. The next few years will determine whether teaching staffs expand to accommodate through direct personal contact the additional students (especially from minority groups) who will seek higher education. If electromechanical devices prevail, the opportunities teaching provides for integration with the research process may decrease. It is a matter of speculation whether the benefit students receive from their university education is affected by the presence of these devices.

We would encourage the research-orient-

ed professor to teach as much as he possibly can—to students, to businessmen, to other professors, and to professional accountants—within the time limits set forth below. If the teaching occurs on a leave of absence to business or another university, so much the better.

The principal benefit the professor receives from outright teaching is the pressure for problem recognition and for devising inspiration or insight to deal with the problem. We speculate that the pressure arises from the intensive give and take with other individuals that is produced by teaching.

How much teaching? That is for the individual himself to decide. It is a question of how much contact with other individuals actually takes place. One would normally expect less exchange in a class of ninety students than in three classes of thirty students each—but in a given instance, the opposite may be true. Non-professors tend to think of a teaching load in terms of contact hours spent per week—and fifteen hours so spent does not seem excessive to them. It may not be excessive for the professor whose teaching style includes neither after-class help for students on an individual basis nor a search for new materials of interest to himself and his classes.

If one is serious about engaging in research, and if one also accepts a 40 to 50 hour work week as desirable, one's teaching load should be such that 5 to 20 hours per week do not have to be spent in direct teaching activities. The writer's experience is that 100–120 students in 2–3 courses may still permit this much time for research. Time should be available in large enough chunks to permit thoughtful review of a problem, including assimilation, integration and other activities necessary to organize the problem into a form suitable for presentation to an interested class. Such presentation most likely will draw the class into the professor's research process.

How often should one seek a leave of absence? We may not be far away from 12-months faculty year, in place of the present 9-months or 10.5 months. If that time comes, the present tolerance of taking 25 percent of one's calendar time away from regular instruction and duties in the summer may disappear. This writer is not prepared to say that one-fourth or one-seventh or one-half is the proper proportion of time to spend at other universities or in accounting experiences.

One's faculty accounting associates figure very prominently in the research process. Professors still find themselves a relatively mobile subculture and have opportunities to change *all* of their faculty associates at once. There are even more frequent opportunities to help select new members for the present faculty.

How can one tell in advance whether one can work successfully with a faculty? The principal things a faculty has to contribute are model elaboration, validation and application. All of these involve criticism, negotiation, compromise and fault-finding. When one finds it impossible to engage in these activities with one's faculty without personal involvement, that faculty is no longer useful in a research capacity (and vice versa). Perhaps such a situation is reversible. So far as this writer knows, there is no way for the individual to anticipate the extent to which his interactions with a faculty will be research-productive.

8. A Footnote—The Professional School of Accounting

This section illustrates use of the conclusion of this paper to evaluate a possible major change in the organization of accounting faculties. A recent President of the AICPA (Louis Kessler) has advocated establishment of independent professional accounting schools. These schools would be located at prominent public and private universities. Graduation from such a school would eventually be one requirement for receiving a CPA certificate.

Without necessarily endorsing Mr. Kessler's proposals, one can admit that the question of change in accounting institutions, and particularly accounting education institutions, is always open for discussion. If new institutions are to be designed, what effect might their unique attributes have on the research process?

Virtually all accounting is presently taught in university business schools. In the majority of such schools, accounting faculty are a minority of all business faculty (although they are the largest group representing a profession). The thrust in most business schools is toward education of the general manager or some management specialist. Three to nine hours of accounting are required for BBA and MBA candidates. These required hours are limited to basics and are presented to persons whose true interests do not necessarily include accounting. At these schools, elective courses in accounting cater to the nonaccounting students. In fact, very few accounting departments are strong enough to disregard the nonaccounting major by devoting a majority of their courses to the curriculum of the future professional accountant as represented by courses such as practice management, etc.

The writer feels that this teaching environment does not offer a proper encouragement to the research process. For the accounting professor, it is a short run diversion *but a long run dead end* to teach students who are only interested in accounting to the extent that it is a decision making tool for managers.

In the "Kessler" professional school, accounting courses would be for students who planned careers in accounting. Such courses should be quite different from those now taught in business schools. They should concentrate on accounting from an accountant's point of view. They should offer the opportunities for exchanges related to research interests and current accounting practice that are necessary to start and sustain the research process in accounting. It is stimulating to anticipate what kind of research this might eventually be.

Naturally, not every school that offers accounting courses will want to be a professional accounting school. Perhaps only a minority of schools will so elect. If this happens, it will present an ideal opportunity to implement the leave-of-absence to teach at another university as a way to encourage research. The faculties of professional schools might contain a proportion of one-fourth to one-half visiting professors. Many professors at business schools would then be afforded opportunities temporarily to teach professional accounting courses at the professional schools. The permanent faculties of the latter could, therefore, be exposed to a rapidly changing variety of scholarly associates.

Academic accountants have traditionally not concerned themselves with structural changes in the accounting profession. The period when this was possible is probably over, for increasing dependence on the profession for financial support has deprived accounting education of uncompromised independence. Educational institutions in accounting will change. The forms, objectives, and participatory patterns of accounting research will change. Those of us who are interested in research in accounting must, by design and directed effort, assure ourselves that there is still room for us in the new institutions that emerge.

Bibliography

1. Allison, David, *The R & D Game: Technical Men, Technical Managers, and Research Productivity,* MIT Press, 1969.

2. Anderson, Harold H. (ed.), *Interdisciplinary Symposia on Creativity,* Harper, 1959.

3. Armstrong, Henry Edward, *The Place of Research in Education,* Smithsonian Institution Annual Report, Washington, 1895, pp. 743–758.

4. Barron, Frank, *Creative Person and Creative Progress,* Holt, Rinehart and Winston, 1969.

5. Barron, Frank, *Creativity and Personal Freedom,* Van Nostrand, 1968.

6. Bernal, John Desmond, *The Social Function of Science,* MIT Press, 1967, 1937.

7. Burch, George Edward, *Of Research People,* Grune & Stratton, 1955.

8. Bush, George Pollock and Lowell H. Hattery, *Scientific Research: Its Administration and Organization,* American University Press, 1950.

9. Bush, George Pollock and Lowell H. Hattery, *Teamwork in Research,* American University Press, 1953.

10. *Changing Patterns of Academic Research,* a symposium sponsored by the Rensselaer Chapter, the Society of Sigma Xi, April 13, 1957.

11. (anon.), *Cooperation in Research,* The Carnegie Institution, 1938.

12. Chambers, Jack A., *Relating Personality and Biographical Factors to Scientific Creativity,* American Psychological Association, 1964.

13. Crawford, Claude C., *The Technique of Research in Education,* University of Southern California, 1928.

14. Deutsch & Shea, Inc., *Company Climate and Creativity,* Industrial Relations News, 1959.

15. _____, *Creativity; A Comprehensive Bibliography on Creativity in Science, Engineering, Business, and the Arts,* Industrial Relations News, 1958.

16. Foundation for Research on Human Behavior, *Creativity and Conformity: A Problem for Organizations,* Ann Arbor, 1958.

17. Gibbs, Barbara, *The Norms of Science and Their Implementation in a University Community,* unpublished thesis, The University of Texas, 1953.

18. Hagstrom, Warren O., *The Scientific Community,* Basic Books, 1965.

19. Harvey, O. J. (ed.), *Experience, Structure & Adaptability,* Springer Publishing Co., 1966.

20. Hill, Karl B. (ed.), *The Management of Scientists,* Beacon Press, 1964.

21. Hinrichs, John R., *Creativity in Industrial Scientific Research,* American Management Association, 1961.

22. Kneller, George Frederick, *The Art and Science of Creativity,* Holt, Rinehart & Winston, 1965.

23. Lowes, John Livingstone, *Teaching and the Spirit of Research,* Phi Beta Kappa, 1933.

24. Lowry, Howard Foster, *Research, Creative Ability and Teaching,* Carnegie Foundation for Advancement of Teaching, 1953.

25. Luszki, Margaret Elizabeth (Butler) Barron, *Interdisciplinary Team Research,* New York University Press, 1958.

26. Nelson, Lois (ed.), *Fostering Creativity,* Selected Academic Readings, 1967.

27. Pelz, Donald C. and Frank M. Andrews, *Scientists in Organizations: Productive Climates for Research and Development,* Wiley, 1966.

28. Pennsylvania University Faculty Research Committee, "Report of the Faculty Research Committee," 1932.

29. Raudsepp, Eugene, *Ideas; How to Create Them, How to Sell Them, How to Manage Creative People,* Hawthorn Books, 1967.

30. Raudsepp, Eugene, *Managing Creative Scientists and Engineers,* Macmillan, 1963.

31. Razik, Taher A., *Bibliography of Creativity Studies and Related Areas,* State University of New York, *1965.*

32. Reeves, Floyd Wesley, *et al., The University Faculty,* University of Chicago Press, 1933.

33. Ruitenbeck, Hendrik M. (ed.), *The Creative Imagination,* Quadrangle Books, 1965.

34. Simon, Herbert A., "On Judging the Plausibility of Theories," in The International Congress for Logic, Methodology, and Philosophy of Science, III, Amsterdam, 1967, J. F. Stall and Bob Van Rootselaar (eds.) *Logic, Methodology and Philosophy of Science,* North Holland Publishing Company, 1968, pp. 457–458.

35. Stein, Morris Isaac and Shirley J. Heinz, *Creativity and the Individual,* Free Press, 1960.

36. Steiner, Gary Albert (ed.), *The Creative Organization,* University of Chicago Press, 1965.

37. Subcommittee on Creative and Research Work, Committee on Curriculum and Educational Policy, Harold Zink, Chairman, De Pauw University, *Creative and Research Work,* 1938 (mimeographed).

38. Taylor, Calvin W. and Frank Barron (eds.), *Scientific Creativity,* Wiley, 1963.

39. *University Research: What It Means to the South,* Southern Regional Education Board, 1959.

40. Von Fange, Eugene K., *Professional Creativity,* Prentice Hall, 1959.

chapter 15

Elements Inducive to Accounting Research at the University Level

Philip H. White

University of British Columbia

Professor Summers deserves our appreciation and respect. His subject is one which openly invites discussion in loose generalities, but he has not merely avoided all such tendencies he has done so in a way which continuously and precisely directs our attention to a large number of facets of the problem. Believing my task is to comment on the paper as written, rather than writing a pocket version of my own, my comments have a rather discrete character which follow the plan of the paper.

Briefly, the method is to identify five stages in the research process and then to assess the importance to these stages of three conditions which are necessary for accounting research to occur. The academic environment is perceived as having nine elements relevant to accounting research, and these elements comprise 47 sub-elements. The relative importance of the environment to research is derived by first assessing the extent to which each sub-element bears on the three conditions for research, and then using these results to compute the significance to the research process. For the purpose of both stages of

the calculations a simple 0-1-2 scale has been used to measure the degrees of importance, although Summers has indicated that the method would probably be improved by the use of ratio scales. As a result of computing the relative importance of environmental factors, there emerge six sub-elements which on the basis of the hypothesis are most important to accounting research.

The hypothesis has not undergone any empirical testing, so that it is, as the author states, highly subjective. Because of this, it is possible to raise questions at various levels. We might, for example, wish to dispute the degrees of importance to the conditions for research which are assigned to particular sub-elements, or to question the relative importance of these conditions to the stages of the research process, but this would be to respond to hypothesis with conjecture. For the present purpose, it will be more useful to concentrate on larger and more basic questions, and it is a tribute to Summers' lucidity that such a choice is possible in a paper of this kind.

Given the refinement of ratio scales and

reliable identification of significant environmental factors, the method has much to commend it for the reason that it compels a more or less precise assessment of each one. And we should not be too quick to charge the method with a pseudo-precision because that would impute to it more than is intended. It is sufficient to agree that the research process has stages of approximately this kind and that there are conditions of this sort which must exist if research is to be undertaken. However, a general weakness of the method is that various items are represented as single entities, whereas they are categories which include several cases of quite different kinds. Thus, research is used to describe a number of activities which are significantly different in methodology and purpose, and it does not necessarily follow that the most favourable environment for one is the same as for another. Moreover, I have difficulty in accepting the idea that each stage of the research process is of equal importance. It seems to me that "inspiration" is crucial and that "problem formulation" is more important than the other three. Observation of the performance of graduate students who are undertaking research for the first time suggests that this is so and Summers' comments about doctoral candidates are confirmatory.

In Table I, conditions are represented to be less important to "problem formulation" and "inspiration" than to the other stages, and this might be accepted. However, if the relative importance of the conditions is considered (i.e., the total of the rows), we might speculate that faculty act as if access to problem solving tools were more important than is represented.

The very detailed treatment of the subject has already been acknowledged, and for this reason it is the more surprising to find that the concept of the environment is not considered or even the rationale of the selection of the nine environmental elements. These comprise: teaching, administration, personal development, associates, community, reward structure, accounting profession, computers and accounting organizations. Some of the elements are activities—teaching and

administration—others are resources—computers—and others could be listed as parts of the environment. It would have made the reasons for this critical selection easier to understand if some impression had been given of the nature of the environment. In the present context it might have been represented as a duality, physical and intellectual. The former might include accommodation, the campus, the community including its geographical position, housing and recreational and cultural facilities. The intellectual environment includes colleagues, faculty at other universities (and the opportunities provided for meeting them), students, university administrators and the organization of work in general in relation to research in particular. The intellectual environment is most important to the quality of life and it is therefore difficult to identify but its importance should not be in doubt. These descriptions have omitted various things which are usually necessary to research such as research assistants, computer facilities and the library. These are seen as resources rather than elements of the environment and have been left out on these grounds. Admittedly, the distinction may well be overdrawn in that resources sometimes represent elements in the environment, thus a forest may be an industrial and recreational resource as well as representing a large and important part of the environment, but the question need not detain us for the only purpose of introducing the idea here is to illustrate my difficulties in accepting the characteristics of the environment which have been adopted. "Personal development," for example, might depend upon the environment, but is it part of it? And if activities like "teaching" and "administration" are part of the environment, why is not "research," itself? All three are included in the work of nearly all faculty members.

As a parting word on this aspect of the paper, I cannot understand why the computer is listed as one of the nine significant elements whereas the library is not mentioned. The omission provokes serious doubts about the nature of accounting research and even accounting knowledge which it would be comforting to have set at rest!

The treatment of and references to teaching are another example of the tendency noted earlier to treat some items as if they were single entities instead of categories of items with significant differences. There is a reference in the paper to the effect of differences in the size of classes and another to the quality of Ph.D. students, but in general no distinction has been drawn between different levels of undergraduate and graduate teaching nor is there any mention of the significance of differences in the quality of students. It is, however, easy to think of cases in which a given amount of teaching would be a negative environmental element and others where a similar amount would make a positive contribution. If the teaching is of the appropriate kind, it seems to me that research and teaching are complementary activities and are not in conflict. This is the principal justification for using university resources in this way and, in general, I do not see the conflict between teaching and research which the paper—and others—present. In the last decade, it has become conventional to represent one as an opportunity cost of the other—faculty claiming that teaching impairs their research and their students the opposite—but this is surely an over-simpification of the problem of allocating resources and in defining the professor's role. Although academic prestige is now heavily dependent on research and therefore faculty like to claim that their potential—unnecessarily constrained—exceeds their performance to date, observation suggests that the maximum time and effort in research of which most faculty are capable are quite low. Research is difficult, hard work which most people can sustain for only limited periods. From this viewpoint, the optimum environment is one which hopefully stimulates the expansion of such periods but at least ensures that there is no impediment to them.

The paper does not refer to the overall importance of the environment to the research process, although this can be deduced. The scale used is 0-1-2 representing effects which are slightly, moderately and highly important. The total score of the 47 environmental sub-elements applied to the three conditions for research is 116, so that the aggregate effect of the environment is something less than moderately important. This effect holds true for each of the three conditions—"mutual constructive critical analysis" has the highest score (44) but the effect is still below the moderately important level, then "curiosity and knowledge about accounting practice" (38) and finally "access to problem solving tools" (34). Apart from the highly subjective evaluation process, it is apparent that these conclusions depend upon how the environment is defined, but they do forestall the temptation to judge the issue by vague general impressions and they compel a solution to the problem of definition.

In the definition of the scale, the equation of zero with "slightly important" is bothersome, and a negative scale indicating environmental elements harmful to research would have been an advantage.

The conclusions included under the heading of "Strategies for the Administrator" are of personal interest, and I agree with Summers that the creation or maintenance of an environment conducive to research is one of the major responsibilities of a university administrator. However, I cannot accept the proposition that the administrator "need not concern himself with who will do (the work)." He must have regard for the quality of what is done and for this reason he may have to be very selective in his allocation of resources. Nor would I agree with the idea that a public university is "an organization paid by the public primarily to teach." In my own view, teaching and research are complementary and primary activities, but it is manifest that the general expectations of public universities include a variety of additional activities. It also follows that I reject the suggestion that public universities "do not provide facilities . . . for research." This is not true in my experience.

Contemplating the administrative difficulties of creating a favourable environment, it is a consolation that Summers has found the influence of the environment to be less than moderately important, and there is further comfort in the knowledge that Wittgenstein wrote a major treatise on logic while serving in the trenches during the First World War. Faculty complaining about the distractions of the embattled campus and harassment by administrators might take note!

chapter 16

Accounting Research:
The Why, The How, The Who

ERNEST L. HICKS

Arthur Young & Company

This paper presents some thoughts of a CPA in public practice about accounting research. The views of other CPAs in public practice have been taken into consideration, but the ideas presented cannot fairly be characterized as research findings. Nevertheless, the ideas expressed are believed to be consonant with those of many practitioners who have thought about the matters discussed.

CPAs in public practice recognize the importance of research and would like for research to have more influence on their practice. This was evidenced by the action of the American Institute of CPAs in 1958 when, in a single action, it established the Accounting Principles Board and the Accounting Research Division. Both were to be important forces—perhaps, in the minds of some, equally important forces—in achieving the Institute's objective of improving generally accepted accounting principles. There is evidence that some practitioners would be better pleased if the system worked better, but I see no evidence that practitioners have given up on research.

With this brief, unscientific background, let us look more closely at accounting research, always, to be sure, from the point of view of a CPA in public practice. Let us consider the objectives, which I have called "the Why," the methods, which I have called "the How" and the instruments, which I have called "the Who."

The Why

From the viewpoint of a practitioner, a discussion of accounting research in a context that does not identify the research objectives is incomplete. Perhaps the objectives are so clear that they do not deserve to be stated. Perhaps the framework is the same for all conceivable objectives. In any event, the following are ways of stating operating objectives for accounting research which appeal to a practitioner.

1. To find out (a) the purposes of accounting and (b) the purposes of financial statements.
2. To find out what accounting conventions can best accomplish the purposes identified as a result of Item 1.
3. To find out (a) whether financial statements made available to the pub-

lic are a communications device, (b) if they are, what they ought to communicate and whether they communicate that as well as can be expected and (c) if they do not communicate adequately, what changes can be made, either in financial statements so that they may better communicate or in the conditioning of readers so that they may better understand.

4. To find out, with respect to reports of CPAs on financial statements, the answers to questions corresponding with those raised about financial statements in Item 3.

5. To find out what transitional steps would best serve to bring present financial reporting practices into conformity with those deemed more desirable as a result of Items 1 through 4.

6. To find out how, until changes resulting from Items 1 through 5 can be made, financial reporting practices can be improved by making relatively minor changes in generally accepted accounting principles.

7. To find out, with respect to financial statements prepared for the use of corporate managements, such of the information described in Item 3 as may be pertinent to such financial statements.

8. To find out (a) whether improvements need to be made in the systems used by corporations to accumulate and use information and (b), if so, (i) what changes would be useful or (ii) whether identified changes would be useful.

9. To find out (a) whether the accounting principles and practices corporations use in reporting to stockholders and the principles they use in reporting to the Internal Revenue Service differ significantly and (b), if so, whether they (i) should be brought into conformity with each other and (ii) can be brought into conformity.

Some of the questions raised or implied by the foregoing listing may already have been answered to the satisfaction of a particular researcher. If so, or perhaps even if not, he might start in the middle, working for example with Item 3 instead of Item 2, with Item 3(c) instead of Item 3(a).

The above list of research objectives is illustrative, rather than exhaustive. Longer lists, and more specific ones, can be drawn of objectives whose achievement could reasonably be expected to have an impact on the development of accounting principles and on the practice of CPAs.

Objectives whose achievement seems to an accounting practitioner to be most needed are those concerned with finding out how different classes or readers perceive financial statements and how, if at all, readers use the information, if any, which they obtain from financial statements.

Accounting practitioners observe, with approval, a trend in accounting research away from a quest for the accounting counterparts of the natural laws with which disciplines such as physics and astronomy are concerned. Practitioners are encouraged also by evidences that the resources of still other disciplines—notably the resources of the behavioral sciences—may, despite recognized difficulties, be brought to bear in accounting research.

The How

This Colloquium deals extensively with how to go about performing research in accounting. In a colloquy so learned, dealing with a topic so esoteric, an accounting practitioner is wont to speak in a soft voice. One is moved, in this mode, to suggest that researchers should not allow themselves to become so absorbed in a concern for methods as to overlook the importance of soundly conceived objectives.

Practitioners recognize, nevertheless, that methods are important. They applaud a trend, which this Colloquium may signal, toward the development of standards by which the adequacy of research may be measured. If such standards were generally accepted and if research were stated to have been performed in accordance with them, the influence of the findings on persons who are not qualified to appraise the research, or are unwilling to do so, might be enhanced.

The Who

The people who may perform accounting research are considered in the three principal classes into which they fall: people in public accounting firms and in the professional societies, people in other business-related organizations and people in universities.

Accounting firms and societies. In accounting firms, there is some research which can be expected to have long-range effect. Some of this occurs in the process of developing policies. Some of it is in support of the representatives of the firms on bodies within the AICPA—principally, the Accounting Principles Board and the Committee on Auditing Procedure. Much of this activity does not meet the standards discussed at this Colloquium. Nevertheless, the interest is in what ought to be, as contrasted with what is.

Much of the "research" in accounting firms is geared to keeping track of what is happening. The objective is to be attuned to the state of generally accepted accounting principles. This activity consists essentially of reviewing selected financial statements and the reports of certified public acountants on them. The statements appear in annual reports to stockholders, in prospectuses and in other publicly-available sources. This is essentially an information-retrieval activity, in which information is classified under subject headings, stored and, when needed, retrieved. Many accounting practitioners have stored in their minds a great deal of information, accumulated through years of practice, about business practices and accounting procedures.

Accounting firms conduct other types of activities that may be classified as research. For example, a firm may conduct studies whose objectives are to develop generalized computer software or to develop auditing procedures that make use, or make better use, of computers or of scientific sampling methods.

The principal long-range research activities of accounting firms are conducted through the AICPA. As to accounting principles, these are conducted through the Accounting Research Division. Its primary function is to contribute to, and to support, the work of the Accounting Principles Board. Other AICPA research activities are conducted in support of the Committee on Auditing Procedure and other Institute committees.

Other business-related organizations. Other organizations have research divisions or sponsor research projects. The National Association of Accountants has published numerous studies, principally on management-oriented subjects. The Financial Executives Institute has established the Financial Executives Research Foundation. This entity sponsored a study by Dr. Robert K. Mautz, published in 1968, entitled "Financial Reporting by Conglomerate Companies." This study was cited by the Securities and Exchange Commission in its proposal to amend certain of its reporting forms to include line-of-business profit and loss information. These and other groups show signs of stepping up their research activities.

Universities. Accounting research performed in universities has made notable contributions to the improvement of accounting principles and of financial reporting practices. The several relevant statements issued by committees of the American Accounting Association have been influential, and so has the work of individual researchers.

Accountants in public practice believe that there is a significant reservoir of accounting talent in universities. They believe that knowledge and insights gained in university research should have an important influence on accounting practices and on the practice of public accounting, and they wish this influence to be intensified.

Accountants in public practice understand, in a limited way, the desire of university researchers not to overemphasize short-term "usefulness," whether of method or of objective. They do not in the least believe that every research activity ought to promise immediate utilitarian advantage. They do believe, however, that accounting exists because, and only because, it serves a purpose. Consequently, they believe that the possible benefits to be gained from the outcome ought to be considered in appraising a proposal for research and in designing the research methods to be applied.

It has been suggested that there is a need to make accounting research more intellectually stimulating. An interesting suggestion for going about this is to challenge researchers to create an entirely new type of bookkeeping (and, presumably, of financial statement presentation); such a system might be the accounting equivalent of three-dimensional tick-tack-toe. To be sure, such a challenge might receive attention, spur interest and stimulate effort. Accountants in public practice believe that some of the pressing questions of the day are equally deserving of attention, interest and effort and may provide equal, or perhaps greater, intellectual stimulation, For example: Does a lack of understanding on the part of readers of financial statements account in part for dissatisfaction with financial statements expressed by some readers? Can the instruc-

tional abilities of accounting educators be put to use in dispelling such misunderstanding, if it exists? Would it be useful, as an accounting educator has suggested, to abandon the single figure of net income as a measure of corporate achievement and to substitute a net income range, in which the extremes are the most conservative and the least conservative determinations that can reasonably be supported?

Coordination. Should the activities of the various classes of researchers somehow be coordinated? Diversity of interest and independence of thought are recognized as essential ingredients of research; cooperative arrangements, if developed, should not introduce constraints. Nevertheless, it would seem that a clearinghouse of some sort ought to be useful. Its principal contribution might be in making possible exchanges of information as to topics on which research is needed. It might also contribute to agreement on questions of research method.

chapter 17

A Practitioner's View of Accounting Research

Philip B. Chenok

Main Lafrentz & Co.

Mr. Hicks' paper suggests a series of operating objectives for accounting research which I found interesting but not necessarily relevant to the needs of the accounting practitioner. Accounting is in crisis. It will take an extended period to resolve the issues. As we move down the fair value road, financial statements will represent a mixture of historical cost and current value.

We cannot depart from historical cost overnight. It will be done on an asset-by-asset, liability-by-liability basis. Problems exist for each item currently reflected in financial statements. Other items, not yet reflected, perhaps should be. One company, for example, has tried to capitalize the fair value of the work force. Others are working to develop the capitalized value of long-term leases.

These are the areas that interest the practitioner. They are the areas of immediate change. While I recognize the need to do long-range research, let me ask that you not ignore the more immediate problems of our profession.

This Colloquium deals extensively with research processes that are under active consideration in colleges and universities. I thought it would be of interest this afternoon to tell you a little of the nature of the research process conducted in a public accounting firm, particularly as it relates to the resolution of difficult practice problems.

Hicks points out that some of the research conducted in public accounting firms is of a long-range nature. That research may involve the development of accounting and auditing manuals, checklists, questionnaires, etc., or it may involve the development of a firm position on general issues. The research-practitioner's most trying moments come, however, when he must decide whether or not a proposed accounting treatment is acceptable for inclusion in financial statements on which his firm is to express an opinion.

Typically, a question comes by telephone at 4:30 on Friday afternoon and must be resolved before 5:00 p.m., since the annual report is about to be issued. Usually the question could have been raised well in advance because it represents an issue about which the partner-in-charge has had nagging doubts for some time. On these occasions the research-practitioner suggests, often in the same soft voice just used by Hicks, that the points at issue may require extensive study and that 5:00 p.m. next Friday might just be about right.

Let me give you an illustration of one of the more perplexing problems with which I am in the process of grappling. Our client, Corporation Pooler, proposes to acquire two companies, Building Company and Operating Company, each owned jointly by three men. Building Company owns the

161

building in which Operating Company operates; it is a special-purpose building and presumably cannot be used for any other purpose. Operating Company pays rent to Building Company at what is represented to be fair rental value. The three owners wish to sell Building Company for cash and to exchange their stock in Operating Company for stock in Corporation Pooler. The question put to us then is whether Corporation Pooler can treat the exchange of stock as a pooling under APB Opinion No. 16. This question is unusual since practice has not yet had a chance to develop under the new Opinion.

In the usual case we apply five basic steps in attempting to resolve problems of this type. These steps are outlined in Armstrong's article, "Some Thoughts on Substantial Authoritative Support." They involve:

1. A definition of the problem. This involves a complete description of the problem including, to the extent determinable, the economic or other objectives sought by the parties, the pertinent facts relating to the event or transaction and a complete description of the proposed accounting treatment.
2. A survey of the relevant literature. This is done to provide evidence of existing standards of practice. It includes a review of AICPA pronouncements, pronouncements of other professional societies, SEC rules and regulations, industry publications, federal and state law and written views of individuals. In reviewing text books, reference books, articles and speeches, we must carefully distinguish between those that reflect "what is" and those that express a view as to "what ought to be."
3. A survey of present practice by organizations with similar problems. This most often involves a review of annual reports, registration statements and the like. I recognize that a determination of what is going on in practice today may not produce the "best answer." (In this context I think the

"best answer" is one which is most responsive to the substance of the transaction or event to be reported.) Nevertheless, it is important to determine the range of existing practice.
4. An evaluation of the information developed.
5. The reaching of a conclusion.

The latter two steps involve establishing a relationship between the information developed in the first three steps and the exercise of judgment. Hopefully, the basis for the conclusion can be objectively presented, but sometimes the solution comes from an intuitive feeling about what is right in the circumstances.

In Corporation Pooler's case the relevant literature is APB Opinion No. 16. Our limited survey of present practice indicated no other instances of this particular problem. Therefore, we sought the views of responsible practitioners in an effort to determine what their position would be faced with a similar problem. The answers are interesting.

Most felt that the payment of cash and stock to the same men constituted a violation of the pooling criteria, and, thus, the whole transaction should be considered a purchase. One practitioner, however, took the position, since the two corporations were not formed in contemplation of the business combination, that the exchange of stock for stock could be considered a pooling if an arms length deal was involved. That is, he would permit this transaction to be accounted for as a pooling, provided that it can be demonstrated that the cash consideration paid for the building represents the fair value of the building, and that the rent agreement is at fair rental value.

In arriving at that conclusion, considerable weight was given to the fact that the individuals could have sold their interest in Building Company to a third party investor for cash, having previously negotiated an arms-length lease between Operating Company and Building Company. It also would be possible to include a purchase option in the lease agreement. Alternatively, the individuals could continue to own Building

Company and receive rental payments over a period of years.

For your information, we have not yet reached a conclusion on this matter.

In closing let me say a few words about the pressures which are exerted on the research-practitioner as he goes through the problem solving process. As I mentioned before, most questions involve time pressures. Often the operating partner will have adopted a preliminary position with his client so that changes in position may reflect on his competence; he, therefore, usu-ally resists change. Our client will have also considered the problem and will have developed weighty arguments in favor of the proposed accounting treatment. Sometimes it is asserted that another firm has approved the proposed treatment. Potential legal liability and possible public embarrassment represent counterbalancing pressures. I mention these pressures only to give you some notion of the environment in which the research-practitioner must operate. I leave it to you to evaluate the results.